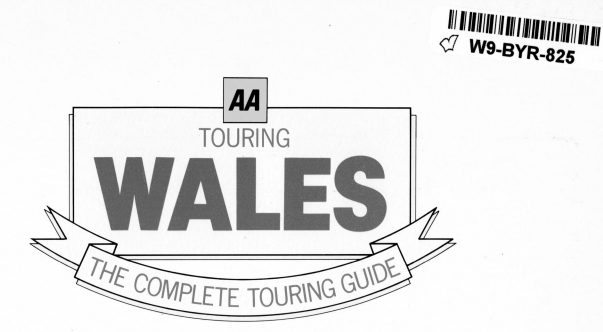

AA

TOURING

WALES

THE COMPLETE TOURING GUIDE

Cover picture:
Gower Peninsula, West Glamorgan,
with the outline of the rocky headland of Worms' Head
in the distance.

Produced by the Publishing Division of the Automobile Association
Editor Allen Stidwill
Designer Neil Roebuck
Picture Researcher Wyn Voysey
Index by D Hancock

Tours compiled and driven by the Publications Research Unit of the Automobile Association.

Photographs by Woodmansterne Picture Library, Jarrolds Colour Library, Barnaby's Picture Library, J Allen Cash Photolibrary, British Tourist Authority, Wales Tourist Board, C Molyneux, The National Trust, J Hunter, Mary Evans Picture Library, Welsh Office, AA Photolibrary, H Williams.

All maps by the Cartographic Department, Publishing Division of the Automobile Association. Based on the Ordnance Survey Maps, with the permission of the Controller of HM Stationery Office. Crown Copyright Reserved.

Town plans produced by the AA's Cartographic Department. ©The Automobile Association.

Filmset by Senator Graphics, Great Suffolk St, London SE1
Printed and bound by New Interlitho SPA, Milan, Italy

Published by the Automobile Association, Fanum House, Basing View, Basingstoke, Hampshire RG21 2EA

ISBN 0 86145 499 5
AA Reference 51923

Touring Wales

CONTENTS

'The Welsh Lakes'. Craig Goch with its elegant dam created to supply Birmingham with water, is one of four man-made lakes in the remote but beautiful Elan Valley.

INTRODUCTION

Wales is magnificent car touring country, with an amazing variety of spectacular scenery. It is a land of lofty mountains, of coal and choirs and mighty castles, a country with its own personality and language, rich in culture and history.

This guide reveals these treasures and more through its carefully planned motoring tours which provide the ideal way to explore this fascinating land. Each self-contained circular tour can be completed within a day and includes magnificent colour pictures to give a foretaste of what is to come.

In past times Wales was not so welcoming and centuries of battles led to the building of mighty castles. Forty eight colourful pages of the guide are therefore devoted to this rich legacy. Also included are 11 pages of invaluable town plans to guide you around the popular towns of Wales. There is also a large scale, 3 miles to the inch atlas of the country.

Touring Wales is just one in a series of six colourful *Regional Guides* which embrace the rich history and varied countryside of Britain. The other five guides in the series are: *Touring the West Country, Touring South and South East England, Touring Central England and East Anglia, Touring the North Country* and *Touring Scotland.* The six regions covered by the series are shown on the adjacent map.

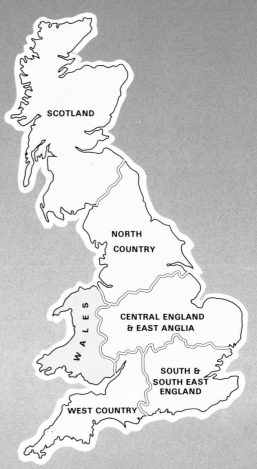

ABOUT THE TOURS

The tours in this guide have been designed for clarity. Each tour occupies two pages and has a clear map accompanying the text. All the places described in the text are shown in **black** on the tour maps and are described as they occur on the road, linked in sequence by route directions. This precise wayfinding information is set in *italic*.

Castles, stately homes and other places of interest described in the tours are not necessarily open to the public or may be open only at certain times. It is therefore advisable to check the opening times of any place before planning a stop there. Properties administered by the National Trust, National Trust for Scotland and the Ancient Monument Scheme (NT, NTS and AM) are generally open most of the year, but this should be checked with the relevant organisation, as should precise opening times.

The Automobile Association's guide *Stately Homes, Museums, Castles and Gardens in Britain* is the most comprehensive annual publication of its kind and describes over 2,000 places of interest, giving details of opening times and admission prices, including many listed in this book.

Backed by downs rising over 600 feet, the golden sands of Rhossili Bay give the Gower Peninsula one of the most spectacular beaches on the Welsh coast.

HOW TO FIND THE TOURS

All the motor tours in the book are shown on the key map below and identified by the towns where they start. The tours are arranged in the book in alphabetical order by start town name. Page numbers are also given on page vii. Each tour begins at a well-known place, but it is possible to join or leave at any point if more convenient.

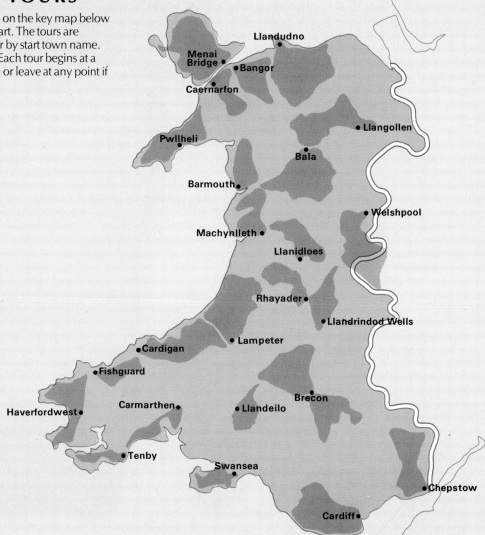

MAPS		Marshland	......	TEXT	
Main Tour Route	═══	Memorial/Monument	m	AM	Ancient Monument
Detour/Diversion from Main Tour Route	▬▬▬	Miscellaneous Places of		c	*circa*
Motorway	══	Interest & Route Landmarks	■	NT	National Trust
Motorway Access	═②═	National Boundary		NTS	National Trust for Scotland
Motorway Service Area	═⑤═	National Trust Property	NT	OACT	Open at Certain Times
Motorway and Junction Under Construction	═╳═	National Trust for Scotland Property	NTS	PH	Public House
A-class Road	A68	Non-gazetteer Placenames	*Thames /Astwood*	RSPB	Royal Society for the
B-class Road	B700	Notable Religious Site	✝		Protection of Birds
Unclassified Road	unclass	Picnic Site	Ⓟ	SP	Signpost (s) (ed)
Dual Carriageway	A70	Prehistoric Site	⌁		
Road Under Construction	= = = =	Racecourse	⬭		
Airport	✈	Radio/TV Mast	⬙		
Battlefield	✕	Railway (BR) with Station	━●━		
Bridge	≍	Railway (Special) with Station	┼┼●┼┼		
Castle	♜	River & Lake	∿◯		
Church as Route Landmark	✝	Woodland Area	◗		
Ferry	– Ⓥ –	Scenic Area	◗		
Folly/Tower	⬙	Seaside Resort	☼		
Forestry Commission Land	⬤	Stately Home	⯅		
Gazetteer Placename	Zoo /Lydstep	Summit/Spot Height	KNOWE HILL 209 ▲		
Industrial Site (Old & New)	⬚		KNOWE HILL 209 ▲		
Level Crossing	LC	Viewpoint	☀		
Lighthouse	⯗				

TOURING WALES

Motor Tours
Pages 2-51

LAKES AMONG THE FORESTS

Rarely level and often winding, the roads taken by this tour
ascend the rocky clefts of mountain streams to summits that
give panoramic views across forest-clad mountains and
tree-bordered lakes. Everywhere is the sparkle
and chatter of water.

BALA, Gwynedd
Behind Bala's cheerful and
unassuming tree-lined High Street is
Tomen-y-Bala, the mound of a
Norman castle. During the 18th
century this was a popular spot for
the local folk to do their knitting.
Hand-knitted stockings from Bala
were once famous, and George III
would wear no others. In the High
Street is a statue of Tom Ellis, a
farmer's son who became Liberal
Chief Whip and a tireless
campaigner for Welsh home rule.
Cyffdy Farm Park (open) is a rare-
breed centre for North Wales.

SNOWDONIA NATIONAL PARK
Much of this route is within the
boundaries of the 845-square-mile
Snowdonia National Park, which
contains some of the most dramatic
and beautiful scenery in Britain and is
famous for its mountain ranges.
The breath-taking valleys between
mountains are often graced by
lovely lakes and reservoirs, or
enlivened with the sound of running
water. In the south are old mine
workings where prehistoric and
modern men have searched
for gold.

*Leave Bala on the B4391 'Llangynog'
road and skirt the northern extremity
of Bala Lake. Cross the River Dee and
follow its valley for several miles.
Climb on to open moorland and the
slopes of the Berwyn Mountains.*

THE BERWYN MOUNTAINS
Stretching from Llangollen to Lake
Vyrnwy, this mountain range is
gradually being changed in
appearance as vast forests of
conifers swallow up its slopes. Views
from the two highest peaks – 2,712ft
Cadair Berwyn and 2,713ft Moel
Sych – open up outstanding
panoramas in all directions.

*Descend into the Eiarth Valley and
enter Llangynog.*

LLANGYNOG, Powys
Remains of once-important slate
quarries and lead mines may be seen
in this area. The church is dedicated
to St Cynog, who was the eldest son
of Brychan, a prince of one of the
ancient Welsh kingdoms.

*Follow SP 'Llanfyllin' along the Tanat
Valley to Penybontfawr.*

PENYBONTFAWR, Powys
Picturesquely set on the southern
slopes of the Berwyn Mountains,
this village has a handsome
Victorian church and a charming
school building. All around is
beautiful countryside.

*Turn right on to the B4396 SP 'Lake
Vyrnwy' and continue along a narrow,
winding road through wooded
country to Llanwddyn.*

The valley which romantic Lake Vyrnwy
occupies was created by a glacier
during the ice ages.

During the 16th century these hills near Dinas Mawddwy were the haunt of
notorious brigands.

LLANWDDYN, Powys
Built to replace the old village of
Llanwddyn, which now lies under
the waters of artificial Lake Vyrnwy,
this village stands in a countryside
dominated by rank upon rank of
dark green coniferous forest. Such
rare creatures as the pine marten
and polecat have been able to make
a comeback because of the new
habitats provided by afforestation,
and are increasing in numbers.
*Turn right on to the B4393 to reach
Lake Vyrnwy. Turn left across the dam
and skirt the wooded south shores of
the lake.*

LAKE VYRNWY, Powys
This lake is 4¾ miles long and was
created in the late 19th century to
supply Liverpool with water. The
gothic water tower on its north-east
side, and thick forests that clothe its
banks to the water's edge, seem to
suggest the depths of the German
Black Forest rather than Wales.

*Continue the circuit of the lake and
return to Llanwddyn. Two alternative
routes leading from the north end of
the lake to Bwlch-y-Groes and
through the Hirnant Pass to Bala
respectively are described at the end
of this tour. Follow the 'Llanfyllin' road
and in 4 miles turn right on to the
B4395 SP 'Pont Llogel'. Later skirt
Dyfnant Forest and cross the Afon
Vyrnwy. Continue to the edge of
Llangadfan. Turn right on to the A458
'Dolgellau' road and climb gradually
out of the Banwy Valley. Descend
along the wooded Dugoed Valley to
Mallwyd.*

MALLWYD, Gwynedd
Mallwyd is set beside the Afon Dyfi
and is the haunt of both artists and
anglers. The rib of a prehistoric
animal handg over the church
porch.
*Turn right on to the A470 and reach
Dinas Mawddwy.*

DINAS MAWDDWY, Gwynedd
During the 16th century this very
Welsh village was at the centre of a
region notorious for its bandits.
Remains of old mines and quarries
dot the area, and one group of
quarry buildings now houses the
Meirion Woollen Mill (open). (An
alternative route to Bala over the
spectacular Bwlch-y-Groes Pass
starts from Dinas Mawddwy and is
described at the end of this tour.)

*Continue on the A470 and climb the
bleak 1,170ft Bwlch Oerddrws Pass.
Descend, with views of Cader Idris
mountain. Beyond the Cross Foxes
Hotel a detour may be taken right on
the B4416 to Brithdir.*

BRITHDIR, Gwynedd
The startling 19th-century church
here was built in memory of Charles
Tooth by his widow, and was
designed so that it appeared to
spring from the soil rather than sit
solidly on it. The interior is simple,
but glows with reflected light from
the beaten copper of the altar and
pulpit. On the approach to the
village is the beautiful Torrent Walk.

*Descend and branch left into
Dolgellau.*

DOLGELLAU, Gwynedd
Granite and boulder stone from the surrounding mountains are the principal materials from which Dolgellau is built. Its narrow, twisting streets are set in a fine position beside the Afon Wnion, and to the south green slopes rise to the craggy summits of Cader Idris. St Mary's

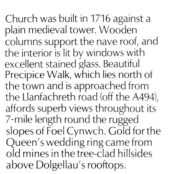

Church was built in 1716 against a plain medieval tower. Wooden columns support the nave roof, and the interior is lit by windows with excellent stained glass. Beautiful Precipice Walk, which lies north of the town and is approached from the Llanfachreth road (off the A494), affords superb views throughout its 7-mile length round the rugged slopes of Foel Cynwch. Gold for the Queen's wedding ring came from old mines in the tree-clad hillsides above Dolgellau's rooftops.

From Dolgellau follow signs 'Bala'. Cross the river then turn right. Later join the A494 and climb the wooded Wnion Valley. To the west is 2,409ft Rhobell Fawr.

RHOBELL FAWR, Gwynedd
Composed of solidified lavas from ancient volcanoes, this 2,409ft mountain is the highest point in the wedge of land between the Wnion and Mawddach Valleys. Fine views

afforded from its summit take in the Rhinog Mountains to the west and the Arans to the east.

COED-Y-BRENIN FOREST, Gwynedd
This Forestry Commission enterprise embraces all the woodlands around and to the north of Dolgellau. It covers an area of nearly 16,000 acres, and access to the woodland and its varied mountain scenery is provided by 100 miles of forest roads; the public is warned against the dangers of leaving litter and especially, carelessly discarded cigarette stubs.

Descend to Llanuwchllyn and the southern end of Bala Lake.

LLANUWCHLLYN, Gwynedd
A road-side memorial here commemorates two great champions of the Welsh language, Sir O M Edwards and his son Sir Ifan ab Owen Edwards. Sir Ifan founded the Welsh League of Youth in 1922. The nearby lakeside mansion of Glanllyn is used as a centre for the league's activities.

Near Brithdir is spectacular Torrent Walk, which follows the Afon Clywedog.

Dolgellau's narrow streets are divided by the Afon Wnion, which is spanned here by an ancient 7-arched bridge.

Bwlch-y-Groes, the Gap of the Cross, is the highest mountain pass in Wales.

BALA LAKE or LLYN TEGID, Gwynedd
Largest natural lake in Wales, Bala is over 4 miles long and in some places measures some 150ft in depth. It is surrounded by mountain scenery and is a popular venue for water-based sports. The narrow-gauge Bala Lake Railway runs along its south-eastern bank from Llanuwchllyn station to Bala, providing a mobile viewpoint from which to enjoy the superb waterside scenery. Originally the route was owned by British Rail, who closed it down in 1965 and sold it to the local council. The potential of the lake-side section was quickly recognised, and a number of steam locomotives were acquired to provide a tourist service.

Return to Bala.

ALTERNATIVE ROUTES
At the north-western end of Lake Vyrnwy are 2 mountain roads. One of these can be taken through the Hirnant Pass to Bala, and the other leads up Cwm Eunant to Bwlch-y-Groes. The latter is described under the Dinas Mawddwy alternative route, which follows later.

HIRNANT PASS, Gwynedd
This alternative route is well worth driving for its scenery. From Lake Vyrnwy it climbs steeply along the valley of the little Afon Nadroedd to a 1,641ft summit at the Hirnant Pass before descending along Cwm Hirnant through the Penllyn Forest to Bala.

From Dinas Mawddwy an alternative route may be taken back to Bala via Llanymawddwy and Bwlch-y-Groes. Leave Dinas Mawddwy by turning right on to an unclassified road and ascend the valley of the Afon Dyfi to Llanymawddwy.

LLANYMAWDDWY, Gwynedd
This remote and mountain-encircled hamlet has a tiny church with an attractive old bellcote.

Ascend a 1 in 4 road to Bwlch-y-Groes.

BWLCH-Y-GROES, Gwynedd
At 1,790ft this is the highest mountain pass in Wales. A road east descends to Lake Vyrnwy through Cwm Eunant, and the road to Bala follows the spectacular and precipitous Cynllwyd Valley.

THE ARANS, Gwynedd
To the west of Bwlch-y-Groes rise the twin peaks – 2,970ft Aran Fawddwy and 2,901ft Aran Benllyn – of the Aran range. Aran Fawddwy is the highest mountain in Wales outside the Snowdon range.

Descend along the Cynllwyd Valley to join the B4403 and drive along the south-eastern shores of Bala Lake to reach the B4391 and Bala.

At the traffic signals keep forward, then branch right, SP 'Sychnant'. Cross the beautiful Sychnant Pass and continue to Conwy.

BANGOR, Gwynedd

Bangor's cathedral is the oldest bishopric in Britain, founded in AD550 by St Deiniol. Bangor means a circular enclosure, or wattle fence, and probably referred to the fence around Deiniol's first church. The present cathedral was rebuilt between 1496 and 1532, after destruction in 1407 by Owain Glyndwr's troops, and its present appearance is due to total restoration by Gilbert Scott in 1866-7. Bangor was not much more than a village until the 19th century, when, during a space of 50 years, Penrhyn's quarries were opened, the docks were built, Telford's road and his suspension bridge were completed, and the railway was laid. The maze of streets and unremarkable architecture of Bangor is dignified by the presence of the University College of North Wales, designed in 1906 by Henry T. Hare. It is a fine English Rennaissance building, unspoilt by the modern extensions added since 1950. Lower Bangor dips down to the shores of the Menai Straits, where a Victorian pier stretches a third of the way to Anglesey. In the town centre, the museum of Welsh Antiquities, housed in the Old Canonry, has exhibits of prehistoric and Bronze-Age implements, Roman and early Christian finds, Welsh furniture and costumes.

Leave Bangor on the A5122, SP 'Conway (A55)', and in 2½ miles pass Penrhyn Castle.

PENRHYN CASTLE, Gwynedd

Penrhyn Castle (NT) is a Victorian extravaganza, financed in 1827 by G. H. Dawkins, the extremely wealthy owner of the Penrhyn slate quarries. The exterior is styled after Norman military architecture — a mass of great walls and crenellated towers built on a fanciful scale. The interior is spacious, lavishly decorated with a richness and complexity that is bewildering and overpowering. Penrhyn Castle was bought by the National Trust in 1951, who have since established a worldwide collection of some 800 dolls, a natural history room, and in the stable block an industrial locomotive museum.

At the roundabout turn left on to the A55 and continue to Aber.

ABER, Gwynedd

Lying just ½ mile from the sea, Aber was a starting point for the journey over the water to Anglesey before the Menai Bridge was built. This involved crossing the vast expanse of Lavan Sands at low tide, beneath which a drowned palace 1,000 years old is alleged to lie, and undergoing a dangerous ferry trip from Beaumaris. Nearby is Coedydd Nature Reserve, set in a beautiful glen, and the spectacular Aber Falls, a 170ft waterfall.

AROUND CARNEDDAU

Encircling the impenetrable bulk of wild Carneddau, the road travels to the mighty fortress at Conwy, meanders along the lush Conwy valley, then twists through the wooded ways of Betws-y-coed: a journey though wild passes, green valleys and coastal plains that sees Wales at her most varied.

Remain on the A55 to Llanfairfechan.

LLANFAIRFECHAN, Gwynedd

The little stream of Afon Llanfairfechan drops 2,000ft over a distance of 3 miles, passing through the old village in the lower and flatter part of its valley. The newer village lies a little to the north where there is a pleasant beach and promenade; good sailing can be had off this coast, and there are fine walks along it.

The tour follows the coast road alongside Conwy Bay to Penmaenmawr.

PENMAENMAWR, Gwynedd

Penmaenmawr has changed very little since it became popular with holidaymakers in the last century, encouraged by William Gladstone, Prime Minister, who made this his summer retreat. The resort offers safe bathing from a good beach backed by a promenade and the pleasant streets and Victorian terraces of the town itself. The headland of Penmaenmawr grows smaller every year, for its stone is continually used in roadbuilding, and quarrying has scarred and disfigured it. An important Iron-Age fort was destroyed in the process, but one of Wales' best-known Bronze-Age stone circles still survives. An urn was

Enchanting Betws-y-coed has attracted tourists since Victorian times when it was a haven for artists and honeymooners

discovered here containing the cremated remains of a child and a bronze dagger, suggesting a ritual sacrifice was performed to consecrate the site.

CONWY, Gwynedd

Three bridges cross the wide estuary of the Conwy on which the town stands; Telford's suspension bridge of 1826; Stephenson's tubular railway bridge; and a modern road bridge. Conwy is the most perfectly preserved of Edward I's walled towns and its castle (AM) is one of the great fortresses of Europe; begun in 1248, it was a key element in Edward I's control of Wales. The town itself began with the building of the castle, and is still largely contained by the medieval walls — 30 ft high with 21 towers built along its length. There are 3 other important survivals from Conwy's past. Plas Mawr (OACT) is a fascinating Elizabethan mansion, built between 1577 and 1580, with courtyards, stepped gables and an octagonal watch-tower, and is now the home of the Royal Cambrian Academy of Art. The Church of St Mary in the town centre incorporates parts of a Cistercian abbey and a worn gravestone to Nicholas Heotes, who died in 1637, 41st child of his father and father of 27 himself. On the corner of High Street and Castle Street is a building, c1500, which is claimed to be the oldest house in Wales, while on the quayside is a tiny house squeezed between 2 terraces, claimed to be the smallest house in Britain (OACT).

From the castle leave on the B5106, SP 'Betws-y-coed'. Continue along the west side of Conwy valley and pass through Tyn-y-groes, Tal-y-bont and Dolgarrog before reaching Trefriw.

Above: Conwy Castle, seen between Telford's bridge and Stephenson's bridge

Below: this 4-poster bed in Penrhyn Castle is made of slate and weighs 4 tons

TREFRIW, Gwynedd

Trefriw was briefly a spa town as the local wells lying a mile north of the village are rich in iron and sulphur. The pump rooms and baths were built in 1835 and by 1867 100 people were visiting the spa each day. Within the village itself is the largest woollen mill in Wales, where visitors can observe all the processes required to turn fleece into woollen products. Llanrhychryn Church, a refreshingly primitive building of ancient timbers, slate floors and whitewashed walls, lies hidden by trees from the village and can be reached by a short climb through woods.

In 1¾ miles turn right with the B5106, still SP 'Betws-y-coed', and pass Gwydir Castle.

GWYDIR CASTLE, Gwynedd

More a Tudor mansion than a castle, Gwydir (OACT) became the seat of the Wynn family around 1500. They altered and added to the original hall over the following 100 years, which resulted in the existing layout. In 1944 the house was bought by Arthur Clegg, who renovated the house which had been greatly damaged by a fire between the 2 world wars. Among the furniture with which Clegg refurnished the house is a magnificient bed, c1570, which bears carvings illustrating scenes from the Bible. Peacocks arrogantly strut around the grounds and there is an arch built to mark the end of the Wars of the Roses, and a 700-year-old yew tree. Nearby are the Gwydir Uchaf Chapel (AM) and house. The house is now used as a Forestry Commission office and exhibition, but the 17th-century chapel retains many of its contemporary features, and possesses a remarkable painted ceiling.

Continue along the valley to Betws-y-coed.

BETWS-Y-COED, Gwynedd

Three rivers meet in the wooded valley that holds Betws-y-coed and the village has 3 attractive bridges. Telford's graceful, iron Waterloo Bridge of 1815 spans the Conwy, and the beautifully-proportioned Ponty-y-Pair dating from about 1470 spans the Llugwy. Downstream, beside the church, is an iron suspension footbridge smartly painted white. Not surprisingly, the area is renowned for its beautiful waterfalls, the most famous being the Swallow Falls, the Conwy Falls and the Fairy Glen Ravine.

At Betws-y-coed join the A5, and follow the wooded valley of the Afon Llugwy. In 2 miles pass (right) the entrance to the Swallow Falls, then in ¼ mile pass (left) a picnic site and arboretum. After another ½ mile is Ty Hyll.

TY HYLL, Gwynedd

In the wooded Afon Llugwy valley, near the Swallow Falls, is the Ty Hyll — the Ugly House — built of massive irregular rocks, thrown together without any cement. This is supposedly an example of hurried construction in order to obtain freehold right on common land. It was used as an overnight stop by Irish drovers taking cattle from Holyhead to the rich markets of England.

Continue to Capel Curig.

CAPEL CURIG, Gwynedd

Capel Curig is a popular resort with climbers, hill walkers and anglers, and there are numerous hotels to accommodate them in this small but somewhat scattered village. Ringed by mountains, it is the natural home for the National Centre for Mountaineering Activities, housed in Plas Y Brenin, formerly the Royal Hotel built by Lord Penrhyn when Capel Curig was developed as a resort.

Remain on the A5 Bangor road, following the Afon Llugwy. Continue through the Nant Ffrancon Pass (NT) before reaching Bethesda.

BETHESDA, Gwynedd

Bethesda takes its name from the Noncomformist chapel which was established here. However, the village is primarily a quarryman's community, for nearby, gouged out of the steep slopes of Bron Llywyd, is the world's largest open-cast slate quarry. It is 1 mile long by 1,200ft deep, covering a total of 560 acres. Richard Pennant was the entrepreneur who created the quarry in 1765, building Port Penryn in 1790 specifically to serve the quarry. By 1875 the quarry employed 2,300 men, but competition from abroad and the increase in production of roofing tiles at the turn of the century caused a decline of the industry.

Continue on the A5 for the return to Bangor.

FROM MAWDDACH TO SNOWDONIA

The wooded mountains of Merioneth hide sparkling waterfalls, deserted gold mines and Iron-Age forts, but the highlight of this tour is undoubtedly the ancient castle at Harlech behind which rise the massive Rhinogs.

BARMOUTH, Gwynedd

Traditional seaside attractions characterise the popular resort of Barmouth with its long, wide promenade that sweeps up to the busy harbour at the estuary mouth and large, sandy beach. From the quayside a ferry plies to Penrhyn Point, linking with the Fairbourne Railway, a narrow-gauge steam line that runs down from the point for 2 miles along the beach to Fairbourne. Splendid views along the way make this a most rewarding outing. One of the most historic buildings in the quaint Victorian town is Ty Gwyn yn y bermo, on the quayside. This 15th-century house is supposed to have been built for Henry Tudor, Earl of Richmond, before he became Henry VII. However, probably the most dominating feature of the town is the wooden railway bridge spanning the estuary. This also carries a footpath, enabling visitors to enjoy the wonderful scenery along the estuary and to enjoy good views of tiny Friar's Island, just off the coast.

Leave Barmouth on the A496 Harlech road and continue for 1¾ miles to Llanaber.

LLANABER, Gwynedd

Perched on the clifftop, just north of Barmouth, is Llanaber's old church which was used rather irreverantly by smugglers in days gone by. Legends say they hid their booty inside the table tombs in the churchyard. The church itself is full of interesting features, such as some 10th-century inscribed stones in the north-west corner, and its doorway is one of the best examples of early English work to be seen anywhere in Britain.

Remain on the coast road and pass through Tal-y-bont to Dyffryn Ardudwy.

DYFFRYN ARDUDWY, Gwynedd

The hills and mountains around this scattered village are full of the remains of Bronze- and Iron-Age settlements. One of the best is Arthur's Quoit, a huge cromlech (prehistoric burial chamber) which can be seen in a field to the west of the village. The capstone is said to have been thrown by King Arthur from the summit of Moelfre (1,932ft), which lies 2 miles away.

Continue to Llanbedr.

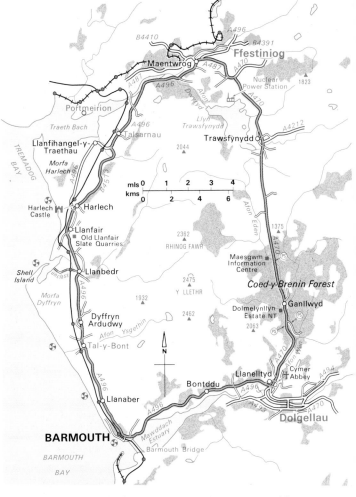

LLANBEDR, Gwynedd

Fascinating shells of all kinds are found in abundance on Mochras, or Shell Island, near Llanbedr, and well over 100 different varieties have been found. The 'island' is actually a peninsula which is cut off from the mainland at high tide — a paradise for children and equally popular with holidaymakers and yachtsmen. The village makes an excellent centre for walking in the area, particularly along the valleys of the Cwm Bychan and Nantcol which lead to the enchanting lakes of Cwm Bychan, Gloyw, Du and Bodlyn. Many of the paths follow the tracks made by miners who worked the local manganese deposits. The Cefn Isaf farm trail, starting near Salem Chapel, winds for 2 miles round a typical Welsh hill farm, the workings of which are fully explained along the way.

Follow the A496, and pass (right) the Old Llanfair Quarry Slate Caverns.

The seaside resort of Barmouth stands at the mouth of the tidal Mawddach estuary, which at low tide reveals acres of golden sands that provide a common feeding ground for many species of birds

Harlech Castle cost nearly £9,000 to build in 1290, an astronomical sum in its time. The builder was Master James of St George, Edward 1's chief architect

OLD LLANFAIR QUARRY SLATE CAVERNS, Gwynedd

Slate mining was an important industry in several areas of North Wales a century ago, and it is possible to recapture something of the grim conditions which prevailed then by visiting the Old Quarry Slate Caverns (OACT). The tunnels and caves which were created by the blasting of the hillsides are now specially illuminated and make a fascinating tour.

In 1¼ miles branch right on to the B4573 for Harlech.

HARLECH, Gwynedd

The name Harlech means 'high rock', an apt description of this small town clinging to the cliffside and overlooked by the majestic 13th-century castle (AM). Edward I built the fortress in 1283 with the purpose of controlling the newly-subjugated Welsh people. Its lofty position, which at that time was right by the sea, guaranteed the castle's impregnability and it successfully resisted rebel attacks for 120 years. The military life of the castle ended during the Civil War when the Royalists who lived there finally surrendered to the Roundhead forces in 1647. The best way to see the layout of the castle is to walk along the walls. Its plan consists of 2 rings of walls and bastions, with the inner wall considerably higher than the outer, a pattern derived from one of the strongest Crusader castles. The nature reserve of Morfa Harlech lies to the north of the town, covering a large plain which was reclaimed from the sea in 1908.

Continue along the B4573 and in 3¼ miles rejoin the A496, SP 'Maentwrog'. (The A496 to the left leads to Llanfihangel-y-traethau).

LLANFIHANGEL-Y-TRAETHAU, Gwynedd

Before the land around it was reclaimed, the old church here was isolated on an island. An inscribed stone pillar stands in the churchyard and inside there is a 17th-century stone inscribed in both Latin and Welsh. On the far side of the Traeth Bach Estuary can be seen the fairytale village of Portmeirion, created by Clough Williams-Ellis in 1926, in the style of the Italian resort, Sorrento.

The main tour passes through Talsarnau then follows the south bank of the Afon Dwyryd to enter the Vale of Ffestiniog at Maentwrog.

MAENTWROG, Gwynedd

This village is reputed to be one of the prettiest in Wales. Most of it was built in the heyday of the local slate industry at Blaenau Ffestiniog, and small quays by the river downstream from here were loading points for the slates. The church of St Twrog was largely rebuilt in 1896, but it is said to date from c 610, possibly because Twrog, a 7th-century giant, is said to have hurled a stone from the hillside into the churchyard, where it still lies buried beneath the turf.

Beyond the village turn right on to the A487. Ascend and continue to Trawsfynydd.

TRAWSFYNYDD, Gwynedd

The huge bulk of Britain's first inland nuclear power station dominates the countryside around Trawsfynydd. Llyn Trawsfynydd is a man-made reservoir and provides all the cooling-water needed by the power station, which can sometimes be visited by arrangement; the parkland around incorporates some nature trails and excellent fishing is available in the lake. The village of Trawsfynydd lies just off the main road where there is the house of a remarkable poet, Hedd Wyn. He was a local shepherd boy who

won the poetry competition in the National Eisteddfod in 1917, but was killed in action on the Somme, in France, before he could collect the award. A bronze statue of him, dressed in gaiters and shirtsleeves, stands in the village main street where it was unveiled in 1923.

Continue southwards on the A470 across a stretch of bleak moorland, then after 4 miles enter the Coed-y-brenin Forest.

COED-Y-BRENIN FOREST, Gwynedd

To either side of the road south of Trawstynydd lies the huge forest of Coed-y-brenin. Its name means King's Forest and it is the fourth largest in Wales, covering an area of more than 16,000 acres. In 1922 the first Douglas fir was planted and this is still the predominant species in the forest, although there are also quantities of larch, spruce and pine. The scenery within the forest is superb, surrounded by a ring of mountains taking in the Rhinogs in the west and Rhobell Fawr in the east. The sparkling river Mawddach and its tributaries flow through the area, breaking out into a series of tumbling waterfalls. An excellent information centre is sited at Maesgwm and this shows what part the forest plays within the local community, what products come from it, the wildlife which inhabits the area and has descriptions of the various facilities available. Planned forest trials start from the picnic sites at Dolgyfeiliau and Tyn-y-groes. This part of Wales used to support a large number of gold mines, and an exhibition of mining machinery can be seen at this information centre.

Near the south end of the forest is the hamlet of Ganllwyd.

GANLLWYD, Gwynedd

The centre of gold mining in the old county of Merioneth used to

be at Ganllwyd and the most prosperous mine, at Gwynfynydd, was the scene of a mini-gold rush in the 1880s, when 250 men worked here. It finally closed in 1917 after producing 40,000 ounces of gold. The Dolmelynllyn Estate (NT) at Gallwyd embraces the superb falls, Rhaiadr-Du, or Black Waterfall. Many rare species of ferns and moss grow in the moist soil around the waterfalls in this nature reserve.

Continue to the outskirts of Llanelltyd.

LLANELLTYD, Gwynedd

Cottages surround the ancient church dedicated to Illtud, a famous Welsh saint of the 6th century. A medieval stone in the church is inscribed in Latin which says that Kenyric's footprint was impressed on it before he set out for foreign parts. Ruins of Cymer Abbey (AM) stand beside the river nearby in a beautiful stretch of the Mawddach valley. The abbey was established by Cistercian monks in the 12th century but was abandoned in about 1350. As well as parts of the south wall of the church there are also the ruins of the refectory and the chapter house.

From Llanelltyd follow the A496 along the Mawddach estuary to Bontddu.

BONTDDU, Gwynedd

Nowadays it is a pleasant holiday village, but about 100 years ago Bontddu was one of the thriving centres of the Welsh gold-mining industry. There were 24 mines in the Merioneth Hills behind the village, and the Clogau mine provided gold for the use of the Royal Family. Nothing now remains of the mine workings, although occasionally fragments of gold may still be found in this area.

The A496 continues beside the estuary for the return to Barmouth.

AMONG THE BEACONS

High moorland that sweeps north from the industrial valleys of South Wales culminates in the sandstone peaks of the Brecon Beacons. Huge reservoirs built to satisfy industry lie to the south, and the crumbling towers of castles rise above the woodlands of the Usk Valley.

Snow and ice add a new dimension of beauty to Llangorse Lake, a place more generally associated with the pastimes of summer.

BRECON, Powys

Streets lined with Georgian and Jacobean houses add much to the beauty and character of Brecon, a mid-Wales town that was raised to the status of cathedral city in 1923. It is an ideal centre from which to explore the Brecon Beacons National Park. The cathedral is situated on the northern outskirts and was originally the church of a Benedictine priory. Dating mainly from the 13th and 14th centuries, the building is cruciform in plan and displays a number of outstanding architectural features. Several priory buildings, including a fine tithe barn, have been restored. A charming walk extends along the banks of the Afon Honddu beyond the cathedral. Remains of Brecon Castle have been incorporated into the Castle Hotel, and parts of the medieval town walls can be seen at Captain's Walk, an area named after French prisoners who exercised there during the Napoleonic wars. St Mary's Church is a greatly restored medieval building in the city centre. The fascinating Brecknock County Museum stands in Glamorgan Street, and the regimental museum of the South Wales Borderers is sited on The Watton. Across the 16th-century bridge which spans the River Usk is Christ College, which was originally built as a Benedictine friary. Restored in the 19th century, it is now a public school.

Crickhowell's beautiful 17th-century bridge is framed by an encircling ring of peaks, including the flat summit of aptly named Table Mountain.

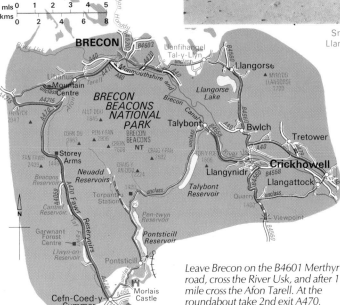

BRECON BEACONS NATIONAL PARK, Powys

From the Black Mountain in the west to the Black Mountains in the east are the 519 square miles of mountain, moor, and pastoral countryside that make up this valuable conservation area. Much of the underlying rock here is Old Red Sandstone, but to the west and south the landscape is built on younger limestones and grits.

Leave Brecon on the B4601 Merthyr road, cross the River Usk, and after 1 mile cross the Afon Tarell. At the roundabout take 2nd exit A470. Proceed to Libanus and there turn right on to an unclassified road SP 'Mountain Centre'. Ascend to moorland and reach the Mountain Centre.

MOUNTAIN CENTRE, Powys

Magnificent views can be enjoyed from the centre, which functions as a meeting place, refreshment room, lecture theatre and comprehensive information office.

Continue and in ½ mile at a T-junction turn left. After 1¾ miles meet crossroads and turn left on to

the A4215 (no SP), then in ¾ mile keep left. Descend to the Tarell Valley and turn right on to the A470 'Merthyr'. Follow a long, easy ascent to a road summit on 1,440ft and the Storey Arms.

STOREY ARMS, Powys

The outdoor pursuits centre here is one of the most convenient points from which to explore the national park's mountain and moorland scenery. To the south-west is 2,409ft Fan Fawr, the highest point of Fforest Fawr, while inside the tour route to the east are the peaks of the Brecon Beacons themselves (NT).

THE BRECON BEACONS, Powys

When seen from a distance the Beacons (NT) present the extraordinary appearance of long, grass-covered swells that break at their apex like frozen waves and fall away to the north in stunning precipices. The highest point is 2,907ft Pen-y-fan, which affords views to the Bristol Channel.

Continue to the Fawr Reservoirs.

THE FAWR RESERVOIRS, Powys

Strung out along the west side of the A470 and fed by the Taf Fawr river are the three Fawr reservoirs — namely Beacons, Cantref, and Llwyn-on. They were constructed during a period between 1892 and 1927 to supply Cardiff with water. Above the Llwyn-on Reservoir is the Garwnant Forest Centre.

Continue past the reservoirs and reach Cefn-coed-y-cymmer.

CEFN-COED-Y-CYMMER, M Glam

The great Cyfarthfa Ironworks were founded here in 1766 by the Crawshay family and Watkin George, one of the foremost of the early ironmasters. Also here is a fine 19th-century railway viaduct.

To visit Cyfarthfa Castle continue on the A470 for 1¼ miles.

CYFARTHFA CASTLE, M Glam

Built in 1825 for 'Iron King' William Crawshay, this rather extravagant latterday castle now houses a museum and art gallery.

From Cefn-coed-y-cymmer turn left on to the unclassified 'Pontsticill and Talybont' road. In 1½ miles at the Aberglais PH turn left. A detour can be made to Morlais Castle by turning right here.

MORLAIS CASTLE, M Glam

Splendidly situated on a 1,200ft hill which affords excellent views of the Brecon Beacons, Morlais Castle (open) was a borderland stronghold built and defended by Gilbert de Clare.

On the main route, continue through Pontsticill and at the end of the village keep left to follow the shores of Pontsticill Reservoir.

PONTSTICILL RESERVOIR, Powys

Excellent views can be enjoyed from a viewpoint at the south end of this extensive reservoir, which was constructed at the beginning of this century as part of a system designed to supply nearby coalfields. Nearby is the present northern terminus of the narrow-gauge Brecon Mountain railway.

Continue for 2¾ miles and turn right. A detour ahead leads to the Neuadd Reservoirs.

The ruined keep of Tretower Castle saw action in the strife that bedevilled Wales during the middle ages.

NEUADD RESERVOIRS, Powys

The two Neuadd Reservoirs form part of the large Taf Fechan system and are beautifully set in the heart of the Brecon Beacons.

On the main tour route, continue across a river and shortly pass a picnic site on the right. Ascend to reach a 1,400ft road summit offering views of Craig-y-fan-ddu and Craig-y-fan. Descend through woodland to the Talybont Valley and the Talybont Reservoir.

TALYBONT RESERVOIR, Powys

Large numbers of waterfowl and other aquatic wildlife may be seen on this 2-mile long reservoir, which supplies Newport with water.

Continue for 1¼ miles beyond the reservoir and turn right (no SP) for Talybont village.

Panoramic views of the magnificent Brecon Beacon mountains are opened up on the roads which follow the Usk Valley between Llangattock and the cathedral city of Brecon.

TALYBONT & THE MONMOUTHSHIRE AND BRECON CANAL, Powys

Winding serenely from Brecon to Pontypool, the Monmouthshire and Brecon Canal offers a leisurely route from which to enjoy the scenery of the Usk Valley. It was built between 1799 and 1812, principally to supply the iron mines of old Monmouthshire (now Gwent), and was originally planned to stretch from Pontypool to Abergavenny. Within months of its commencement the decision was made to extend it to Brecon. Talybont has a modern bridge crossing the canal and makes an ideal centre from which to walk the towpaths and explore the surrounding countryside. East of Talybont the canal passes through the 375-yard Ashford Tunnel.

Cross the canal bridge at Talybont and turn right on to the B4558. Beyond the village keep forward SP 'Crickhowell'. Drive along the wooded Usk Valley to reach Llangynidr.

LLANGYNIDR, Powys

A fine old bridge of c1600 spans the Usk at Llangynidr, and five of the Monmouthshire and Brecon Canal's six locks are in this village.

Drive 1 mile beyond the canal bridge at Llangynidr and turn right on to the B4560 'Beaufort' road. Climb through sharp bends to 1,460ft for magnificent views. Continue past a quarry and turn left on to an unclassified road SP 'Llangattock'. (For a detour to 1,694ft with superb views continue the ascent on the B4560 for another 1 mile.) Continue on the main route and descend to Llangattock.

LLANGATTOCK, Powys

St Catwg's Church, on the edge of the village, carries a massive 15th-century tower and contains some interesting memorials. Old limestone quarries exist south on the slopes of Mynydd Llangattock, where there is also a National Nature Reserve.

Turn left into Llangattock then keep forward to the end and turn left on to the A4077. Turn right to cross the Usk into Crickhowell.

CRICKHOWELL, Powys

A magnificent 13-arched bridge dating from the 17th century spans the River Usk at Crickhowell. All that remains of the local castle is a mound and some battered-looking masonry, but there are some attractive houses in the town and the church has a pleasing 19th-century broach spire. Sir George Everest, who gave his name to the Himalayan mountain, was born here in 1790.

Leave Crickhowell on the A40 'Brecon' road. After 1¾ miles the A479 to the right leads to Tretower and its castle.

TRETOWER, Powys

A sturdy keep surrounded by a many-sided stone wall comprises the remains of Tretower Castle (AM), which was usurped as a habitation in the 14th century by nearby Tretower Court (AM). The latter is considered a very fine example of a fortified mansion and was the home of the Vaughan family for three centuries.

Continue on the A40 to Bwlch.

BWLCH, Powys

Fine views of the Usk Valley and the surrounding mountains are afforded from the road as it approaches this little hamlet. The name 'Bwlch' means 'The Pass'.

Drive beyond the war memorial and turn right on to the B4560 'Llangorse' road. Continue to Llangorse.

LLANGORSE, Powys

Restoration and so-called improvement during the 19th century destroyed much of the character of the little local church, but its 15th-century wagon roof has survived. An ancient inscribed stone has been preserved here.

Continue to the end of the village and turn left on to an unclassified road SP 'Brecon'. Shortly pass a road leading to the lovely expanse of Llangorse Lake.

LLANGORSE LAKE, Powys

This, the largest natural lake in South Wales, is a haven for many kinds of flora and fauna. It is also a centre for many water-based leisure activities, including fishing and boating.

On the main route, continue and in 1½ miles turn left into Llanfihangel Tal-y-Llyn. Keep forward and after 2½ miles turn left. Go under the road bridge then turn right to join the A40. In ¾ mile at roundabout take 2nd exit B4601 to re-enter Brecon.

The graceful 15-arched viaduct at Cefn-coed-y-cymmer was built in 1866 to carry the Brecon and Merthyr Railway. Today it stands as an impressive example of 19th-century invention and engineering skill.

THE BRECON BEACONS AND MYNYDD EPPYNT

Steep hills sweep down to verdant valleys where farmsteads are scattered over the wooded slopes and small towns occupy strategic crossing points on the swift-flowing rivers. North of the Brecon Beacons rises the harsh moorland plateau of the Mynydd Eppynt, an island of high ground bordered on all sides by rivers.

BRECON, Powys
Encircled by hills, the old county town of Brecknockshire lies at the meeting point of 2 rivers, the Usk and the Honddu. The narrow streets and elegant town houses are imbued with the atmosphere of the 18th and 19th centuries. At an inn in the High Street, the celebrated actress, Sarah Siddons (née Kemble) was born in 1755. Captain's Walk owes its name to the period of the Napoleonic Wars when it was a favourite place of exercise for captured French officers imprisoned here. The church of St John, raised to cathedral status in 1923, was originally the church of a Benedictine priory founded in 1091. Most of the present building, however, belongs to the 13th and 14th centuries. The aisles were formerly filled with craft-guild chapels, of which only one, that of the corvizors (shoemakers).

remains. The Brecknock Museum contains an outstanding collection of local history and the barracks of the South Wales Borderers houses their Regimental Museum here.

From Brecon town centre follow SP, 'Upper Chapel B4520', and in ¼ mile turn left on to the B4520. Continue along the Honddu valley and later pass Lower Chapel at the southern edge of Mynydd Eppynt hills.

MYNYDD EPPYNT HILLS, Powys
Access to the high moorland summits of the Mynydd Eppynt hills is restricted because of an army firing range, but some roads and tracks do cross this exhilarating expanse of wild, bleak countryside. In the north the high sandstone scarps look down over Builth Wells; in the west, the dense woods of the Crychan Forest sweep down to the valley

of the River Bran, and in the south, the hillsides are studded with small farms interspersed with scattered trees.

½ mile beyond Upper Chapel keep forward on the steep (1 in 6) Builth Wells road. Later reach a summit of 1,370ft before a long descent into Builth Wells.

BUILTH WELLS, Powys
The mound of the 13th-century castle of Builth is all that is left, and from this period dates a shameful episode in the town's history, which earned the inhabitants the nick-name 'the traitors of Builth.' In 1282 a prince of Wales, Llewellyn the Last, hunted by the English, asked for shelter from the townspeople. They refused and he was later killed near Cilmeri. Builth today owes much of its character to the medicinal springs that made the town fashionable in the 18th century when it was a spa town. Its earliest buildings date from this period, as the town was totally destroyed by a fire in 1691 and money was sent from all parts of Britain to help the reconstruction. The River Wye, spanned by a graceful 6-arched bridge, and the River Irfon meet at Builth, and a little further up the Irfon valley is a delightful brook called the Nant-yr-arian, meaning the 'brook of silver'. In times of plague farmers brought produce to the brook and the townspeople threw coins into the water as payment.

Turn left on to the A483 and shortly cross the River Irfon by the Iron Bridge. Continue to Garth.

GARTH, Powys
Magnesium springs led to the establishment of a small pump room at Garth, but the village was never able to compete with its neighbours Builth, Llangammarch and Llanwrtyd Wells.

At the end of the village turn left for Llangammarch Wells.

LLANGAMMARCH WELLS, Powys
The smallest of the Welsh spas, Llangammarch was renowned for its success with heart complaints. Its springs were not sulphurous like those of many spas, but rich in barium chloride. For such a little village the unusually well-appointed hotel had its own lake, golf-course, tennis and shooting facilities. Just outside the village at Llwyn Einon, a charming triple-gabled house (not open), lived Theophilus Jones, whose classic history of Brecknockshire was published in the early part of the 19th century. He is buried in the churchyard.

By the church at the edge of the village turn right on to the Llanwrtyd Wells road and cross the Afon Cammarch. In 1 mile turn left.

The Brecon Beacons, seen from Llanhamdach
Inset: cattle market day at Llandovery

can make vacationers long for the city.

One exception is the Beekman Arms Hotel in Rhine beck, which dates to 1766 and holds claim to being the oldest continuously operated hostelry in the United States. Rhinebeck, midway between Manhattan and Albany, is a historic river town known for its architecture, antiques and a vintage airplane museum.

The hotel's restaurant, called The Beekman 1766 Tavern, is an enchanting spot, with a stone hearth in the lobby and a wood-paneled, low-ceilinged tavern with a long wooden bar and simple wooden tables. A nook off the side, called the Wine Cellar, has six high-backed wooden booths, while a glass-enclosed front porch faces the center of town.

Until about two-and-a-half years ago The Beekman Arms served nondescript tourist rations. Then the restaurant was taken over by Larry Forgione, the owner of An American Place in Manhattan, and things turned around dramatically — yet prices remained modest. Mr Forgione, and his talented resident chef, Melissa Kelly, have introduced some classic American winners like Yankee pot roast with mashed potatoes and root vegetables, pot pies (one of venison with a peppered cranberry crust; another of smoked turkey and vegetables), as well as regional dishes like planked salmon.

For more contemporary fare, try the napoleon appetizer, constructed of lightly smoked salmon, lemon cream drizzled with chive oil and homemade potato chips. Food like this is the biggest thing to hit Rhinebeck since George Washington considered (but changed his mind) sleeping over in town (but decided against it).

Desserts worth sampling include the irresistible chocolate pudding, the Hudson Valley apple crisp with vanilla ice cream, and, in season, the towering strawberry shortcake. A three-course dinner at The Beekman 1766 Tavern runs about $40 per person with a glass of wine and tax, but not tip.

The Beekman 1766 Tavern, 4 Mill Street, Rhinebeck

BRECON BEACONS

ho... ...ith rambles along the ban... the lovely River Irfon or more energetic walks in the surrounding hills.

Turn left on to the A483. There is a gradual climb through the edge of the Crychan Forest to a 950ft summit below the easily-climbed Sugar Loaf (1,000ft) which stands at the head of the Bran valley and can be seen on the descent to Llandovery.

LLANDOVERY, Dyfed
Llanymddyfri, 'the church amid the waters', aptly describes the delightful little town with its picturesque ruined castle on a mound overlooking the River

The Tywi valley near Llandovery

..., the market centre of the Upper Tywi valley. Pleasant Georgian and Victorian buildings are interspersed with a remarkable number of public houses, and historians will point out that in the days of Richard III the town charter gave Llandovery the sole right of keeping taverns in the area. The present bank stands on the site of the famous Bank of the Black Ox, founded in 1799 by cattle-drover David Jones when the town was the centre of the cattle trade and herds of black cattle passed through on their way to the English markets. Llandovery has 2 churches, both on the outskirts. The parish church is much restored but St Mary's-on-the-hill (Llanfair-ar-y-bryn) retains an atmosphere of great antiquity with its fine tie-beam roof and barrel-vaulted chancel.

In the town an unclassified road on the right, SP 'Rhandirmwyn', follows the Tywi valley for 11½ miles to the Llyn Brianne Reservoir and Dam. From the viewing point, a narrow road with passing places leads high above the shores for 7 miles into the Tywi Forest. On the way, another detour may be made to Cilycwm, SP to the left across the Tywi valley, 3 miles from Llandovery.

TYWI VALLEY, Dyfed
Hemmed in on either side by steep wooded hills, the River Tywi flows through one of the most beautiful of South Wales' valleys. Near Llandovery, the famous Dolauhirion bridge spans the river, a graceful single-arched stone structure built in 1773 by the self-taught builder William Edwards. Llyn Brianne reservoir was formed in 1972 by drowing part of the valley. Nearly 3 square miles of water are confined by a dam some 250ft high.

CILYCWM, Dyfed
On the west side of the Tywi valley nestles the village of Cilycwm, its little streets bright with white and colour-washed old cottages and its 15th-century church framed by ancient yew trees; inside the church are medieval frescoes and old box pews. The Methodist chapel is believed to be the first meeting house ever established in Wales.

Follow SP 'Brecon A40' from Llandovery, shortly joining the deep, wooded valley of the Afon Gwydderig. There is a long, gradual climb passing, after 2½ miles, the Mail Monument set in a lay-by on the right.

THE MAIL MONUMENT, Dyfed
This simple stone obelisk is a reminder that drunkenness was sometimes a hazard of travelling even before the invention of the motor car, for here a coach and its passengers were driven off the road by an intoxicated driver and all were killed.

The tour continues up the Gwydderig valley past Halfway and the south-western corner of the Mynydd Eppynt to reach Trecastle on the upper reaches of the Usk valley. Continue to Sennybridge.

SENNYBRIDGE, Powys
Situated at the confluence of the Rivers Usk and Senni, Sennybridge was mainly developed in the 19th century when the large sheep and cattle market was transferred here from Defynnog after the turnpike road was opened. Sennybridge sheep sales became a major event in the area. They were started by Scottish farmers who bought large sections of sheep grazing in Fforest Fawr when it was sold in 1815, having been Crown property since the Middle Ages.

Beyond the village turn right on to the A4067 and shortly reach Defynnog. Here bear left on to the A4215, continuing along the Senni valley with views ahead of Fan Frynych (2,047ft). After 2¼ miles turn left, SP 'Mountain Centre', on to a narrow road which crosses the 1,100ft Mynydd Illtyd. To the right are excellent views of the Brecon Beacons, and to the right of the road is the Brecon Beacon Mountain Centre.

BRECON BEACONS, Powys
More than 500 square miles of wild mountainous country, stretching from the Black Mountains in the west to the Black Mountains in the east, were designated in 1957 as the Brecon Beacons National Park. From the highest of the red sandstone peaks, Pen-y-fan (2,906ft) and Corn-Du (2,863ft) there are wonderful views northwards over the bleak plateau of Mynydd Eppynt and westwards to the rugged grandeur of the Black Mountains. The Beacons are so called because in the days before telecommunications, they formed part of a chain of prominent hilltops on which beacon fires were lit to give warning of important events.

Gradually descend, with views of the Black Mountains ahead, and on reaching the roundabout take the B4601 for the return to Brecon town centre.

SNOWDON AND THE SEA

The name Gwynedd lives again as a modern county.
Gwynedd the fortress, the strong land dominated by the great
star of Snowdon and moated by the Menai Strait, has never
died. It is still as majestically severe as it was
under the Celtic princes.

CAERNARFON, Gwynedd

Workaday Caernarfon is a
comfortable small town which has
become the most important tourist
centre in Snowdonia. Above its
jumbled roofs rise the massive
towers of Edward I's 13th-century
castle (AM), acknowledged as the
finest of its type in Britain, while
nearby is the old walled town and,
in the harbour area, a maritime
museum. East of the town centre is
the Roman fort of Segontium, with
its own museum. Although host to
thousands, the town preserves a
parochial 'Welshness' that is implicit
in the gesticulating statue of Lloyd
George opposite the castle balcony
from which newly invested Princes
of Wales greet their subjects. The
sheltered waters of the Menai Strait
abound with small craft from the
town's sailing clubs, and offer some
of the finest fishing in Britain.

*Leave Caernarfon on the A487 SP
'Bangor', and drive alongside the
Menai Strait to port Dinorwic.*

PORT DINORWIC, Gwynedd

Once a busy port concerned with
the export of Dinorwic slate, it is
now a well-known yachting centre
with a large marina.

*Continue and in 1½ miles at a
roundabout take 1st exit SP
'Holyhead'. In ¾ mile at another
roundabout take 1st exit to join the
A5. Cross the Britannia Bridge into
Anglesey and immediately branch left
then turn right A4080 to reach Menai
Bridge town. Here follow signs
Bangor and cross Telford's suspension
bridge then at roundabout take 1st
exit A5122 to enter Bangor.*

BANGOR, Gwynedd

Old Bangor is a delightfully
undistinguished maze in which the
Cathedral of St Deiniol (claimed to
be the oldest bishopric in Britain)
crouches with unassuming
modesty. The handsome buildings
of the University College of North
Wales were officially opened in
1911. There is a town museum and
art gallery. On the seaward side
Bangor's streets dip down to the city
shore and a superb pier.

*Leave Bangor on the A5122 'Betws-y-
coed' road and continue to the
entrance of Penrhyn Castle Estate.*

PENRHYN CASTLE, Gwynedd

Although the site of Penrhyn Castle
(NT) can lay claim to antiquity, the
improbable extravaganza that rears
its battlements above the park's

Caernarfon Castle, one of a series built to subjugate the Welsh, is arguably the finest
example of medieval fortification in Britain.

wooded acres has its roots set firmly
in 19th-century gothic fantasy. Parts
of the edifice bear more than an
accidental likeness to other great
houses, and the combinations of
revived styles favoured by architect
Thomas Hopper are bewildering but
effective. Inside are interesting
exhibits, displays, and impressive
chambers open to the public.

*In ¾ mile at roundabout take 2nd exit
A5 and almost immediately turn right
on to the B4409 'SP Caernarfon'. In
3½ miles at a roundabout turn left on
to the B4547 SP 'Llanberis'. After 2
miles turn right and descend to a T-
junction with the A4086. A detour
can be taken from here by turning
right on the A4086 to the edge of
Llanrug, then left on to an unclassified
road for Bryn Bras Castle.*

BRYN BRAS CASTLE, Gwynedd

Bryn Bras Castle (open) is a piece of
19th-century romanticism which
presides over Llanrug village. It
stands in grounds noted for their
peaceful lawns and embowered
walks through tranquil mature
woodland.

*The main drive turns left on to the
A4086 to skirt the shore of Llyn
Padarn.*

LLYN PADARN, Gwynedd

Once part of a much larger water,
Llyn Padarn is separated from its
sister lake Peris by a natural dam
formed by the gradual accumulation
of material washed down in a
mountain stream. Its north-eastern
shore carries the narrow-gauge line
of the steam-powered Llanberis
Lake Railway, whose predecessor
transported slate from the Dinorwic
slate quarries to Port Dinorwic.
There is also a country park.

Shortly branch right into Llanberis.

LLANBERIS, Gwynedd

Terraced houses built on sites
blasted from the rock huddle
together to form Llanberis, a typical
village of the slate-working
communities of North Wales. A
route which ascends to the main
summit of Snowdon from here is
considered the easiest of the
mountain's 3 main paths. Close to
the village is the lower terminus of
the Snowdon Mountain Railway.
Also here is the Oriel Eryn Welsh
Environment Interpretation Centre,
and across the valley at Gilfach Ddu
is the Welsh Slate Museum housed
in the works buildings of the former
Dinorwic Quarry. This is also the
starting point of the Llanberis Lake
Railway.

SNOWDON MOUNTAIN RAILWAY, Gwynedd

Unlike its close neighbour, the
Llanberis Lake Railway, Snowdon's
hard-working little rack-and-pinion
steam line was created as a tourist
aid and owes nothing to heavy
industry. It was an enormous success
during the 19th-century tourist
boom, and still carries a huge
number of armchair mountaineers.
About ½ mile or so from the lower
terminus is Ceunant Mawr, one of
the finest waterfalls in North Wales,
and by the second viaduct the River
Arddu twists in a 120 ft fall from the
lip of a spectacular gorge.

*Continue along the A4086. Pass
Dolbadarn Castle and skirt Llyn Peris.*

DOLBADARN CASTLE, Gwynedd

The 13th-century castle represented
by these gaunt, strangely attractive
ruins (AM) was a stronghold of the
Welsh princes and has nothing to do
with Anglo-Norman design. Its task
was to guard the entrance of
brooding Llanberis Pass; its bloody
history testifies to the single-
mindedness with which its native
garrisons fulfilled this rôle.

LLYN PERIS, Gwynedd

Smaller and narrower than Padarn,
Llyn Peris is a secretive place entirely
dominated by the moonscape
devastation of the enormous
Dinorwic slate workings.

Llyn Padarn is one of many jewel-like
lakes which encircle Snowdon.

The Great Hall at Penrhyn Castle displays the mixture of styles favoured by romantic Victorian architects.

Radiating from the main peak of Snowdon are the knife-edged ridges of Crib Goch and Y Lliwedd.

This view from Snowdon's summit encompasses the lesser peak of Yr Aran and distant Moel Hebog.

Since it was opened in 1896 the Snowdon Mountain Railway has carried millions of passengers to the mountain's summit.

DINORWIC SLATE QUARRY, Gwynedd
The vast disused Dinorwic slate quarry rises terrace upon grey terrace from the shore of gentle Llyn Peris, a large monument to the scale of disruption caused by man in the search for materials. The effects of slate extraction might be considered appalling, but workings such as these provided much-needed employmemt.

Continue past Nant Peris and ascend to the summit of Llanberis Pass.

LLANBERIS PASS, Gwynedd
Snowdonia's great mountain masses tower above this narrow pass. To the north are the Glyders, whose highest point is 3,279ft Glyder Fawr, and to the south is the Snowdon massif, crowned by 3,560ft Yr Wyddfa.

PEN-Y-PASS, Gwynedd
Situated at the 1,169ft summit of the Llanberis Pass, this is the starting point of the Miner's Track nature trail and path to Snowdon.

SNOWDON, Gwynedd
Snowdonia National Park covers some 845 square miles and comprises large tracts of mountain and moor divided by deep valleys. Within this area is the star-like Snowdon range, with Snowdon itself culminating in the peak of Yr Wyddfa

– the highest land south of the Scottish border. Radiating from the main peak are the knife-edged summits of Crib Goch and Y Lliwedd, which encircle lakes Glaslyn and Llydaw. Although all the paths to Snowdon are well trodden, no walker should set out without being properly dressed and equipped as sudden changes in the weather can prove fatal, even to the experienced.

Descend to the Pen-y-Gwryd Hotel situated at the head of the Gwryd Valley, and at the T-junction turn right on to the A498, SP 'Beddgelert'. Continue to the viewpoint above Llyn Gwynant.

LLYN GWYNANT AND NANT GWYNANT, Gwynedd
From the viewpoint Llyn Gwynant appears as a jewel surrounded by the tree-covered flanks of mountains, with the craggy, waterfall-threaded slopes of 2,032ft Gallt-y-Wenallt on the north side. Nant Gwynant, which connects lakes Gwynant and Dinas, is often described as the finest mountain valley in Snowdonia. From its northern side the Watkin Path winds up a wooded valley on to open mountainside to reach the summit of Snowdon.

Continue along the valley and reach Llyn Dinas.

LLYN DINAS, Gwynedd
Beautiful Llyn Dinas derives its name from the ancient fort of Dinas Emrys, which stands near the lake's west end, and is traditionally associated with Merlin the magician. Legend has it that the true throne of Britain is hidden in the waters of the lake, and will one day be revealed by a youth treading on a certain stone. Rising to the north-west is 2,451ft Yr Aran, which is a superb pinnacle from which to appreciate the majesty of the Snowdon range.

Skirt the shores of Llyn Dinas and continue to Beddgelert.

BEDDGELERT, Gwynedd
Alpine-style Beddgelert is completely surrounded by mountains and echoes their permanence in the solid stone of its architecture. Its name (Gelert's Grave) refers to the legend that Welsh hero Llywelyn the Great killed his dog Gelert because he thought that it had savaged his son. In fact the dog had just saved the baby boy from wolves. Historians have thoroughly debunked this story, which has since been laid at the door of an inventive local innkeeper, but its telling rarely leaves a dry eye in the schools of North Wales. Moel Hebog–'The Mountain of the

Hawk'–dominates the landscape to the south-west of Beddgelert.

Keep forward on the A4085 'Caernarfon' road and reach Beddgelert Forest and picnic site.

BEDDGELERT FOREST, Gwynedd
Attractive trails laid out by the Forestry Commission lead up through varied stands of conifers to tree-shrouded Llyn Llywelyn from the picnic site here.

Continue past Llyn-y-Gadair to Rhyd Ddu, where a path leads to Snowdon. Skirt Llyn Cwellyn and follow the Afon Gwyrfai (known for its excellent game fishing). Pass through Betws Garmon and Waunfawr to re-enter Caernarfon.

CARDIFF, S Glam

Utilitarian in parts, though not depressingly so, Cardiff displays the mixture of dignity and pragmatism to be expected from the capital city and cultural centre of Wales. Massive expansion resulted in the city becoming the world's principal coal port by the start of the 20th century, but its present-day appearance is almost totally modern. One family particularly

BESIDE THE BRISTOL CHANNEL

For many centuries the Bristol Channel has admitted traders and invaders to the heartlands of the Severn Valley, and more recently it has provided a route for the export of Welsh coal. Picturesquely ruined castles recall troubled times; great harbours recall the industrial prosperity of the past.

considered to be one of architect William Butterfield's finest achievements. The Turner House Art Gallery, a branch of the National Museum, is in Plymouth Road.

At the roundabout take 2nd exit SP 'Sea Front' on to an unclassified road. Descend to the Esplanade and drive forward into Raisdale Road. Cross a railway bridge and at crossroads, turn left. After ¼ mile turn left on to the B4267 SP 'Sully, Barry'. After 1 mile a detour can be made by turning left on to the unclassified 'Swanbridge' road for Sully Island.

involved in the city's growth was the Butes, who built the vast docks, sank a fortune into the development of the city as a living and working community, and restored the castle. The latter, an appealing mixture of genuine period remains and 19th-century reconstruction, was the brainchild of the 3rd Marquess, working with the architect William Burges. Inside the perimeter walls the handsome Norman keep surmounts a motte surrounded by a defensive moat. In direct contrast, and well distant in a 'gothick' complex, are 19th-century living quarters that reveal the full expression of romantic medievalism so loved by Bute and the famous Burges. Cardiff's principal buildings stand quite close to the castle in Cathays Park and include the City Hall and County Hall, the University College and the National Museum of Wales. The Llandarf district north-west of the city centre can be reached through some of Cardiff's elegant parks. Here, in a village-like setting, is the city's cathedral, an historic building which was almost destroyed by the ravages of war but is now fully restored to its old splendour. Its south-east tower and spire form a delicate and familiar local landmark. Other features in the city include quaint Victorian arcades, the world famous Cardiff Arms Park Rugby Ground, the new St David's concert and conference hall, Welsh Industrial and Maritime Museum and the Bute Road Station Trust.
Leave Cardiff via the A4160 'Penarth' road. After 3 miles at a roundabout take 2nd exit, and at the next roundabout bear right to enter Penarth.

The Norman keep and later, 19th-century, buildings at Cardiff Castle stand within walls that date partly from Roman times.

Real gold adds splendour to the 19th-century buildings at Cardiff Castle.

Ogmore Castle was founded by a Norman knight called William de Londres.

PENARTH, S Glam

During the second half of the 19th century Penarth was adopted by well-to-do Victorians and transformed into a seaside resort. Gardens and lawns lend quiet charm to the pleasant atmosphere of the town, and the old harbour has found a new lease of life with water ski-ing and sailing enthusiasts. Dangerous currents make bathing hazardous. St Augustine's Church, on the headland, was built in 1865 and is

SWANBRIDGE, S Glam

At low tide Sully Island becomes accessible from here. Views from the island encompass much of the Bristol Channel and are constantly changing with the coming and going of sea traffic.

On the main route pass through Sully and in 1 mile turn left on to the A5055 and enter Barry. After 1 mile turn right under a railway bridge, then keep forward at ensuing roundabouts SP 'Barry Island'. Pass Barry Station, bear left, and shortly turn left to reach Barry Island.

BARRY, S Glam

In the 19th century Barry's population expanded from 500 to a staggering 12,665, and side by side with the development of docks that were to become among the largest in the world came the popularization of the Barry Island holiday resort. Park Road leads to Porthkerry Country Park, passing scant remains of Barry Castle on the way. Scrapped British Rail steam locomotives rust away in a metal breaker's yard here. Over 2,000 birds of prey can be seen at the Welsh Hawking Centre.

Return across the causeway and keep forward then ascend on the A4050 'Cardiff' road. In ½ mile at a roundabout take the 1st exit SP 'Cowbridge'. At the next roundabout take the 1st exit A4226 SP 'Llantwit Major'. After a mile turn left on to the unclassified 'Rhoose' road. In ¾ mile enter a roundabout and leave by the 1st exit. Cardiff (Wales) Airport to the right is the home of the Wales Aircraft Museum. Continue, with views left across the Bristol Channel through Rhoose, dominated by a cement works, to Aberthaw. After ¾ mile meet a T-junction and turn left on to the the B4265. Cross the River Thaw and enter St Athan.

ST ATHAN, S Glam
Two 14th-century effigies and a window commemorating the coronation of George VI can be seen in St Athan's medieval church. An RAF airfield lies to the north-west.

Continue on the B4265 to Boverton, turn left on to an unclassified road, for Llantwit Major.

LLANTWIT MAJOR, S Glam
Once this quiet place was one of the most important and influential centres of learning in British Christendom. The school founded here by 5th century St Illtud attracted scholars from distant parts and fostered some of the greatest minds of early Welsh history. A faint echo of the foundation survives in the 13th- and 15th-century Church of St Illtud — a remarkable structure formed by two churches joined end to end. Inside are a richly-carved Jesse Tree, depicting Christ's descent from the line of David, and a collection of ancient stone crosses. Other features of the town include an old dovecote and monastery gateway, a 15th-century town hall, the Old Swann Inn, and the imposing Great House (open to the public on application).

Follow signs Bridgend and at the bypass roundabout take 1st exit rejoining the B4265. Pass through typical Vale of Glamorgan scenery to St Bride's Major. Turn left on to the B4524 'Southerndown' road, and continue to Southerndown.

SOUTHERNDOWN, M Glam
This small resort is a good starting point for exhilarating walks to Ogsmore-by-Sea or the windy

headland of Trwyn-y-Witch (Witches Nose). Curious blowholes and wave-carved caves are features of the local cliffs.

Continue to Ogmore-by-Sea.

OGMORE-BY-SEA, M Glam
Sandy beaches and pleasant cliff walks make this a pleasant Bristol Channel resort; at low tide a more sinister side is revealed in the shape of Tusker Rock — notorious cause of dozens of shipwrecks.

Continue past the Merthyr-Mawr Warren at the mouth of the Ogmore River to reach Ogmore Castle.

OGMORE CASTLE, M Glam
This Norman castle (AM), on the River Ewenny has a somewhat battered stone keep that is one of the earliest of its type.

CANDLESTON CASTLE, M Glam
A footpath and stepping stones across the River Ewenny lead from Ogmore Castle to the tree-shrouded and dilapidated remains of Candleston. During the 15th century it overlooked a wide fertile plain, which has since been overwhelmed by sand dunes.

Continue on the B4524. After 1½ miles meet a junction and turn left on to the B4265, passing the edge of Ewenny.

EWENNY, M Glam
In 1141 Maurice de Londres, of Ogmore Castle, founded a priory here. Its remains (AM) are in beautiful surroundings and comprise the virtually complete 13th-century circuit walls, fragments of various buildings, and a Norman church considered to be the finest of its kind in Wales. Massive defensive details are reminders of the precarious balance that existed between war and peace in medieval Wales.

Cross the Ewenny River and in 1 mile at the roundabout take 3rd exit SP 'Cardiff' on to the Bridgend Bypass A48. At the next roundabout take 2nd exit A473 SP 'Llantrisant' and in a further 1 mile at a roundabout take 2nd exit on to the B4181 SP 'Coity'. Go under the railway bridge then keep forward unclassified for Coity. Turn right on to the 'Bryncethin' road, and pass the entrance to Coity Castle.

Stryt Lydan Barn at St Fagan's Folk Museum originally stood in the one-time Welsh county of Flintshire.

Many locomotives stand in Woodham Brothers' scrapyard on Barry Island.

COITY, M Glam
Coity Castle (AM) dominates the centre of its namesake village. Nearby St Mary's Church contains several interesting monuments, and features a beautiful east window made by William Morris' company.

Ascend with hill views and cross the M4. Descend to join the B4280, turn right SP 'Blackhill' on to the A4061 under a railway bridge, and bear right into Bryncethin. Continue along the wooded Ogmore Valley to Blackmill, and turn right on to the A4093 'Tonyrefail' road. Continue through farm and moorland scenery to the edge of Tonyrefail. Turn right on to the unclassified 'Thomastown, Llantrisant' road, and after 1¼ miles turn right again. In 1 mile at roundabout take 1st exit on to the A4119. Follow the Ely River, then pass Llantrisant Forest and enter Llantrisant.

LLANTRISANT, M Glam
Both church and castle command dominating hilltop sites above the steep attractive streets of Llantrisant. The Royal Mint was moved here in 1967.

Enter the roundabout in Llantrisant and take the 2nd exit on to the A4119 SP 'Cardiff'. After 1½ miles turn left SP 'Groes-faen'. Pass through Groes-faen and in 3 miles turn right on to an unclassified road SP 'St Fagan's'. In 1¾ miles enter St. Fagan's.

ST FAGAN'S, S Glam
Attractive thatched cottages and a waterside church are charming features of this River Ely village, but St Fagan's is best known for the amazing collection of buildings that has been gathered round its 16th-century castle to form the Welsh Folk Museum. Complete buildings of many different periods have been rescued from all over Wales and painstakingly rebuilt in the grounds. Even the furnished interiors are authentic, and in some cases the buildings still fulfil their original functions.

Turn left, following the river, then keep forward through the Cardiff suburbs to reach the city centre.

CORACLES ON THE TEIFI

Seaward lies the coast of Cardigan Bay, where Victorians transformed quiet Welsh villages into prosperous ports, now the playgrounds of yachtsmen and tourists. Inland the salmon waters of the Teifi cascade through a luscious valley to the town of Cardigan and flow on to swell the Irish Sea.

CARDIGAN, Dyfed

On the banks of one of the loveliest rivers in Wales — the Teifi — stands Cardigan, once the headquarters of Welsh princes. In the past there has been many a bloody battle in the defence of the town's nationality, and it was here that Rhys ap Gruffydd won a rousing victory against a Norman-Flemish army in 1136. Perhaps the most outstanding architectural feature of Cardigan is the fine medieval 7-arched bridge over the Teifi. Old warehouses by the river are a reminder of Cardigan's former importance as a port, which flourished on the trade supplied by Cardiganshire's lead mines. Unfortunately, the Teifi silted up in the 19th century, and gradually trade died away. Today Cardigan is most concerned with its own affairs, generated through the rich farmland and forest which surrounds it, engendering in the town an air of independence. But this friendly town welcomes visitors, who come from the little seaside resorts up and down the coast to shop at the market which is still held beneath the arches of the Guildhall, and simply to enjoy the old-fashioned atmosphere and beautiful riverside setting. Two miles south off the A478 is the Cardigan Wildlife Park. This unusual mixture of Park and Sanctuary has a diverse range of mammals, birds and plants. Other features include fishing on the River Teifi, nature walks and disused slate quarries.

Leave Cardigan on the A487 Aberaeron and Aberystwyth road and gradually ascend to high ground beyond Penparc. In 2½ miles turn left on to the B4333 and continue, with views of the sea, to Aberporth.

CARDIGAN BAY, Dyfed

It is said that beneath the waters of Cardigan Bay lies a lost Atlantis. The seas were apparently kept from the Bay by a great embankment, which was put in the care of Siethenyn ap Siethenyn Sardi — one of Wales' greatest drunkards. He let the wall decay, and eventually it broke down altogether, destroying, so legend has it, 16 fortified towns. The plateau which meets the sea in a series of high cliffs is cut by narrow, wooded river valleys, such as the Teifi valley at Cenarth. The coastline itself is pierced at intervals by small, steep-sided river valleys which shelter fishing villages like Llangranog, where a small beach has formed at the river mouth. The people of Cardigan Bay are Welsh speaking, perpetuating a Welsh culture of fishermen and farmers.

ABERPORTH, Dyfed

Overlooking 2 sandy coves, this popular village is well sheltered from prevailing winds and so attracts flocks of visitors every year. Eastwards high cliffs stretch away to Tresaith, while westwards the coast climbs to the 400ft headland of Pencribach. The headland is inaccessible, and is used as a missile testing range.

Continue on the B4333 and after 2¼ miles turn left to rejoin the A487, SP 'Aberystwyth', for Tan-y-groes. For several miles there are views on both sides as the road keeps to high ground. At Brynhoffnant, the B4334 to the left leads to the attractive coastal village of Llangranog.

LLANGRANOG, Dyfed

A strange rock formation, likened to a lizard's head, overlooks the yellow sands of Llangranog where rocky outcrops are revealed at low tide. The slate-roofed houses of the village lie cramped by the walls of the narrow valley which shelters them. Up on the coastal hills cliff-top walks, preserved by the National Trust, give magnificent views along the coast.

Ornamental ducks in Aberaeron's attractive harbour

The main tour continues on the A487 to Plwmp.

In 2½ miles, at Synod Inn, turn left on to the A486. Pass through Cross Inn before the descent (1 in 8), with coastal views ahead, into New Quay.

NEW QUAY, Dyfed

The New Quay Harbour Company, formed in 1833, developed a newly-established shipbuilding industry, which by 1860 employed some 600 shipwrights. However, road and rail gradually took away the coastal trade the port relied on, and although small fishing boats still land mackerel, herring and shellfish here, the amateur yachtsman has taken over the harbour. Yachting, and the sands revealed at low tide, have been the salvation of New Quay. During the summer months the neat, brightly painted Georgian and Victorian houses up on their terraced hillside look down upon a gay and lively scene and despite the tourist boom, New Quay remains one of the most charming little towns on the west coast.

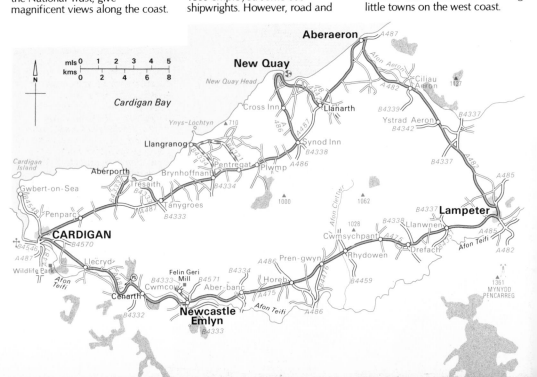

Continue on the B4342 Aberaeron road through a pretty wooded stretch. In 3 miles turn left on to the A487 to Llanarth.

LLANARTH, Dyfed
Llanarth lies partly alongside the road and partly up on the hillside above a steep ravine where the old village church stands. This holds objects of considerable antiquity within its walls: an 11th-century font; an ancient stone with an Ogham (ancient alphabet of the Celts) inscription superimposed with a carved Irish Celtic cross of the 9th century; and a collection of early English and Welsh bibles. Nearby, at Wern, is where Henry VII is said to have spent the night on his way to Bosworth Field, and to have had an affair with the daughter of the house from which the family, the Parry ap Harrys of Cardiganshire, claimed royal blood.

Continue on the A487 with excellent coastal views on the approach to Aberaeron.

ABERAERON, Dyfed
Aberaeron is a delightful town purposefully and attractively laid out by 19th-century planners who turned a small fishing hamlet into a flourishing trading port. Colour-washed Regency houses stand gathered about a square in orderly array and lined up on terraces overlooking the harbour. The earliest development provided the inner and outer harbours, the Harbour-Master's house, now a hotel, and the elegent brown-stone town hall. The town was renowned for its ship-builders, and schooners built here by master shipwright David Jones were highly prized. However the railways eventually took away the trade, and today the harbour is used primarily by yachtsmen and the quayside by holidaymakers.

At the far end of the town, turn right on to the A482, SP 'Lampeter', and follow the pleasantly wooded Aeron valley to Ystrad Aeron. Beyond the village a winding road leads through hill country before entering Lampeter.

LAMPETER, Dyfed
Lampeter is a busy trading centre at the confluence of several main roads, and market day, Tuesday, is a good time to experience the friendly atmosphere of this truly Welsh town. It is best known for St David's College, founded in 1822 by an Englishman, Bishop Burgess. The building, designed by C. R. Cockerell, was described by Sir Gilbert Scott as 'a most charming example of the early Gothic revival'. The original quadrangular building has not been marred by the modern additions and the remarkable library of some 80,000 books, medieval manuscripts and

This fine stained-glass portrait of St Christopher in Lampeter parish church is by R. J. Newberry, c1901

The Falls of Cenarth, a famous beauty spot on the River Teifi

first editions is housed here. A mound in the college grounds marks the site of a medieval castle, and on the opposite bank of the Teifi runs a stretch of Sarn Helen — a Roman road named after the Welsh wife of Magnus Maximus, who unsuccessfully attempted to become Emperor in AD 383.

In the town centre turn right into the High Street and leave on the A475 along the north side of the Teifi valley. Follow a 'switchback' road through several small villages. At Horeb, cross the A486 and later rejoin the Teifi valley before Newcastle Emlyn.

NEWCASTLE EMLYN, Dyfed
The castle, built in the 13th century, regularly changed hands between the Welsh and the English until 1403, when it finally fell to Owain Glyndwr's troops, but was almost destroyed in the process. Having fallen into disrepair, the castle was given to Sir Rhys ap Thomas by Henry VII, who rebuilt it for comfort rather than for security. It went the same way as its predecessor, however, when in 1645 Cromwell's troops found the castle in Royalist hands, won it, and then rendered it useless. So today little remains, except part of the walls and a ruined gatehouse standing on a grassy hillock. The town itself, although architecturally unassuming, is attractive. There is a town hall of 1892, and the Victorian church where slate from the Cilgerran quarries is used for the paving stones, the pillars, the chancel arch, the font, and even the sundial outside. A plaque on a house near the bridge over the Teifi commemorates Isaac Carter, who set up the first printing press here in Wales in 1718.

To the north-east near Cwmcoy is Felin Geri Mill.

FELIN GERI MILL, Dyfed
This watermill (OACT), built in the 16th century, was the last one in Wales to use the original production process for grinding wholemeal flour as a commercial concern. Visitors can see each stage of this ancient method and there is a museum, a water-powered saw mill, a shop and a bakery here as well.

The main tour turns left across the river bridge into the town centre, then right, SP 'Cardigan'. At the next T-junction turn right on to the A484 for Cenarth.

RIVER TEIFI, Dyfed
Flowing south and then west across the Cardigan plateau, the Teifi has beautiful carved valleys and steep gorges where waterfalls and rapids, such as those at Cenarth, challenge even the salmon's prowess. The Teifi and the Tywi are the only rivers where salmon are still fished from the coracle. These craft have been in use since prehistoric times. Built of interwoven ribs of ash, hazel or willow, and covered in a skin of tarred canvas, the coracles work in pairs with a net cast between them to trap the salmon. The Teifi also has the distinction of being the last refuge of the beaver, which probably became extinct in Britain during the 16th century.

CENARTH, Dyfed
The beauty of Cenarth Bridge and the Falls attract thousands of visitors every year. The Teifi cascades over a series of rocky ledges into swirling pools where sheep are washed prior to shearing during spring. Coracle men wait downstream to catch any luckless animals swept away by the current. Stone and colour-washed cottages around a simple church blend harmoniously with the delightful scenery surrounding the village.

Continue on the A484 along the Teifi valley through Llechryd to return to Cardigan.

THE HINTERLAND OF CARMARTHEN BAY

Ruined fortresses along the sandy coast of Carmarthen Bay stand guard over this peaceful corner of South Wales that inspired the poetry of Dylan Thomas. Carmarthen, at one end of the tour, reflects the antiquity of Wales, while Tenby at the other is a bustling tourist town.

CARMARTHEN, Dyfed

An important local centre with a busy food and cattle market, Carmarthen is believed to be the oldest town in Wales. Narrow, winding streets thread between old houses up to the ruins of the 14th-century castle, now almost completely masked by the imposing modern county hall. Down below, on the River Tywi, traditional Welsh coracles are still used for salmon fishing. The town has a long history going back to Celtic times and cAD75 the Romans built a major fort, *Moridunum,* here: the remains of an amphitheatre have been unearthed near Priory Street. Many fine Roman remains are now displayed in the Carmarthen Museum in the old Bishop's Palace (OACT) at Abergwili, to the north-east of the town. Of the many fine buildings in Carmarthen, the oldest is St Peter's Church, probably dating from the 12th century. The splendid houses beside the church and the elegant Guildhall of 1770 testify to the town's distinguished past. Carmarthen has always been associated with the Arthurian wizard Merlin. He was, reputedly, born near Carmarthen and hid in a crystal cave in Merlin's Hill. The decayed stump of Merlin's Oak is carefully preserved by the townspeople against the prophecy that 'When Merlin's oak shall tumble down then shall fall Carmarthen town'.

Leave Carmarthen on the A40, SP 'Haverfordwest' and 'St Clears'. In 1 mile turn left on to the B4312, SP 'Llanstephan', and at the T-junction turn right. Later run alongside the attractive estuary of the Afon Tywi to reach Llanstephan.

LLANSTEPHAN, Dyfed

The approach to Llanstephan is heralded by a glimpse of the ruined battlements of an impressive medieval castle. Its strategic position at the mouth of the River Tywi ensured a violent and cruel history for this most imposing fortress (OACT). The large, sandy beach below the castle runs up to the waterfront in the village marked by a pleasant, grassy area called The Green. In bygone days cockle-pickers and their donkeys tramped over the sands.

At the church keep forward along an unclassified road, then bear right, SP 'St Clears' and 'Llanybri'. At Llanybri keep forward, SP 'Bancyfelin'. Continue, then keep left and follow a sharply undulating byroad (narrow in places). Nearly 2 miles farther, at the Wern Inn, turn right, then at the war memorial keep left and pass through Llangynog. In 1¼ miles turn left, then ½ mile farther at the main road turn left on to the A40. In 2½ miles join the St Clears Bypass

ST CLEARS, Dyfed

This small agricultural town was famed as one of the centres of the Rebecca Riots in the 1840s (see Rhayader tour). The riots obviously had some effect because in 1884 the toll system was reformed. St Clears' church is one of the oldest in the area and contains some fragments of Norman work, including a font and the carved chancel arch. It was originally the church of the Cluniac Priory, founded by the first Norman Lord of St Clears, of which nothing remains.

From the bypass branch left, SP 'Pendine', and at the T-junction turn right on to the A4066 for Laugharne.

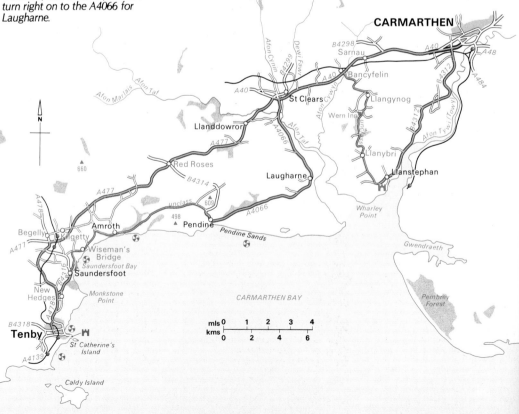

Dylan Thomas's garden-shed workroom at his boathouse in Laugharne

Above: the River Tywi snakes its way across its flood plain, passing Carmarthen to the right

Left: Saundersfoot — busy port turned holiday resort.

LAUGHARNE, Dyfed

Dylan Thomas said of Laugharne, 'this timeless, mild, beguiling island of a town . . .', and he will always be linked with this charming, modest place where he lived happily for 16 years in the Georgian boathouse romantically perched on Cliff Walk. Photographs, furniture and mementoes constitute a small museum here now. Many characters in his poem *Under Milk Wood* were probably based on local people and the play is still regularly performed in the town. The poet is buried in a simple grave in the churchyard. The ruined castle on the water's edge was once an important strategic bastion, like that at Llanstephan, but was subsequently converted into a lavish Tudor residence by Sir John Perrot, illegitimate son of Henry VIII. In addition to the castle, the town has an attractive old harbour, a 13th-century church and a smart 18th-century town hall with a white tower and belfry. It is here that the Portreeve resides — an official post left over from Norman times. He wears a chain of golden cockleshells and has a retinue who attend him at town functions.

Continue on the A4066, passing on the right steep wooded slopes and on the left dunes and marshy land, to Pendine.

PENDINE, Dyfed

Five miles of firm, smooth sand form the extensive beach which made this resort a magnet in the 1920s for those seeking a seaside holiday. However, the hitherto peacefulness was shattered when motor speed trials were introduced to the area. Sir Malcolm Campbell broke the existing land speed record here in 1924, and a tragic accident in 1927 killed Parry Thomas when his car *Babs* crashed. The car was buried in the sand until 1969 when it was exhumed for restoration. Unfortunately peace has still not returned to Pendine Sands, for part of them are now used for missile testing.

Ascend steeply from the village on the B4314 and at the top turn left on to the unclassified road for Amroth.

AMROTH, Dyfed

Strangely-shaped petrified tree stumps can be seen here sticking out of the blue clay at exceptionally low tides. This forest was buried over 1,000 years ago, and the sea still eats away at the village. Several cottages and the old coast road have been washed away over the centuries. Amroth Castle (not open), an 18th-century house, was visited by Lord Nelson in 1802.

Continue for ½ mile then turn left, SP 'Tenby' and descend to Wiseman's Bridge. Continue through a wooded stretch and at the top of the ascent keep left, then descend to Saundersfoot.

SAUNDERSFOOT, Dyfed

During the 19th century Saundersfoot was a busy port shipping the local anthracite coal, but today it is an attractive and popular yachting and fishing village. The splendid sandy beaches either side of the harbour are ideal for safe bathing.

Go forward on to the B4316 and in 1 mile (at the roundabout) turn left on to the A478 for Tenby.

TENBY, Dyfed

Tenby's busy but sheltered harbour is the focal point of the town's narrow, winding streets bounded by remnants of the 13th-century town walls. Castle Hill is crowned by the remains of a Norman keep, and is also the home of the local museum, which houses a splendid collection of displays relating to the Tenby district. The Tudor gabled Merchant's House (NT) is a relic of the town's important seafaring history. It has been beautifully restored, revealing original beams and large areas of wall paintings and has a Tudor period museum. St Mary's Church in Quay Hill is a Norman building and is the largest parish church in Wales. Robert Recorde, the mathematician who devised the 'equals' sign, is buried inside it. The town was also the birthplace of the painter Augustus John in 1878. Just off the coast lies St Catherine's Island, which is accessible on foot at low tide. The fort on the island was originally built by Lord Palmerston as a defence against possible attack by Napoleon III. On Harbour beach is the tiny St Julian's Seamen's Chapel.

CALDY ISLAND, Dyfed

Motor launches run from Tenby harbour to Caldy Island, about 2½ miles offshore. The island is populated by Cistercian monks who farm the land and produce Caldy Island perfume, which they sell. The medieval church on the island contains a stone inscribed with Ogham lettering — and alphabet used by Irish Celts in the 6th century.

Return along the A478, SP 'Camarthen', to the Begelly roundabout and take the A477, SP 'St Clears'. Continue through a pretty wooded inlet and beyond Red Roses gradually descend through pleasant wooded country to Llanddowror.

LLANDDOWROR, Dyfed

The quiet atmosphere in this peaceful village of whitewashed houses gives no hint of the frenzy which was generated here in the 18th-century by the local vicar. Distressed by the ignorance and illiteracy of his parishioners, and of Welsh people in general, he started a system of travelling schools. Teachers travelled from parish to parish teaching children and adults of all ages to read the Bible and it was claimed that about 150,000 people learned to read through this scheme.

Continue on the A477 and in 1½ miles, at the roundabout, take the A40 for the return to Carmarthen.

A WELSH BORDERLAND

From the cliff-edged River Wye on the long-contested Welsh border, travel along the outstandingly beautiful valley to White Castle and ancient Monmouth, historic bastion of Norman power. Continue on through the broad Usk valley to Caerleon, past powerhouse of Rome's legions in South Wales.

Monmouth's 13th-century gateway was originally used as a tollhouse, prison and watchtower

CHEPSTOW, Gwent

Chepstow, a border town, stands with its feet in the Wye on a stretch of the river that is distinguished by the high cliffs of its banks, and it was upon one of these natural fortresses that the castle (AM) was built — the first Norman stone castle in Wales. The cellar and the lower 2 storeys of the Great Tower survive from the original building erected by William Fitz Osbern. His castle was added to by later generations of the powerful de Clare family. After the Restoration, Henry Marten, one of those who signed the death warrant of Charles I, was subsequently kept a prisoner for 20 years, in the tower which now bears his name, until his death at the age of 78 in 1680. Another survivor from the Middle Ages is Westgate, part of the substantial town wall, where duty was collected on all goods which passed through it for the Lord of the Manor.

Follow SP 'Monmouth' and at the end of the town join the A466. Pass Chepstow Racecourse to reach St Arvans. Here, turn left, SP 'Trellech'. Later climb through wooded countryside to reach Devauden. Join the B4293 and continue through Llanishen to Trellech.

TRELLECH, Gwent

The village of Trellech takes its name from the 3 mysterious leaning standing stones by the village crossroads. Once part of a larger complex, their purpose is not really known, but perhaps, like Stonehenge, they were used for measuring time, or as the site of ancient religious rites. The stones appear again in carved relief on the remarkable sundial given to the church in 1689.

Continue on the B4293. In 4¼ miles bear right and later cross the A40. At the next T-junction turn left, then at the roundabout turn right and cross the Monnow Bridge to enter Monmouth.

MONMOUTH, Gwent

The Normans realised that to hold Monmouth, strategically placed on the Wye and Monnow, was virtually to control the whole of South Wales. The fortified bridge gateway (AM) which they built over the river in 1262, and guarded the town for centuries, is the only one now left in Britain. The castle has not lasted so well, being mostly destroyed in the Civil War of 1646. Harry of Monmouth, who became Henry V, was born within its walls. Such was his popularity that in 1673 the Duke of Beaufort built Great Castle House (exterior AM), in order that his first grandson could be born near the birthplace of his greatest hero, Henry V; he built the house from the stones of the castle and the interior has fine woodwork and

plasterwork. St Mary's Church stands on the site of Monmouth Priory, built by the same Fitz Osbern who founded the castle. A Monmouth Cap, the woollen headgear reputedly worn by the Monmouth archers at Agincourt on whom Henry V relied heavily for his victory, can be seen in the local museum. Today a statue of Henry V stands high up on the façade of the neo-Classical Shire Hall of 1724, overlooking Agincourt Square where there stands a statue of C. S. Rolls, co-founder of Rolls-Royce, pioneer aviator and the first man to fly the channel in both directions. A collection of Nelson's mementoes can also be seen in the town museum.

Return across the Monnow Bridge and at the roundabout turn right on to the B4233. At Rockfield bear left, SP 'Abergavenny', and later pass through Hendre. After 4¼ miles, at the edge of Llantilio Crossenny, a detour can be made by turning right on to an unclassified road to White Castle.

WHITE CASTLE, Gwent

Small, but powerful, White Castle (AM) is one of 3 fortresses which, in the 12th and 13th centuries, formed a strategic triangle of such importance that the Crown always

kept direct control over them, lest they should be turned against the reigning monarch. The isolated castle gets its name from the white plaster which once adorned it, remains of which can still be found on the stone work. At the end of the 12th century the castle consisted merely of a stone tower surrounded by a curtain wall, but in the following century, in which the Welsh rose under the 2 Llewellyns, the castle was considerably refortified. Semi-circular towers were added, a gatehouse was built, and the outer ward enclosed by another curtain wall with attendant towers. Domestic buildings were built within, enabling many servants to be housed here in reasonable comfort. However, the castle was never tested in war, and after the Welsh retreat of 1277, it became a purely administrative centre, collecting tithes and levies from the residents of the surrounding countryside. With the decline of the feudal system, the castle finally fell into ruins through disuse.

Continue on the B4233 through Llanfapley to Abergavenny.

ABERGAVENNY, Gwent

Abergavenny stands upon the banks of the River Usk within a great green bowl, guarded by 4 hills. The Romans had a fort here, but the earliest evidence of Abergavenny's history is the Norman castle. It was founded before 1090 by Hamelin de Balun, but William de Breos is the name remembered by the Welsh. He came to the castle in 1176, and one of his first acts was to invite all the leading local chieftans to a Christmas banquet. While the chieftans ate, William ordered his soldiers to slay them all. The ruins consist of fragments of the curtain wall; the ruined gatehouse and a few other remnants and are now part of a pleasantly wooded park. The museum located within the castle grounds, houses many interesting exhibits associated with the history of Abergavenny. These include rural craft tools, Welsh kitchen, saddlers shop, costumes and Roman coins. St Mary's Church is built on the site of a Benedictine priory founded at the same time as the castle, and contains some outstanding relics of the past. Among these are the splendid tombs of the Herbert family, but outshining all their finery is a simple wooden effigy of a 13th-century knight. One mile west of Abergavenny off the A40 is the Sugar Loaf viewpoint offering wide views over the Usk valley and the Blorenge.

Leave the town centre on the A40, SP 'Raglan'. In 1¼ miles, at the roundabout, take the A4042, SP 'Newport'. Pass through Llanellen, Llanover and Penperlleni, then in 1¼ miles turn left on to the A472, SP 'Usk'. After another 4¼ miles, across the river bridge on the left, is the town of Usk.

USK, Gwent

Usk, meaning 'water', is, not surprisingly, named after the river on which it stands. It overlooks the broad meadows of the Usk valley, and is known for its excellent salmon fishing and inns; those around Twyn Square attest to Usk long being a market centre for the surrounding rural area. *Burrium,* the Roman station which stood here before the town, was an important fort from where the legions made unsuccessful sorties into the Welsh mountains. The Normans came and went, leaving behind them a castle and a church. The former stands ruined, just a gateway, a keep, round tower and remnants of the living quarters, yet still retains the grace and dignity of the finest Norman architecture. The castle suffered terribly during the 15th-century Glyndwr rebellion and was slighted in the Civil War.

The main tour continues forward on to the unclassified Llangybi/Caerleon road to Llangybi.

LLANGYBI, Gwent

An ancient mineralised spring here is dedicated to St Cybi, and was a place of pilgrimage to which people came seeking miraculous cures from its waters. The well chamber has a paved walk around it and niches in its walls for offerings. The beehive vault is thought to be unique in Wales. In this area there are a number of standing stones, cists and cromlechs, which mark the site of ancient burial sites.

Remain on the unclassified road to Caerleon.

CAERLEON, Gwent

This was *Isca,* home of the 2nd Augustinian Legion, one of 3 permanent legionary bases in Britain. It is estimated a population of some 6,000 lived here, and excavations have revealed a hospital, kitchens, baths, and outside the walls, a granary. Perhaps the most remarkable remain here is the amphitheatre (AM), the only one completely excavated in Britain. It is oval, and an earth bank, originally 8 yards high, held tiers of wooden seats that could seat several thousands. Ships from all over the world were said to dock at the Roman quays, bringing gold to decorate the palaces and churches, and finance the 200 schools which were said to thrive here. In the Middle Ages considerably more of the fort was visible, and these signs of a sophisticated civilisation gave rise to legends of King Arthur's Court.

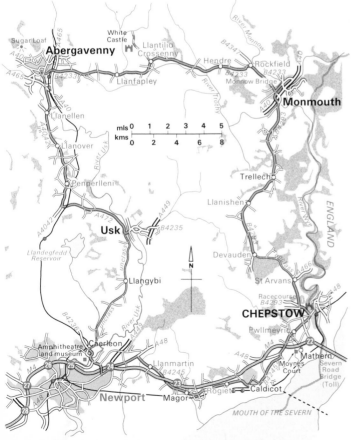

Chepstow Castle, guarded on one side by the Wye and on the other by a ditch

From the one-way system follow SP 'Newport'. Cross the River Usk then turn left on to the B4236, SP 'Christchurch'. In ¾ mile turn right, then keep left. At the A48 turn left then ½ mile farther, at the roundabout, take the 3rd exit, SP 'Langstone'. In 1½ miles turn right on to the B4245 for Magor.

MAGOR, Gwent

Cadwaldwr, the last Welsh prince also to be king of England, founded Magor's spacious church in the 7th century. The Cathedral of the Moors, as the church is known, is mainly Norman, with a 13th-century tower which overlooks the Bristol Channel. In the churchyard lie the ivy-clad remains of a priory.

At the Wheatsheaf Inn turn left. In 2¼ miles skirt Rogiet, then 1¼ miles farther turn left on to an unclassified road to enter Caldicot.

CALDICOT, Gwent

New shops and industrial estates have turned Caldicot from a village into a sizeable town in little over a decade. The Romans had a pottery here when it stood on the busy *Via Julia,* and the Normans a castle. This was built in the late

12th century, but by the 17th century had fallen into decay. It was restored this century and medieval banquets and traditional musical entertainment take place within its walls.

At the roundabout take the 3rd exit, then in ½ mile turn left to rejoin the B4245. In 2 miles turn right on to the A48. After crossing the M4 a short diversion can be made by taking the 2nd turning right on to an unclassified road to Mathern.

MATHERN, Gwent

The old church at Mathern is dedicated to St Tewdric, a 6th-century king who ended his days as a hermit. Bishop Godwin buried his coffin in the chancel that was built in 1610. The nearby Bishops Palace (not open) was the residence of the Bishops of Llandaff from the time of the Glyndwr rebellion in the 1400s up until 1705. It has medieval and Tudor features and a glorious garden. Also near the village is Moynes Court (not open), a 17th-century building with a much older gatehouse, once the home of Bishop Godwin.

The main tour returns along the A48 by way of Pwllmeyric to Chepstow.

THE STONEHENGE QUARRY

Between placid Cardigan and bustling Fishguard is a jagged coast backed by the craggy, rock-strewn block of Mynydd Prescelly. In prehistoric times the great bluestones of Wiltshire's Stonehenge were hewn from these slopes and somehow hauled to Salisbury Plain.

FISHGUARD & GOODWICK, Dyfed

Lower Town, as the oldest part of Fishguard is called, is a delightfully unspoilt fishing village. It was chosen as the setting for the film version of Dylan Thomas' *Under Milk Wood*, and is connected to Upper Town by a steep hill. The square in Upper Town features a Market Hall and the attractive Royal Oak Inn. During the 18th century Fishguard witnessed the signing of a treaty that ended the last invasion of British soil. In reality the so-called 'invasion' was a fiasco perpetrated by a motley band of French soldiers and convicts bent on pillage. Unable to reach and destroy Bristol, which had been their mission, they landed at Carregwastad Bay and quickly discovered large amounts of alcohol from a recent shipwreck. Incapably drunk, the invaders were easily captured by the local militia – aided (it is said) by stout-hearted Welsh women dressed in traditional costumes that the French took to be soldiers' uniforms. Goodwick, almost joined to Fishguard, is a resort with sandy beaches; it is also the embarkation point for one of the principal ferry services to Eire. East and west of Fishguard is the breathtaking seaboard and shore scenery of the Pembrokeshire Coast National Park.

PEMBROKESHIRE COAST NATIONAL PARK (NORTH), Dyfed

Two outstanding features of the northern part of this superb national park are its grand coastal scenery and its rugged upland typified by the Mynydd Prescelly range. Pencaer Peninsula, to the west of Fishguard, is characterized by a wind-torn landscape and precipitous cliffs that make it as daunting as it is exhilarating. Much of Pencaer Peninsula and the northern part of Mynydd Prescelly are made up of volcanic rocks, but farther east at Dinas Head and Cemaes Head are gentler sedimentary rocks from a less traumatic period of the earth's history. National Park information is available in Fishguard.

Leave Fishguard by the A487 'Cardigan' road. Descend from Upper to Lower Town with views across the old harbour to Fishguard Bay. Continue to Dinas.

DINAS, Dyfed

This small village features the handsome Tabor Chapel and is connected to the cove and cliff scenery of Dinas Island by several little roads and footpaths. The 'island' is isolated only in name nowadays, but at the end of the ice age it was separated from the mainland by a true channel. The local church, at Cwm-yr-eglwys, was built in 1860 after its predecessor was destroyed in a violent storm. The cove here is considered one of the most beautiful in Wales and the tip of the headland falls away in the impressive 500ft cliffs of Dinas Head. Strange impressions found on a slab of rock here are traditionally held to be the Devil's footprints. Seals are very numerous along the coast. Pwllgwaelod, on the west side of Dinas Island, is a quiet bay with an old lime kiln and an inn.

Continue on the A487 for 1¼ miles to reach Cerrig-y-Gof.

CERRIG-Y-GOF, Dyfed

Overgrown though this important prehistoric monument may be, it is worth exploring because it is the only one of its kind in England and Wales. It is in a field off the main A458 road (OS ref SN037389), and comprises the remains of five rectangular burial chambers set in a circle. The name can be translated into English as 'Blacksmith's Stones'.

Continue on the A487 to Newport.

NEWPORT, Dyfed

Ever since the 13th century, when this pretty little town received its first charter, the Lord (or Lady) Marchers of Cemais have had the right to select the town mayor. Remains of the original Norman castle were incorporated into a mansion during the 19th century. Newport, as its name implies, was once an important seaport, but today its main function seems to be as a quiet resort taking full advantage of its superb sands. To the west lies Parrog, which once received coastal trade at a quay whose crumbling remains are

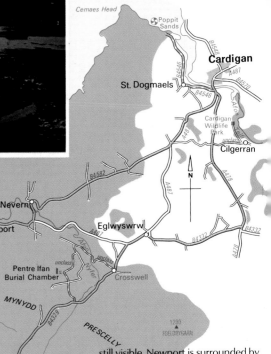

Once a haven for small fishing boats, picturesque Fishguard Harbour, situated in Lower Town, now provides safe anchorage for holiday craft.

still visible. Newport is surrounded by reminders of man's prehistoric past, including the remains of an iron-age fort above the town on the peak of Carningli, and a cromlech called Carreg Coetan Arthur, upstream from Gwaun bridge.

The huge stones which make up the distinctive outline of Pentre Ifan burial chamber were originally covered by a large cairn that has long since disappeared.

By tradition the first cuckoo of spring sings from Nevern's ancient cross.

Continue on the A487 for 2 miles and meet crossroads. Turn left on to the B4582, drive through woodlands, and cross the Afon Nyfer to enter Nevern.

NEVERN, Dyfed
Not only is Nevern one of the most attractive and beautifully-set villages in Wales, it is also the guardian of a great treasure in the shape of a Celtic cross which stands outside the local church. Almost 13ft high and carved with intricate patterns, the cross carries a number of obscure inscriptions that have never been deciphered. Also in the churchyard is an avenue of Irish yews leading to the rugged old building itself, which contains other carved stones. One of the trees exudes a blood-like sap and is known as the 'Bleeding Yew'.

Follow the 'Cardigan' road B4582 between high banks for 5 miles, then meet the A487 and turn left. Descend into Cardigan with panoramic views. Shortly before entering the town the route allows a detour to be made to St Dogmaels via a left turn on the B4546.

ST DOGMAELS, Dyfed
The old Welsh county of Cardiganshire was named after the influential Ceredig, whose descendant St Dogmael founded a hermitage here in the 6th century. The abbey was established in 1115 by Robert Fitz-Martin, Lord of Cemais, and the ruins (AM) that survive today comprise fragments dating from the 14th to 16th centuries. A collection of carved stones is housed on the site of the former abbey infirmary, and other examples may be seen in the adjoining 19th-century parish church. One of these, known as the Sagranus Stone, was inscribed in both Latin and Ogham and proved an invaluable key to mid-19th-century historians working to decipher the ancient Ogham script. The road to St Dogmaels can be followed beyond the village to the excellent beach at Poppit Sands. Good walks from here lead through lovely countryside to the wild cliffs of Cemaes Head.
Enter Cardigan.

CARDIGAN, Dyfed
Poets of all periods have waxed lyrical over the beautiful Afon Teifi, which flows into the sea at Cardigan. The salmon and sea trout that thrive in its tree-shaded waters are fished for from coracles, small traditional craft that have continued to use the river while relative newcomers have been forced elsewhere by the silting of Cardigan's port. The town is no longer of maritime significance, but the observant visitor will find many reminders of its sea-faring past. A fine 17th-century 6-arched bridge spans the Teifi beneath the remains of a Norman castle. Cardigan nowadays has a mainly Victorian character and appearance typified by its notable 19th-century guildhall, the venue for a regular market held among its basement arches.

Recross the Teifi bridge and in ¼ mile branch left on to the A478 'Tenby' road. After 2 miles note a left turn leading to fascinating Cilgerran Castle.

CILGERRAN, Dyfed
Legions of artists have been inspired by the craggy situation and romantic air of Cilgerran Castle. The Afon Teifi, itself the subject of poetry and song, flows beneath the castle walls and once a year is the scene of competitive bustle and the display of ancient skills in a picturesque coracle regatta. The pretty little village of Cilgerran is somewhat overshadowed by its 13th-century guardian (AM). North of the village is the Cardigan Wildlife Park.

On the main route proceed along the A478. After 3 miles turn right on to the B4332 'Fishguard' road and continue with fine views of the Prescelly Mountains. Drive into Eglwyswrw.

EGLWYSWRW, Dyfed
In medieval times the body of St Wrw was entombed in a chantry chapel of the local church, after which the parishioners would allow nobody else to be buried there because they believed that the virgin saint 'would not have any bedfellows' – even in death.

Meet a T-junction and turn left on to the A487 SP 'Fishguard'. After ¾ mile turn left again on the B4329 SP 'Haverfordwest' and drive to Crosswell. Here a detour can be made to Pentre Ifan burial chamber; turn right on to an unclassified road and follow a stretch of the wooded Afon Nyfer, then in 1½ miles turn left.

PENTRE IFAN BURIAL CHAMBER, Dyfed
Undoubtedly one of the finest megalithic monuments in Britain, Pentre Ifan (AM) stands on a slope overlooking vast tracts of the Pembrokeshire National Park and the distant waters of Cardigan Bay. To the west is 1,138ft Mynydd Carningli, on which St Brynach is said to have been ministered to by

Nest, whose beauty was legendary in medieval Wales, was abducted from Cilgerran Castle by one of her admirers.

angels. The monument itself consists of a 16-ton capstone supported by three spindly uprights and is thought to be some 5,000 years old.

On the main route, continue along the B4329. Climb steadily on to high moorland and reach a 1,328ft road summit. This viewpoint affords fine panoramas of the Mynydd Prescelly range.

MYNYDD PRESCELLY, Dyfed
Gentle moorland slopes dotted with outcrops of stone typify the scenery of Mynydd Prescelly, an ancient mountain range which culminates in 1,760ft Foel Cwmcerwyn east of the B4329. Beyond Foel Cwmcerwyn and 1,531ft Foel Feddau is 1,200ft Foeldrygarn, whose slopes are said to have provided the famous blue stones of Stonehenge, in Wiltshire.

The slopes of Mynydd Prescelly rise to rock-strewn summits from 1,535ft Foeleryr.

Descend to Greenway and crossroads at the New Inn. Opposite is Rosebush Reservoir.

ROSEBUSH RESERVOIR, Dyfed
Completed in 1932, this reservoir holds 170 million gallons and is an excellent leisure amenity for fishing and boating enthusiasts.

Turn right on to the B4313 'Fishguard' road. After 1 mile pass an unclassified right turn leading to the delightful countryside of the Gwaun Valley.

GWAUN VALLEY, Dyfed
Words like magical, secret and enchanting come easily to mind when describing the Gwaun Valley. Its little river flows through a thickly-wooded coomb, which rises on the northern side to the lower slopes of the Prescelly Mountains.

Return to Fishguard on the B4313, passing through attractive countryside.

HAVERFORDWEST, Dyfed

Houses crowd the steep slopes of Haverfordwest under the stern gaze of the old castle which overlooks them all. Built in the 13th century by William de Valence, a Fleming, it has always been a centre of power. Haverfordwest, isolated from England by the southern valleys and constant battles, was ruled by Norman lords, who, unlike their fellow invaders elsewhere in the country, refused to inter-marry. Thus this part of Pembrokeshire became known as Little England beyond Wales. In 1405 Owain Glyndwr burnt the town during his bid to reassert Welsh independence, but the castle survived. Unscathed, it did surrender to Parliament in the Civil War, but when a fresh revolt against the Puritans broke out, Cromwell had the castle 'slighted'. The noble keep which remains is now the county museum and art gallery. Once the main sea-link with Ireland, before the growth of Milford Haven in the 19th century, Haverfordwest is now an important market and administrative centre. The old Butter Market survives, and of the 3 churches, St Mary's is the finest.

Leave Haverfordwest on the A4076, SP 'Milford Haven'. Pass through Johnston and Steynton to reach the coast at Milford Haven.

MILFORD HAVEN, Dyfed

Nelson called this drowned valley the best harbour in the world, and to it the town of Milford Haven owes its existence. In the late 18th century Milford was developed as a fishing port and naval dockyard by Charles Greville. Disaster struck in 1814 when the naval dockyard was moved to Pembroke Dock, but Milford retaliated by rapidly becoming a deep-sea fishing port with the fourth largest catch in Britain. The town's closely-ranked houses climb a smooth rounded hill, and from their perches witnessed the departure of 170,000 ships in convoys during World War II, and saw the growth of 4 great oil refineries and a massive power station along the Haven's shores. Yet despite this tremendous development, which obviously has had some effect on the natural surroundings, the greater proportion of the Haven has remained undisturbed and in fact the upper reaches have been designated a nature reserve. The town itself retains a neat harbour used by fishing trawlers, pleasant gardens and an excellent shopping centre.

Turn right along the promenade and at the war memorial turn left. At the end of the town turn left across the bridge then right, SP 'Hubberston' and 'Dale'. At the edge of Herbrandston turn right, SP 'Dale', and continue along a high-banked road. After 5 miles turn left on to the B4327 for Dale.

LITTLE ENGLAND BEYOND WALES

This is England's Wales, where the Normans settled and the Welsh never regained supremacy. Place-names in both languages appear in this corner of Wales that is mostly a National Park, catering for seaside tourists yet caring for the rare wildlife.

The Fishguard Bay Yacht Club has its headquarters at Fishguard's Lower Town, where the Gwaun joins the sea

DALE, Dyfed

Dale is a pleasant little village lying just within the mouth of Milford Haven. It has all the atmosphere, sights and sounds of a small yachting centre, and is conveniently placed near some fine sandy beaches; Musselwick Sands, Martin's Haven from where boats sail to Skomer Island, Marloes Sands and Westdale Bay. Henry VII landed from France at nearby Mill Bay in 1485, to begin a venture which brought him victory over Richard III at Bosworth and consequently the throne of England.

Return along the B4327 and in 1 1/2 miles pass a turning to the left for Martin's Haven. In 3/4 mile keep left, then bear right with the Haverfordwest road. Nearly 2 miles farther go forward SP 'Talbenny' and 'Little Haven'. Pass through Talbenny and later turn left for the descent to Little Haven. On the steep ascent turn sharp left, SP 'Broad Haven', then descend to Broad Haven.

BROAD HAVEN, Dyfed

A silver strand of sand a mile wide make Broad Haven and its neighbour, Little Haven, ideal stopping places for a day on the beach. Strangely-folded cliffs border the bay and this beautiful remote area is renowned for its rare wild flowers, sea-birds and magnificent coastal scenery. Broad Haven itself is a busy place and in the car park is the countryside unit of the Pembrokeshire Coast National Park, which provides information on talks, walks and excursions for those who would like to know more of this delightful countryside.

PEMBROKESHIRE COAST NATIONAL PARK, Dyfed

The upper reaches of Milford Haven, the Preseli Hills, the coast and its outlying islands are all included in a National Park covering about a third of Pembrokeshire. The wild coastline where seals breed and hundreds of seabirds feed is a naturalists' paradise — home of the peregrine falcon and the rare chough. The best way to explore the coastal areas is by way of the 167-mile coastal path which can be joined at almost any point along its length between Amroth and St Dogmaels. The path was officially opened in 1970.

At the end of Broad Haven keep forward (no SP) along highbanked roads. In 2 3/4 miles, at a crossroads, turn left, SP 'Nolton'. Pass through Nolton and bear right for Nolton Haven.

NOLTON HAVEN, Dyfed

In this narrow inlet of St Bride's Bay, high cliffs shelter a farm, a chapel, a few sleepy cottages and a sandy beach which is exposed only at low tide. A tradition associated with this coastline is the collection of seaweed for the making of laver bread, best eaten with bacon or, some say, with porridge.

Continue, passing the long, sandy beaches of Newgale Sands and at the main road turn left on to the A487 for Newgale.

NEWGALE, Dyfed

This modern holiday village faces 2 1/2 miles of sandy beach backed by a pebble bank. At the north-east end of St Bride's Bay the winds whip up some fine surf, which has made Newgale a popular surfing resort. Very low tides reveal the stumps of a prehistoric forest.

Continue for 3 miles to Solva.

SOLVA, Dyfed

Solva appears at its best — a huddle of white, typically-Welsh cottages, hugging the hillside along the half mile of Solva Creek — from Gribin Head (NT). The village was favoured by smugglers, but this sheltered spot in an otherwise rocky and inhospitable coastline, was soon sought out by ships carrying lime and coal. Some disused lime kilns of the 19th century still stand near the road bridge. Today the amateur sailor reigns in the harbour, and the sailing club offers excellent facilities in St Bride's Bay. The Middle Mill at Solva, a watermill open to visitors, produces woollen weaves and hand-made furniture.

Continue on the A487 to St David's.

The Pembrokeshire Coast path near Solva

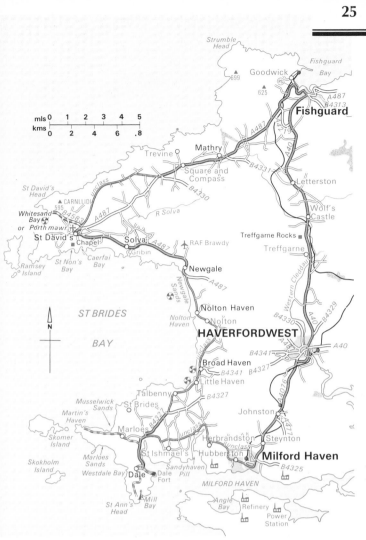

ST DAVID'S, Dyfed

Hardly more than a village, yet to every Welshman St David's is a hallowed place. St David, a descendant of the ancient Kings of Wales and patron saint of Wales, was born and lived here. Now his bones lie in the great cathedral, begun in 1180, which was some 500 years after his death. It was thought to be built in the shallow vale where it stands to hide it from the sea and possible invaders. The plain exterior belies the richly decorated interior. The floor slopes about 3ft from west to east, and the piers of the nave lean outward — an earthquake in 1248 was the cause of that. In front of the high altar lies the tomb of Edmund Tudor, father of Henry VII and between it and the Holy Trinity Chapel is an iron-bound chest containing the bones of St David and his teacher, St Justinian. Remnants of St David's original shrine are kept on the north side of the presbytery. It was badly damaged during the years in which the cathedral suffered neglect until Sir Gilbert Scott was commissioned in 1826 to renovate the building. The Bishop's Palace (AM) was built in 1340 to house pilgrims visiting the shrine, and there are extensive remains.

Leave on the A487 Fishguard road and in ½ mile turn left on to the B4583, SP 'Whitesands', then pass on the left the road which leads to Whitesand Bay.

WHITESAND BAY, Dyfed

Whitesand Bay, or Porth Mawr, is well-known for its excellent surfing and sweep of beautiful sands. In the early days of Christianity the bay saw many comings and goings to Ireland, and it is said St Patrick himself journeyed from here. The ancient chapel, excavated in 1924, is called St Patrick's Chapel in recognition of this.

The main tour continues forward along the unclassified road. In 4¼ miles bear right, SP 'Fishguard', then 1¼ miles further turn left on to the A487 for the outskirts of Mathry.

MATHRY, Dyfed

There is a legend here which tells of a father whose wife bore him 7 children at once; unable to support them and his already large family, he took them to a river to drown them, but they were saved by St Teilo, and thereafter the children were known as the Seven Saints of Mathry.

Continue on the A487, SP 'Fishguard'. At the edge of Goodwick turn right on to the A40 and ascend to Fishguard.

FISHGUARD, Dyfed

In the past herring fishing and pilchard curing were Fishguard's main industries: but in 1906 a new harbour was built, and in the following year so was a breakwater out to sea, both in the expectation that the new Atlantic liners would make Fishguard their first port of call. With the outbreak of World War I these hopes faded and the great liners never came. Fishguard is divided into 2; Upper Fishguard stands back from the sea and from it the road falls steeply to Lower Fishguard, which nestles beside the winding creek, indistinguishable from its counterparts in Cornwall or Brittany. Fishguard is noted in history as the scene of the last invasion of British soil. A French force landed here in 1797: the story goes that the French surrendered to a group of Welsh women in red cloaks and traditional tall hats; the French had thought they were Redcoats. There is a memorial in the churchyard to the heroine Jemima Nicholas, who rounded up a number of the French single-handed armed with only a pitch-fork. Fishguard is an ideal centre for touring, as the coastline here is truly magnificent, especially around Strumble Head and the beautiful Gwaum valley.

Leave on the A40 Haverfordwest road and continue through Wolf's Castle. The drive then enters a narrow Gorge and to the right are the prominent Treffgarne Rocks. From some angles these take on the fantastic shapes of a giant, a lion and a unicorn. Continue on the A40 for the return to Haverfordwest.

WESTERN BAYS

Retired seamen favour the quiet towns and villages of Cardigan Bay, and their neat cottages fit in well with the pastel shades of the omnipresent Welsh chapels. Inland is neat farming country crossed by small streams that suddenly waken into angry rapids and waterfalls.

LAMPETER, Dyfed

Neat rectangular fields bounded by hedges cover the gentle hills around Lampeter like a giant patchwork quilt. The town itself preserves a distinctive Welsh character coloured by its own personality. Small shops interspersed with dapper private houses, two Georgian hotels, and a proud Victorian town hall occupy the main street under the eye of the parish church. The latter was rebuilt in 1869, but contains memorials from earlier ages. Lampeter is best known for St David's College, which was founded in 1822 so that Welsh students (prohibited by expense from attending Oxford or Cambridge) could acquire a university education. The founder was Thomas Burgess, Bishop of St David's and the son of a Hampshire grocer. Although integrated with the University of Wales in 1971, the college remains a complete university in miniature.

Leave Lampeter on the A482 SP 'Aberaeron'. Drive through pleasant hill country and join the Aeron Valley at the combined villages of Felin Fach and Ystrad Aeron. Continue with the river through wooded country to reach Aberaeron.

ABERAERON, Dyfed

Lampeter is not alone in being connected with that most English of counties, Hampshire. At the turn of the 18th century an Aberaeron heiress called Susannah Jones married a widowed Hampshire curate. Some years later the couple inherited a fortune and commenced to plan and build Aberaeron. The Development, which included the construction of harbours, quays, stores, a town hall, and numerous dwellings, continued well into the middle of the 19th century and resulted in an extremely pleasing Georgian-style town with a charm enhanced by the Welsh habit of highlighting architectural details with brightly-coloured paint. Aberaeron's days as a busy seaport are long gone, and today it performs a useful service as an elegant and unspoilt holiday resort.

Leave Aberaeron on the A487 'Aberystwyth' road. Drive through Aberarth, with glimpses of coastal scenery to the left, and continue to Llanon.

LLANON, Dyfed

Memories of Dylan Thomas' *Under Milk Wood* are awoken here. Like the setting for that famous play, the village seems to be a retirement place for old sea captains with shipshape little cottages named after the craft they once commanded. Llanon is certainly of the sea and grew from the nearby fishing village of Llansantffraid, where the remains of fish traps said to have been constructed by the monks of Strata Florida Abbey can still be seen in places on the beach.

Continue to Llanrhystud.

LLANRHYSTUD, Dyfed

No less than three castle mounds, the best of which is Caer Penrhos, survive near this attractive 19th-century village.

Climb inland and descend through Llanfarian to the Ystwyth Valley. Continue through Rhyd-y-Felin and later cross the Afon Rheidol into Aberystwyth.

ABERYSTWYTH, Dyfed

Seat of government and a holiday resort with a shopping area that serves a large locality, Aberystwyth grew to real importance with the establishment of its Norman castle by Edmund Crouchback in 1277. It is still a place of significance, and opposite the ruins of the castle is a Victorian hotel building that was bought in 1870 to form the nucleus of the University of Wales. Modern university buildings stand east of the town on Penglais Hill and include the National Library of Wales, which houses an incomparable collection of early Welsh manuscripts. Also of interest are the varied exhibits of the Ceredigion Museum. Notable among the many superb 18th- and 19th-century buildings preserved in the town are the fine houses that stand in Laura Place. A Victorian funicular railway operates on Constitution Hill, and echoes from the more distant past are evoked by the well-preserved iron-age earthworks that lie south of the town on Pen Dinas. The church at Llanbadarn Fawr – now a suburb of Aberystwyth – was founded in the 6th century by St Padarn, but the building that now occupies the site dates from the 13th century. Two beautiful Celtic crosses are preserved inside.

VALE OF RHEIDOL LIGHT RAILWAY, Dyfed

British Rail's only narrow gauge line uses steam locomotives along 12 miles of the lovely Rheidol Valley between Aberystwyth and the spectacular Devil's Bridge. Originally opened in 1902 to carry local lead ore and the occasional passenger, the line's route through the breathtaking scenery of the 'Vale' has ensured success as a major tourist attraction and probably assured its future as a centre for steam-engine nostalgia.

To leave Aberystwyth, return over Afon Rheidol on the A487 SP 'Cardigan' and after 1¼ miles branch left on to the A4120 'Devil's Bridge' road. Climb steadily, pass through Capel Seion, then 5 miles beyond the latter reach a 990ft road summit affording splendid views into the thickly-wooded Rheidol Valley. Continue to Devil's Bridge.

DEVIL'S BRIDGE, Dyfed

A spectacular wooded gorge, tremendous waterfalls, and three bridges stacked on top of each other in a 700-year sequence are to be seen here.

Leave Devil's Bridge on the B4343 'Tregaron' road. Continue through hilly country and descend into the Ystwyth Valley. Cross a river and enter Pontrhydygroes.

PONTRHYDYGROES, Dyfed

The neat cottages in this village were once occupied by employees of the important local lead-mining industry. Ruins of the mine buildings stand empty and useless on the surrounding hillsides — a comment on 'robber' mineral industries.

Continue, and at the post office bear right on to an unclassified road SP 'Trawscoed'. Drive along a thickly-wooded valley and pass the Tyn-y-Bedw picnic site. After a short distance turn left on to the B4340 and proceed to Ystrad Meurig.

Whitewashed farm buildings dotted amongst gentle hills typify the countryside of old Cardiganshire.

Little remains of once-powerful Strata Florida Abbey, except a beautiful doorway and these medieval floor tiles.

This staunch little steam engine was specially built for the Vale of Rheidol Railway in 1902.

STRATA FLORIDA ABBEY, Dyfed

Low foundations and a beautiful west doorway (AM) opening on to grass are all that remain of the once great and noble abbey of Strata Florida. In the 13th century, when the abbey was at the height of its power, it ran huge flocks of sheep on the vast upland areas of Mid Wales under its control. The Welsh prince Rhys ap Gruffydd started the abbey in 1184; an extensive group of attractive 18th-century farm buildings now covers much of the site eventually occupied by the abbey buildings. The refreshingly plain, early 19th-century parish church of Pontrhydfendigaid stands in the abbey grounds. Its yard is said to contain the grave of Dafydd ap Gwilym, who lived during the 14th century and is considered one of the greatest Welsh poets.

Return to Pontrhydfendigaid and turn left on to the B4343. Skirt Tregaron Bog.

YSTRAD MEURIG, Dyfed

The now closed St John's College had been a famous educational establishment since the mid-18th century. Also of interest here are the slight remains of a Norman castle.

Continue to Caradog Falls, with the extensive Tregaron Bog to the right.

CARADOG FALLS, Dyfed

These picturesque falls are situated on a tributary stream of the Afon Teifi, just south of the tour route.

Continue to Pontrhydfendigaid.

PONTRHYDFENDIGAID, Dyfed

A quaint old bridge spans the Teifi here. Once a year the village is the venue of a popular and well-endowed eisteddfod – a traditional Welsh festival of poetry and music.

Leave Pontrhydfendigaid on the B4343 'Tregaron' road. Cross the Afon Teifi and shortly turn left on to an unclassified road for a detour to Strata Florida Abbey.

TREGARON BOG (CORS TREGARON), Dyfed

The 1,898-acre extent of this National Nature Reserve makes it the largest peat bog in Wales. In spring it is loud with the cries of curlew and plover, in summer it is white with the fluffy tufts of bog cotton grass, and in winter its sedges turn the glowing red that must have inspired its full Welsh name – 'Cors Goch Glanteifi', or the 'Red Bog Along the Teifi'.

Continue to Tregaron.

TREGARON, Dyfed

Dominating the square of this unspoilt Welsh town is a bright-green statue of Henry Richard. Born in 1812, he became the Liberal MP for Merthyr and was such an outspoken supporter of disarmament that he became known as the 'Apostle of Peace'. The church of St Caron dates basically from the 14th century, but was restored during the 19th century. On Tuesdays Tregaron fulfils its prime function as a market town and fills with farmers, traders and sheep.

Leave Tregaron with SP 'Llanddewi Brefi, B4343'. Drive along the Teifi Valley to reach Llanddewi Brefi.

LLANDDEWI BREFI, Dyfed

A great synod was held here in AD 519 to debate the *Heresy of Pelagius*, which denied the biblical doctrine of original sin. One of those refuting Pelagius was St David, beneath whom the ground is said to have risen so that those around could hear what he was saying. The village's 13th-century church stands on a mound which tradition holds to be the same miraculous eminence that provided the saint with his vantage point. Several interesting old stones can be seen inside the church.

Continue on the B4343 SP 'Lampeter' to reach Llanfair Clydogau.

LLANFAIR CLYDOGAU, Dyfed

Sarn Helen, a Roman road, passes through this scattered little parish. The local church stands within a circular graveyard and contains a strangely-carved font. Other features of the village include a handsome bridge and an elegant chapel.

Drive through Cellan, and within 2 miles meet a junction. Turn right on to the A482 and return to Lampeter.

Aberaeron's brightly painted Georgian cottages overlook Cardigan Bay.

ON THE BLACK MOUNTAIN

Infinite shades of green colour this tour: pale hillsides rise from ruined Talley Abbey; lush farmland borders the winding Afon Tywi; and the light-shifting subtlety of moorland sedges surrounds the giant Llyn Brianne Reservoir and climbs the Black Mountain.

LLANDEILO, Dyfed

This riverside market town stands amid rich farming land and is a good centre for fishing and touring. Many places of interest exist in the surrounding area. A 19th-century stone bridge in the town arches over the River Tywi in a magnificent single span of 145ft. Llandeilo's church, virtually rebuilt between 1848 and 1851, contains two attractive cross heads of Celtic origin.

Leave Llandeilo on the A40 'Llandovery' road and in ¼ mile reach the B4302 turnoff on the left. This may be taken as a detour to picturesque Talley by turning left SP 'Talley' and driving 6 miles through the hamlets of Maerdy and Hallway.

TALLEY, Dyfed

Neat cottages and an attractive church protectively cluster round the remains of once-famous Talley Abbey (AM) deep in the green folds of the Dyfed hills. Little of the abbey's 12th-century fabric has survived pillaging for building material that has gone on unchecked through the centuries, but an undeniable air of sanctity still exists. A path through the yard of the adjacent church leads to the two lakes of Talley, where clouds of dragonflies hover over the placid waters during the summer months.

On the main route continue along the A40 and pass through pleasant hill scenery to Llandovery.

LLANDOVERY, Dyfed

Llandovery's name means 'Church amid the waters' and derives from its position at the confluence of the Bran, Gwydderig, and Tywi. The town has been a place of some significance at least since Roman

Coarse grass and moorland sedges blanket the undulating ridges of the Black Mountain, which is traversed by twisting mountain roads.

Beautiful Dolauhirion Bridge spans the Afon Tywi north of Llandovery.

times, a fact highlighted by the siting of Llanfair-ar-y-Bryn Church within the ramparts of a Roman fort. Roman tiles are incorporated in the fabric of the church. A monument to William Williams, a local man who is most remembered as being the composer of the hymn *Guide Me O Thou Great Jehovah* stands in the churchyard. Another notable inhabitant of Llandovery was Rhys Pritchard, who wrote a collection of simple verses collectively called *The Welshman's Candle*. This work became as popular in Wales as Bunyan's *Pilgrim's Progress* did in

England. A reminder of the town's important connexions with cattle droving is the building which houses Lloyd's Bank. Until 1909 this was the Black Ox Bank, founded in 1799 by a drover named David Jones. The nearby Market Hall is a low 19th-century building capped by an extraordinary pepper-pot turret. Llandovery College, a public school founded in 1848, was created for the express purpose of providing an education entirely in the Welsh language. Overgrown remains of a Norman castle surmount a mound above the cattle market.

Rhys ap Gruffydd founded Talley Abbey during the 12th century.

Drive over the level crossing in Llandovery and turn left on to the A483 SP 'Builth Wells'. In ¼ mile meet crossroads and turn left on to the unclassified 'Llyn Brianne' road. One mile farther reach the bridge by Dolauhirion.

DOLAUHIRION BRIDGE, Dyfed

Designed by William Edwards and built in 1773, this splendid bridge spans the Tywi in a single graceful arch of 84ft.

Continue through increasingly spectacular scenery, with Crychan Forest behind a high ridge to the east.

CRYCHAN FOREST, Dyfed & Powys

This large forest is named after the little Afon Crychan. The forest itself extends almost from Llandovery to Llanwrtyd Wells and is bounded in the east by the moorland of Mynydd Eppynt.

About 1¾ miles from Dolauhirion pass a left turn from the main tour rout which leads to Cilycwm village.

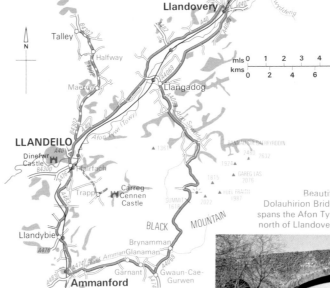

CILYCWM, Dyfed
Situated in one of the tributary valleys of the Tywi, Cilycwm is surrounded by some of the wildest scenery in South Wales and is noted for the old wall paintings in its 15th-century church. The village chapel is claimed to be the first Methodist meeting place to have existed in Wales.
Continue through Rhandirmwyn on the main route. Three miles on the left is a signposted footpath leading to Twm Sion Catti's Cave.

TWM SION CATTI'S CAVE, Dyfed
A short nature trail up Dinas Hill leads to the one-time hideout of Twm Sion Catti, a famous early 16th-century outlaw whose modern reputation has a lot in common with England's tales of Robin Hood.
Continue through a wooded gorge to reach the carpark and viewing area at Llyn Brianne Reservoir. A narrow but excellently surfaced road may be taken through magnificent scenery to the reservoir's farthest arm and Towy Forest.

LLYN BRIANNE RESERVOIR, Dyfed & Powys
The creation of this huge reservoir in the early 1970s was greeted with mixed emotions, as the area flooded had previously been considered one of the most remote and beautiful in Wales – if not all Britain. New roads to the lake have made it easily accessible, and the spectacular scenery that surrounds its great expanse can be enjoyed by all. The last British nesting sites of the kite exist in closely-guarded and highly-secret locations in this area.

TOWY FOREST, Dyfed & Powys
On the northern slopes of Llyn Brianne, accessible via the new reservoir road, are the coniferous ranks of Towy Forest. The Afon Tywi has its source some miles north in the wild moors of central Wales.
Return along the Llyn Brianne access road to the crossroads at Llandovery. Turn right on to the A483 and then left on to the A40 SP 'Brecon'. In ¼ mile turn right on to the A4069, SP 'Llangadog', and continue along the Tywi Valley to reach Llangadog.

LLANGADOG, Dyfed
Llangadog was once an important town, with a 12th-century native Welsh castle unusual in that it was probably using defensive techniques learned from the Norman conquerors. The overlords, ever wary of opposition, completely destroyed it in 1277. All that remains today is a mound sited about ½ mile south of the village. Carn Goch, the largest iron-age hillfort in Wales, lies 3 miles south-west at OS SN689243.
At the T-junction turn left, SP 'Brynamman'. Follow the pretty Afon Sawdde Valley with the river on the left and ascend on to the slopes of the Black Mountain. Continue to the 1,600ft viewpoint.

BLACK MOUNTAIN, Dyfed
West from the A4069 viewpoint the Black Mountain falls away in ridges to the fertile Tywi Valley. In the middle distance Carreg Cennen Castle can be seen perched on its craggy limestone cliff, and to the east the grass-covered peaks of 1,987ft Foel Fraith and 2,076ft Gareg Las rise against a long backdrop provided by the ridge of Bannau Sir Gaerfyrddin – The Carmarthen Van. Geologically the Black Mountain is made up of very ancient red sandstone in the north and younger millstone grit in the south, the two beds being separated by a band of limestone. It is a lonely windswept land inhabited only by sheep and a thriving population of indigenous wild animals.
Descend, with views over a partly industrial area, to Brynamman. Turn right for Gwaun-cae-gurwen. On the nearside of the ensuing level crossing turn right again on to the A474 SP 'Ammanford'. Drive through Garnant and Glanaman to Ammanford.

AMMANFORD, Dyfed
Until the late 19th century the Cross Inn at the centre of this town was almost the only building here, but discovery of a local anthracite coalfield quickly brought the mixed blessing of industrial prosperity. Nowadays the area is dotted with slag heaps from the workings, but the essentially agricultural character of the local countryside remains.
At traffic signals turn right on to the A483 SP 'Llandeilo'. Proceed to Llandybie.

LLANDYBIE, Dyfed
This small town stands on the edge of the local coalfield and is justifiably proud of its splendid early Victorian railway station. The church preserves a medieval barrel roof and carries an imposing battlemented tower. Inside are a number of interesting monuments. A lane leads east from Llandybie to beautiful river scenery and the waterfall of Glynhir.

Associated in legend with one of King Arthur's knights, Carreg Cennen Castle is perched dramatically on a limestone cliff overlooking the Black Mountain.

Continue to Ffairfach. A slight detour for splendid Carreg Cennen Castle can be made from here by taking a right turn on to an unclassified road, then turning right again and ascending. Follow the subsequent descent and keep left at the edge of Trapp.

CARREG CENNEN CASTLE, Dyfed
No description of this most romantic of castles can better that given by A C Bradley, who wrote: 'It looks for all the world like an Arthurian Castle one might see in dreams....' A steep approach via a farmyard leads to the imposing pile of walls and turrets perched on a limestone cliff which drops a breathtaking 200ft into the attractive valley below. The existing building fabric dates from the 13th century, but a fortress existed here long before that. The atmosphere of permanence about the castle inspired Dylan Thomas to refer to it reverently, in the prayers of one of his characters, as 'Carreg Cennen, King of Time'.
Return to Ffairfach on the main route and continue to Llandeilo with views to the left of Dinefwr Castle.

DINEFWR CASTLE, Dyfed
As Llandeilo is approached from the south, the ivy-clad tower of a castle can be seen rising from trees on a hill directly west of the town. This is Dinefwr (Dynevor) Castle (AM), which was once the seat of Welsh princes. Ruins comprising the keep and part of the curtain wall are situated in a private park near a 19th-century mansion. The ruins will be open to the public when necessary repairs are completed.

Llyn Brianne serves as a storage reservoir for the Afon Tywi water supply scheme.

LLANDRINDOD WELLS, Powys

Llandrindod stands just above the junction between the Rivers Ithon and Aran and the Church of the Trinity, built in the Middle Ages, marks the founding of the community. Llandrindod was no more than a scattered hamlet until 1749, when a hotel was built and the fashions of Bath were introduced — ballrooms, dining salons and gaming places. 1867 saw the arrival of the railway, and by the turn of the century Llandrindod had some 80,000 visitors a year and the town retains its spacious Edwardian streets and fine hotels from this heyday. In the War Memorial Gardens is the Llandrindod Wells Museum, which is chiefly devoted to finds from nearby Castell Collen, a Roman fort whose inhabitants may well have known of the curative properties of Llandrindod's waters. The Automobile Palace, in Temple Street, is a more contemporary museum. Here the Tom Norton Collection of bicycles and tricycles is kept. The waters which put Llandrindod on the map can still be taken at the pump room in Rock Park, now privately owned.

Leave on the A483 Newtown road. Pass through Crossgates and later reach Llanddewi.

LLANDDEWI, Powys

The village lies amid the beautiful scenery of the Ithon valley, and may be a site of ancient fortification as traces of tumuli and old defence systems have been found in the area. The church was rebuilt in 1890 on the site of a much earlier building, and preserves a walled-up Norman doorway and a 14th-century font. Perhaps the best building is Llanddewi Hall, now a farmhouse, opposite the church. This displays the simple, strong lines which gave it its authority in the days when it was the most important manor in the district.

Continue along the A483 to Llanbister.

LLANBISTER, Powys

Llanbister stands on a steep hill above the River Ithon and copes with the slope by a series of steps. It was the scene of bloody revenge in the 15th century; a quarrel among members of the Vaughan family resulted in a fight in which John Vaughan killed David Vaughan. David's sister took revenge by attending an archery competition, in Llanbister, dressed as a man. When her turn came to shoot, she turned from the target and shot John, and escaped during the ensuing confusion.

Continue along the valley to Llanbadarn Fynydd.

Penygarreg Dam holds back the waters of a 240-acre lake, which can be fished for trout by permit holders

AROUND THE WELSH LAKES

Victorian business acumen was responsible for the charming spa town of Llandrindod Wells; the 19th century created the lovely Elan Valley — the Welsh Lake District — and Newtown sprang up in the 20th century, but ancient Welsh culture marks the surrounding towns and hamlets with an indelible stamp of its own.

The red dragon of Wales has made the Dragon Pottery at Rhayader famous

DOLFOR, Powys

Dolfor stands at over 1,000ft above sea level, and from the hill above the village there are magnificent views, and from the summit of nearby Kerry Hill (1,565ft) the Brecon Beacons are visible to the south. The Rivers Teme, Ithon and Mule all have their sources in this area. The village inn is so unspoilt that from the outside it still looks like an ordinary house.

Garreg Ddu Reservoir, one of the Elan Valley reservoirs built between 1892 and 1907. Claerwen Reservoir was opened by Elizabeth II in 1952

Keep forward on this road, climbing to 1,200ft with magnificent views over the Severn valley and distant mountains. After a long descent turn left at the crossroads on to the A489 and descend into the Severn valley to Newtown.

LLANBADARN FYNYDD, Powys

Closeby the River Ithon stands the village church, rebuilt, but still with its original east window, remnants of its rood screen, and an altar rail of 1716. This lovely spot was once an isolated mountain village, and retains some of this character, but its position on the main Llandrindod Wells to Newtown road has inevitably resulted in development. The road was said to possess a bend for every day in the year — 365. An important cattle sale is held in the village street during late summer.

Pass the New Inn PH then turn right SP 'Dolfor'. Gradually ascend on to high moorland and later go forward on to the B4355, SP 'Newtown'. Descend to Dolfor and turn right on to the A483, then right again on to the narrow unclassified road past the church.

NEWTOWN, Powys

Although originally established in 1279, the 20th century has virtually seen another Newtown arise. Extensive building, including a theatre and civic offices, have appeared in a variety of styles, ranging from Tudor to contemporary; such diversity imparts its own charm. In Llanllwchaiarn, a district of Newtown where some of the old town still exists, the Newtown Textile Museum has established itself in one of the blocks where weavers used to work. The museum includes exhibits of the wool trade, old tools and machinery and other general items of local history, giving a picture of Newtown life in the past. In 1885, the little stone and half-timbered building in which Owain Glyndwr held one of his parliaments during the first decade of the 15th

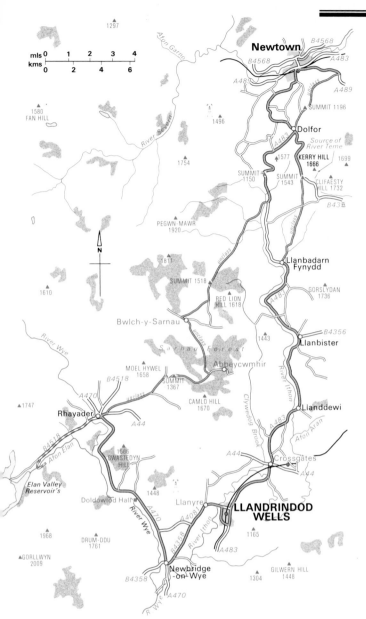

century, was brought from Dolgellau and re-erected on its present site in Newtown. The most honoured native of Newtown is Robert Owen, the great social reformer who is known as the father of trade unionism. He is buried in the churchyard of the old parish church. Also buried here are a boy and girl, lovers who were denied marriage by their families and consequently made a suicide pact and took poison. Thousands attended the funeral: in death the couple were allowed to be together and were buried in the same grave.

At the crossroads in the town centre turn left on to the A483. A long, winding ascent leads past Dolfor to a 1,200ft summit. In 1 mile, on the descent, go forward on to the Bwlch-y-sarnau road (main road bears sharply left, care required), and cross the River Ithon. In 5¼ miles bear right to reach Bwlch-y-sarnau. Here go forward at the crossroads and at the T-junction turn right, SP 'Rhayader'. At the next T-junction turn left and in 1 mile turn right and continue to Rhayader, joining the A44 on entering the town.

RHAYADER, Powys
A busy, bustling little town which has kept a 19th-century atmosphere even though many of its shop fronts have been modernised. Far below, the River Wye bounces over boulders and rocky platforms towards pretty falls below the bridge. Although some light industy has grown up, Rhayader is essentially a market town noted for its sheep fairs, nestling as it does above the River Wye on the edge of vast moorlands, often referred to as the Welsh desert. The most notable

historical event at Rhayader was the Rebecca Riots during the 19th century. Men, dressed as women and calling themselves Rebecca's Daughters, tore down the turnpike gates in protest against high toll charges. They took their name from the biblical quotation Genesis 24:60 'And they blessed Rebekah, and said unto her, Thou art our sister, be thou the mother of thousands of millions, and let thy seed possess the gate of those which hate them'.

From Rhayader, a detour can be made to the Elan Valley Reservoirs. At the crossroads go forward on to the B4518, SP 'Elan Valley', cross the Wye and in ¼ mile bear left. Later pass the Elan Valley Hotel and in ½ mile go forward for Caban Coch, Garreg Ddu and the other reservoirs.

ELAN VALLEY, Powys
During the 19th century a new reservoir complex constructed by the Corporation of Birmingham created a beautiful series of lakes and wooded slopes known as the Welsh Lake District. Before the Elan Valley was flooded, it was famous for its wild, haunting beauty. Beneath the waters of Caban Coch lies a house in which the poet Shelley lived for a while with his young wife Harriet.

The main tour turns left at the crossroads on to the A470 following the Wye valley.

WYE VALLEY, Powys
Running along the southern boundary of old Radnorshire, the Wye is a delightful river to either fish in or walk beside. It is a true mountain stream, its bed strewn with great boulders interspersed with deep, swirling pools, rapids and falls and it is a paradise for trout fishermen, as well as being famous for salmon. In 1308 Edward II took with him 3,000 dried salmon for his Scottish Campaign and many of them came from the Wye.

5 miles from Rhayader, pass Doldowlod Hall (not open), where the famous engineer James Watt spent his retirement, and continue to Newbridge-on-Wye.

NEWBRIDGE-ON-WYE, Powys
This pretty village beside the sparkling waters of the River Wye is a very popular base for fishermen as both the Wye and nearby Ithon offer excellent sport. In the village itself is the Mid Wales House Gallery — an art gallery and craft shop.

Turn left on to the B4358, SP 'Llandrindod', then in 2½ miles go forward on to the A4081. Shortly beyond Llanyre cross the River Ithon then bear right to re-enter Llandrindod Wells.

Rhayader's 2 main streets meet at the town's clock-tower war memorial

LLANDUDNO, Gwynedd
Justifiably known as the 'Queen of Welsh Resorts', Llandudno developed in the 1850s from a cluster of fishermen's cottages to a Victorian seaside resort which is a classic of its kind. The town was the brainchild of Liverpool surveyor Owen Williams, who planned the great sweep of the Promenade and the majestically wide streets. Great Orme's Head, with its gardens, cable railway, an ancient church, and windswept grassy slopes, separates the resort's two superb beaches.

Leave Llandudno on the A546, SP 'Deganwy'. Pass through Deganwy and in 1¼ miles reach a roundabout and take the 1st exit on to the A55 'Betws-y-coed'. A detour to Conwy may be made from the main route by crossing the Afon Conwy from this roundabout.

CONWY, Gwynedd
Three bridges span the Conwy estuary for access to the town, which is squeezed between the mountains and the sea. The oldest of the bridges was built by Thomas Telford in 1826 to carry traffic previously forced to use the perilous ferry. In 1848 Stephenson built a tubular railway bridge across the estuary, and in 1958 a new road bridge took the load from Telford's original. All three bridges seem to lead straight into Edward I's magnificent castle, which, along with the complete town walls, is a supreme example of 13th-century defensive architecture (all AM). The original medieval street plan is preserved, but only a few old buildings survive. Outstanding amongst these are Aberconwy (NT), which was built in 1400, and houses the Conwy Exhibition and the lovely Tudor house of Plas Mawr. Also of interest are the Visitor Centre, and 'Britain's Smallest House'.

Continue on the main route through Llandudno Junction. After ¾ mile at

NORTHERN RESORTS AND MOUNTAIN LANES

Children's laughter is as common as the cries of gulls on the North Wales coast, but away from the sea the sounds diminish and change till all that is heard is the breeze through sedges and the murmur of mountain streams.

The weathered rock of Great Orme's Head is typical of limestone scenery.

roundabout follow signs Betws-y-coed on to the A470. Drive through Glan Conwy, pass the Felin Isaf Watermill (open) and 1¼ miles farther reach the entrance to Bodnant Gardens.

BODNANT GARDENS, Gwynedd
The finest garden in Wales, and one of the best in Britain, Bodnant (NT) occupies a superb terraced site on the east side of the Conwy Valley and is open from March to October. It is best seen early in the year when its celebrated azaleas and rhododendrons are in bloom. The gardens were first laid out in 1875 by Henry Pochin, and have been considerably extended since.

Follow the beautiful Vale of Conwy to Llanrwst.

LLANRWST, Gwynedd
A graceful 3-arched bridge that spans the Conwy here is dated 1636 and (probably wrongly) attributed to architect Inigo Jones. Near by is Ty Hwnt i'r Bont, a 15th-century house (NT) which is open as a café. In the parish church are an elaborate 15th-century rood loft and screen which were brought from Maenan Abbey at the Dissolution. Across the river are the beautiful Gwydir Chapel of 1633, which houses memorials to one of Wales' greatest land-owning families, the Wynnes, and the Tudor

Gwydir Castle (open), which was once one of their family seats.

Continue on the A470, cross a railway bridge then turn left on to the B5427 SP 'Nebo'. In 3½ miles reach a T-junction and turn right on to the B5113. Pass through Nebo and later descend into Pentrefoelas.

PENTREFOELAS, Clwyd
Mountain scenery starts to give way to moorland near this hamlet. An

8ft-high inscribed pillar known as the Levelinus Stone marks the spot where Llywelyn ap Sisyll, a prince of Gwynedd, fell in battle in 1023.

Turn left on to the A5, and after ¼ mile turn left again on to the A543 'Denbigh' road. Ascend on to the Denbigh Moors.

DENBIGH MOORS, Clwyd
Forestry plantations and huge reservoirs have dramatically changed the character of this moorland region in recent years. The latest enterprise is the construction of the vast Brenig Reservoir.

Continue past the lonely Sportsman's Arms – the highest inn in Wales – and drive through Bylchau to reach Denbigh.

DENBIGH, Clwyd
Overlooking the town's attractive streets are the ruins of Edward I's great castle (AM). It was begun in 1282 with the construction of town walls that have remained remarkably intact to the present day. Perhaps the most impressive feature of the fortress is its tripartite gatehouse. Inside the town walls are remains of St Hilary's Tower (AM), which formed part of the original garrison chapel, and Leicester's Folly (AM). The latter is part of a church that was to have replaced the Cathedral of St Asaph, but was never completed. In the lower part of the town are the remains of a Carmelite friary (AM).

Continue on the A525 'Rhyl' road, with the ridge of the Clwydian Range prominent to the right. Enter Trefnant.

Conwy Castle is arguably one of the greatest works by Edward I's military architect, Master James of St George.

TREFNANT, Clwyd
Church, parsonage, and school here were built by architect Sir Gilbert Scott during the 19th century. The capitals of the columns inside the church are decorated with carved leaves typical of tree species found in the countryside round Trefnant.

Keep forward for St Asaph.

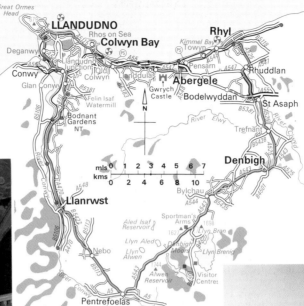

Delightfully naive 17th-century paintings decorate the roof of Gwydir Uchaf Chapel at Gwydir Castle, Llanrwst.

ST ASAPH, Clwyd
Both a village and a city, little St Asaph stands beside the River Elwy and has a cathedral that was founded by St Kentigern in AD 560. This has subsequently been rebuilt several times, and major restoration work was carried out during the 19th century by architect Sir Gilbert Scott. The building, no bigger than a large parish church, is the smallest cathedral in England and Wales.

Follow SP 'Rhyl', and after ¾ mile meet a roundabout and keep forward. A detour to Bodelwyddan can be made from the main route by turning left on to the Conwy road A55.

BODELWYDDAN, Clwyd
Rising gracefully above the village roof tops like the tip of a giant white spear is the 202ft spire of the parish church. Its prominence as a landmark that can be seen miles around must have been planned by Lady Margaret Willoughby de Broke, who built it in 1856 as a giant memorial to her husband. The interior of the building has earnt it the name 'The Marble Church', for no less than 14 different kinds of that stone were used in its construction.

Continue on the main route and turn right into Rhuddlan.

RHUDDLAN, Clwyd
The princes of Wales and their Norman conquerors recognised Rhuddlan's position in the Vale of Clywd as being of military significance, and both forces built castles here. The mound, or motte (AM), of the first invasion stronghold

Fish eagles, hawks, and many other birds of prey can be seen at Colwyn Bay's Mountain Zoo.

The graceful lines of the bridge at Llanrwst have led to its being attributed to Inigo Jones.

still exists but it is the great castle of Edward I (AM) that really captures the eye. This was his headquarters whilst conducting the campaign to conquer Wales, and it was the Statute of Rhuddlan that confirmed his sovereignty in 1284. The parish church dates originally from the 13th century, and the bridge (AM) over the Clwyd has 16th-century arches.

At the roundabout take the 1st exit for Rhyl.

RHYL, Clwyd
'Sunny Rhyl' offers 3 miles of sandy beach and almost all the entertainments expected of a seaside resort as popular as this. Few other British holiday towns cater better for the family holiday, and Rhyl has been a confirmed success ever since its development from a pair of fishermen's cottages in 1833.

Leave Rhyl promenade on the 'Abergele' road and shortly turn right on to the A548. Follow the coast through Kinmel Bay and Towyn to Pensarn.

PENSARN, Clwyd
This resort, linked with Abergele, is at the centre of a 5-mile sand and shingle beach.

Reach a roundabout and turn left to enter Abergele.

ABERGELE, Clwyd
No longer simply a market town but also a busy resort, Abergele is surrounded by caravan sites, chalets, and all the paraphernalia associated with the seaside. Its Tudor church features a double nave.

Turn right on to the A547 'Conwy' road and pass the road to Gwrych Castle.

Partial demolition after the Civil War reduced Rhuddlan Castle's 13th-century fabric to a picturesque ruin.

GWRYCH CASTLE, Clwyd
This mock-Norman extravagance with castellated walls and fairy-tale turrets was built in 1814. It now serves as a holiday centre, offering medieval banquets and jousting among its attractions.

Continue to Llanddulas.

LLANDDULAS, Clwyd
Llanddulas is both a holiday village and a loading point for limestone worked in local quarries.

Remain on the A547 SP 'Old Colwyn' and continue to Colwyn Bay.

COLWYN BAY, Clwyd
Lovers of Victorian architecture will find much to please them in Colwyn Bay. The resort is hardly more than a century old, and is somewhat more restrained in character than many of its neighbours. Excellent parks soften the character of the town, and the Welsh Mountain Zoo is a post-war development featuring a good variety of wild animals.

Continue forward and follow signs 'Rhos on Sea' then 'Llandudno' on to the B5115. Pass through Rhos then cross Little Orme's Head and return to Llandudno.

THE DEE VALLEY AND THE VALE OF CLWYD

From the small town of Llangollen, where streets are filled with the sound of music from the International Eisteddfod every July, the drive crosses by the lofty Horseshoe Pass into the rich farmland of the Vale of Clwyd and carries on through Clocaenog Forest to the pretty lakeside town of Bala and the picturesque Dee valley.

LLANGOLLEN, Clwyd
In July every year this small Welsh town on the River Dee plays host to thousands of visitors and competitors who flock to the International Musical Eisteddfod, which was instituted in 1947. Llangollen's old stone bridge dates from 1345-6 and is doubly acclaimed: firstly as one of the Thri Thlws Cymru, the 3 beauties of Wales; secondly in a traditional rhyme as one of the Seven Wonders of Wales. 'Pystyll Rhaeadr and Wrixham Steeple/ Snowdon's Mountain without its people;/Overton Yewtrees, Saint Winifred Wells,/Llangollen Bridge and Gresford Bells.' A source of wonder in their own lifetimes were the Ladies of Llangollen, Miss Sarah Ponsonby and Lady Eleanor Butler. These eccentric ladies left their native Ireland and defied convention by setting up house together in 1778 at Plas Newydd, a handsome black and white timbered house (OACT), inaccurately described by the poet Wordsworth as a 'low-browed cott'. The ladies always wore severely masculine dress and were often mistaken for men. It became fashionable to visit them and among their distinguished guests were Sir Walter Scott and the Duke of Wellington. To the west of the town are the Horseshoe Falls, not a tumbling cascade, but an elegant semi-circular weir designed by Thomas Telford to take water from the Dee to his canal. There is a small canal museum on the town wharf.

Leave Llangollen on the A542 Ruthin road, and follow the Eglwyseg valley to pass ruined Valle Crucis Abbey.

VALLE CRUCIS ABBEY, Clwyd
Set amid hill and valley, the original majestic ruins (AM) evoke the splendour of the abbey. It was built by Madog ap Gruffydd Maelor, Prince of Powys, and destroyed by order of Henry VIII 3 centuries later. Of the abbey church only the west front, with its beautifully carved doorway, survives. The Cistercian monks ate fish not meat, and had fishing rights in the River Dee.

Continue on the A542 and shortly pass (right) the Pillar of Eliseg.

PILLAR OF ELISEG, Clwyd
Prince Eliseg fought a great battle against the Saxons in 603 to reclaim his inheritance of Powys. Concenn, his great grandson, had the 12ft-high pillar cross erected on the hillside in Valle Crucis 2 centuries later to commemorate the victory, and its history was inscribed in Latin on the stone. This is one of the oldest surviving records of pre-Norman Britain. During the Civil War, Cromwell's soldiers threw the cross down and broke it. The remaining portion was re-erected in the 18th century.

Continue up to the Horseshoe Pass.

HORSESHOE PASS, Clwyd
The spectacular Horseshoe Pass (1,367ft) leads over the eastern edge of Llantysilio Mountain into the undulating pastures of the Vale of Clwyd. From the summit there are superb views of the rocky ridge of Eglwyseg Mountain and the wooded Dee valley.

2½ miles beyond the summit go forward at the roundabout, then in ½ mile turn left on to the A525. Descend the wooded Nant-y-garth Pass into the Vale of Clwyd and continue to Ruthin.

RUTHIN, Clwyd
'Rhyl, St Asaph, Denbigh and Ruthin lie along the Vale of Clwyd like beads threaded on a string and the fairest of these is Ruthin', wrote the novelist Stanley Weyman in 1928. Ruthin, encircled by wooded hills, is an old market town where Edward I built a stronghold in the 13th century to keep the troublesome Welsh in check. In September 1400 however, the Welsh prince Owain Glyndwr rebelled against the English and sacked Ruthin in September 1400. After the Civil War the medieval castle fell in ruins and the present structure, now a hotel, dates from the 19th century. A number of attractive 16th- and 17th-century timbered houses stand in the old streets which meander up to the little square. Here the Maen Huail stone is kept, where, according to legend, King Arthur slew Huail, his rival in love. The old court house and prison is now a bank; projecting from the eaves is the stump of a gibbet last used in the reign of Elizabeth I.

At the roundabout in the town centre go forward, SP 'Cerrig-y drudion', then keep forward on to the B5105. Cross rolling countryside and pass through Clawdd-newydd, before entering Clocaenog Forest.

CLOCAENOG FOREST, Clwyd
The vast green expanse of Clocaenog Forest clothes the slopes of the Denbigh moors. Like many of the woodlands in North Wales, this is the creation of the Forestry Commission, who started planting in the 1930s: the trees are mostly conifers — larch and sitka spruce. There are picnic areas and way-marked forest trails.

Descend to Llanfihangel Glyn Myfyr and cross the Afon Alwen then continue to Cerrigydrudion.

The 4-arched medieval bridge over the River Dee at Llangollen

CERRIGYDRUDION, Clwyd
English author George Borrow describes Cerrigydrudion in his book *Wild Wales* as a 'small village near a rocky elevation from which no doubt the place takes its name . . . the rock of heroes.' The rocky elevation is the nearby hill of Pen y gaer, crowned by an Iron-Age hill fort where it is said that King Caractacus was betrayed to the Romans by Cartimandua and taken in chains to Rome. His bearing so impressed his captors that they set him free.

Pont Cysyllte aquaduct is still used, 176 years after its completion, by pleasure craft on the Llangollen Canal

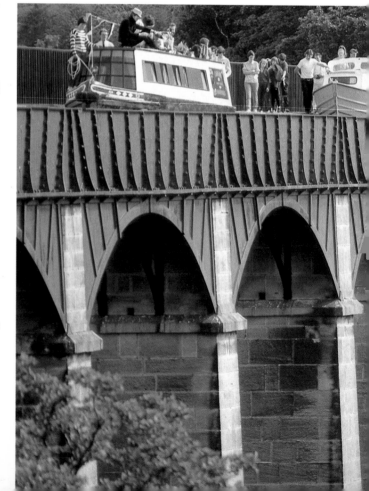

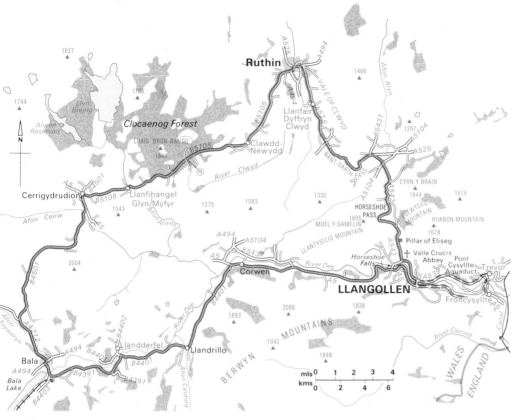

Not at all legendary is the rare fish, the gwyniad, whose only known habitat is the deep waters of the lake; its name comes from the whiteness of its scales. Along one shore of Bala Lake runs the Rheilffordd Llyn Tegid, the Bala Lake narrow-gauge railway which was opened in 1972.

Cross the River Dee and follow the valley, then in 3¼ miles turn left on to the B4402, SP 'Corwen'. In 1 mile turn right on to the B4401 for Llandrillo.

LLANDRILLO, Clwyd
This small village on the Afon Ceidiog, which flows down a narrow valley into the River Dee, is an excellent starting point for walks in the Berwyn Mountains, one of the 3 great mountain ranges of North Wales. The lowest pass over these hills is higher than 900ft, and many of the summits top 2,000ft.

Continue through pleasant countryside and after 7¾ miles turn right on to the A5, SP 'Llangollen', to reach Corwen.

CORWEN, Clwyd
Corwen lies amid the beautiful scenery of the wooded Dee valley, overlooked by the Berwyn Mountains. The Welsh hero Owain Glyndwr, who raised a revolt against Henry IV, had estates near Corwen from which he took his name. A groove in the lintel of the church doorway was reputedly made by Glyndwr hurling his dagger at it in a fit of rage. Some of the gravestones in the churchyard are hollowed out to allow mourners to kneel and pray over the dead.

Remain on the A5 through the beautiful wooded Dee valley for the return to Llangollen.

A 9 mile extension to the drive can be made as follows: from Llangollen follow the A5 to Froncysyllte. Here, turn sharp left on to the B5434, SP 'Trevor', and descend into the valley. On the right is Pont Cysyllte.

PONT CYSYLLTE, Clwyd
The wonder of Pont Cysyllte is the spectacular aqueduct, built by Thomas Telford in 1805 to carry the Llangollen branch of the Shropshire Union canal over the Dee valley. The 1,007ft-long aqueduct is the longest in the country, supporting a cast-iron trough on 18 tapering stone piers 127ft above the river. At the time, people scoffed at Telford, but boats still cross the aqueduct and after all this time there is scarcely any leakage of water from the dovetailed joints of the iron trough.

Cross the River Dee, then bear right. At the T-junction turn left on to the A539 (no SP) and return along the north side of the valley to Llangollen.

Ringed by hills, 140ft-deep Bala Lake is said to conceal a drowned city

In Cerrigydrudion turn left on to the Llangollen road, then left again on to the A5. In ½ mile turn right on the B4501, SP 'Bala'. After 7 miles turn left on to the A4212 and continue to Bala.

BALA, Gwynedd
Knitting warm woollen stockings was Bala's main industry in the 18th century: they were so famous that George III insisted on having a pair to ease his rheumatism. Bala is a pretty town on the northern shore of Bala Lake, and was made an important centre of Welsh Nonconformism by its minister, Thomas Charles, born in 1755. His aim was to provide Bibles for his people, and hearing of this, a village girl, Mary Jones, made an epic journey in 1800 on foot, 25 miles across the mountains, to obtain a Bible from him. Her determination inspired him to become one of the founders of the British and Foreign Bible Society, an organisation dedicated to the dissemination of Bibles throughout the world.

Leave on the B4391, SP 'Llangynog', and pass the northernmost end of Bala Lake.

BALA LAKE, Gwynedd
This 4 mile-long lake is the largest natural expanse of water in Wales. Its Welsh name is Llyn Tegid, and it is also known as Pimble Mere — the lake of 5 parishes. Legends include the story that the Dee flows through the lake without its waters mingling with those of the lake. Tradition gives the source of the Dee as 2 fountains, Dwy Fawr and Dwy Fach, named after 2 people who escaped the Great Flood, represented by Bala Lake.

MOORLANDS OF CENTRAL WALES

Towns are few and far between in mid Wales, and villages tend to be scattered round chapel or church buildings. Much of the area is open moorland scored by the occasional river valley, a wild, underpopulated region haunted by the cries of curlews and buzzards.

LLANIDLOES, Powys
Tree-lined streets, a happy blend of old and new architecture, and a few venerable shop fronts combine to form Llanidloes' unique character. The 16th-century Market Hall in the centre of the town is a rare survivor of a type of building that was once common all over the country. Its arcaded lower floor is open to the street and once sheltered market stalls. The floor above now houses a folk museum, but has variously functioned as an assize court, Quaker meeting place, Wesleyan and Baptist premises, public library and working men's institute. John Wesley preached from a stone preserved beside the hall. A beautiful arcade of five bays in the parish church was brought from Abbey Cwmhir at the time of the Dissolution of the Monasteries, and was installed in 1542. Also from the abbey are the timbers of the hammer-beam roof, but the gilded angels are not original and were added to the ends of the beams at the time of their transfer. Llanidloes stands at the confluence of Afon Clywedog and the River Severn.

Leave Llanidloes on the B4518 'Llyn Clywedog' road. Cross the Severn and turn left to follow the Clywedog Valley. After 2 miles, with views of 1,580ft Fan Hill on the right, turn left on to an unclassified road. Cross the valley and ascend to Clywedog Dam.

LLYN CLYWEDOG RESERVOIR, Powys
Excellent views of the reservoir can be enjoyed from the dam, whose curving 237ft wall is the highest of its kind in Britain. The reservoir itself was opened in 1968 and is a popular sailing venue. Nearby Fan Hill commands extensive views to Plynlimon Mountain and south into the old county of Radnorshire.

Continue with the Clywedog Reservoir on the right and Hafren Forest on the left.

HAFREN FOREST, Powys
Comprising large plantations between Clywedog Reservoir and the slopes of Plynlimon Mountain, this forest was started by the Forestry Commission in 1937, and is named from the Welsh equivalent of 'Severn'. The River Severn flows from the eastern flank of Plynlimon, where it rises in company with the Wye and several other vigorous waters. A picnic site is situated in the forest opposite the extreme western arm of the reservoir.

Continue to a T-junction and turn right on to the 'Llanbrynmair' road. After 2½ miles reach the edge of Staylittle.

Bare moorland slopes crossed by winding roads typify the scenery of the mid-Wales wilderness, a place of rolling hills and deep valleys.

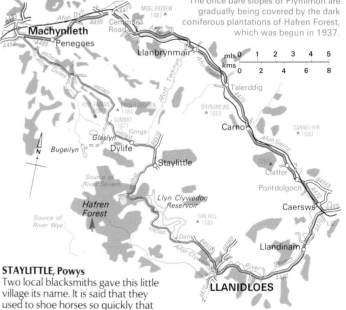

The once bare slopes of Plynlimon are gradually being covered by the dark coniferous plantations of Hafren Forest, which was begun in 1937.

STAYLITTLE, Powys
Two local blacksmiths gave this little village its name. It is said that they used to shoe horses so quickly that customers only needed to stay-a-little. On the hillside above the village is a Quaker burial ground with a nearby chapel overlooking the Clywedog Reservoir.

At Staylittle turn left on to the B4518. After 1 mile turn left on to the unclassified 'Machynlleth' road, which is unguarded and must be driven with care. After a short distance pass high above the deep gorge of the Afon Twymyn, and continue to Dylife.

DYLIFE, Powys
A few haphazard ruins, spoil tips, and an air of desolation are all that remain of an enormous lead-mining community that once flourished at Dylife. Huge numbers of men lived and worked here under awful conditions until the 1870s, but all that exist now are an inn and a tiny group of houses set back off the road. A little east of Dylife the infant Afon Twymyn plunges down spectacular Ffrwyd Fawr waterfall.

Continue for about 2 miles to a track leading left from the route to lakes Glaslyn and Bugeilyn.

LAKES GLASLYN & BUGEILYN, Powys

Care should be taken to stay on the footpath access to these two lakes, as the area is made dangerous by deep peat bogs and several precipitous drops. This is a wild and lonely landscape, once extensively mined for lead, but now inhabited only by sheep, birds, and the occasional fox. Glaslyn lies on private land, and Bugeilyn (which means Shepherd's Lake), is situated in the foothills of the Plynlimon range. Small flint arrowheads, presumably once used by people now buried in nearby prehistoric cairns, have been found washed out of the peat.

Continue towards Machynlleth and shortly reach a 1,671ft road summit. Views south and east from here take in extensive moorland, with 1,850ft Foel Fadian to the left and 1,784ft Bryn-y-Fedwen to the right. Descend, with impressive views north-west to Cader Idris and Aran Fawddwy, then drive down a long descent and keep forward at all road junctions to reach Machynlleth.

MACHYNLLETH, Powys

On market days Machynlleth's Maengwyn Street is packed with stalls selling a wide variety of wares. On the north side of the same street is the Owain Glyndwr Institute, which stands on the site of a building where Welsh revolutionary Owain Glyndwr held Wales' last independent parliament in 1404. On the other side of the street is the timbered Court House, with an inscription dated 1628. The road as a whole is dominated by an ornate Victorian clock tower which was erected by public subscription to mark the coming of age of Lord Castlereagh, heir to the Marquess of Londonderry. The marquess owned Plas Machynlleth, a 17th-century

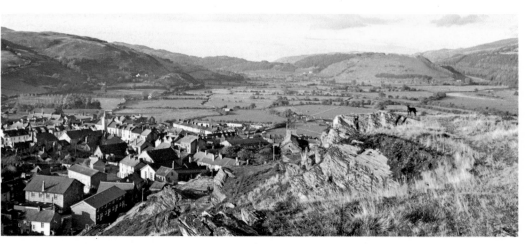

mansion which stands at the end of Pentrerhedyn Street and now houses the council offices. The grounds in which the house stands have been adopted as a public park.

Leave Machynlleth on the A489 'Newtown' road and proceed to Penegoes.

PENEGOES, Powys

A tradition that the head of a Welsh chieftain, executed in this village, is buried under a local tree has proved so tenacious that in 1950 there was a serious proposal to dig for the skull. Penegoes once had a tiny curative bath that was fed from a spring whose waters were said to bring relief from rheumatism. Richard Wilson, painter of landscapes, was born in the village in 1714. His birthplace is said to have been the Rectory, but the building occupying this site now dates only from c 1800.

Follow the Dyfi Valley to Cemmaes Road and turn right on to the A470 'Newtown' road. Continue along the Twymyn Valley to Llanbrynmair.

Situated in the Dyfi Valley, Machynlleth is the principal market town for this part of Mid Wales and has associations with the popular Welsh folk hero, Owain Glyndwr.

LLANBRYNMAIR, Powys

Roughly divided into half old and half new, this small scattered village enjoys a rural setting threaded by little rivers and was the site of an important castle during the 12th century. Only the castle mound survives today. The local church is sited in the old part of the village and contains ancient oak timbers. Abraham Rees, preacher and scholar, was born in the village in 1743. In 1778 he embarked on the preparation of information for *Chambers' Encyclopaedia*, a mammoth task that took 9 years to complete and won Rees election as a Fellow of the Royal Society. He was later made a Doctor of Divinity by Edinburgh University for his work on a further encyclopaedia.

Continue through the wooded gorge of the Afon Iaen to reach a road and rail summit at Talerddig, where there is a natural arch beside the road. Continue to Carno.

Left: the valley at Dylife was once exploited for its mineral wealth. Below: this statue of engineer David Davies stands at Llandinam.

CARNO, Powys

Opposite Carno's church, which contains an ancient cross-incised slab that saw many years' service as a gatepost, is the Aleppo Merchant Inn. This unusual title was given to the pub by a retired sea captain who had been in charge of a ship of that name. A Roman fort was situated here, and later in history several fierce battles between the ruling princes of north and south Wales were fought near Carno.

Drive along the broad valley of the Afon Carno and pass through Clatter and Pont-dolgoch to reach Caersws.

CAERSWS, Powys

Earthworks of a large Roman installation may be seen near the railway here, forming a hub from which the raised causeways of ancient roads still radiate in recognizable form. The village itself is laid on a typically Roman grid-iron pattern at the meeting of two rivers with the Severn. John Ceiriog Hughes, a famous 19th-century bard, was manager of a narrow-gauge railway here for many years. A memorial plaque marks the house where he lived, and his remains lie north-west at Llanwnog. The latter boasts a fascinating old church.

Continue on the A470 and after ½ mile meet a T-junction. Turn right on to the 'Llangurig' road and shortly go over a level crossing, then follow the River Severn to reach Llandinam.

LLANDINAM, Powys

Green hills rising to the lower slopes of mountains spread from the Severn Valley site of this pretty village. Close to a handsome iron bridge that spans the river is a statue of Llandinam's most famous native, David Davies. After starting from a modest beginning Davies worked to become a railway contractor, then went on to make a fortune with the construction of Barry Docks. The local church has been extensively restored and stands on the site of a hillfort which is still faintly visible. Ancient carvings preserved in the church include an interesting illustration of Adam and Eve.

Remain on the A470 for the return to Llanidloes.

CADER IDRIS

Between the wide watery expanses of the Dyfi and Mawdacch estuaries lies the unyielding massif of Cader Idris. The tour winds in a figure of eight round both these startlingly contrasting landscapes, introducing each with stretches of seaside motoring.

MACHYNLLETH, Powys
Magnificent scenery surrounds the historic market town of Machynlleth. Its attractive tree-lined main street, Maen Gwyn, takes its name from a direction stone of extremely ancient date, no doubt used by the earliest inhabitants, who made a prehistoric trackway along the Dyfi valley. The stone, now in 2 fragments, is set against the wall of a house in the street. The pinnacled Victorian clock tower in the centre of the street was erected by the Marquess of Londonderry in the 1870s. He had aquired the local Plas (manor), now used as council offices, and where sheepdog trials are held annually in the grounds.

Leave Machynlleth on the A487, SP 'Dolgellau'. In ¾ mile cross the River Dyfi and turn left on to the A493 and in 3 miles enter Pennal.

PENNAL, Powys
Low, slate-roofed cottages cluster about a church rebuilt, in early Classical style, during the 19th century, with a hipped roof and gilded weathercock. It stands within a circular enclosure which in turn acts as Pennal's central roundabout. The salmon of the Dyfi and trout from neighbouring streams are a great attraction for anglers, and the peaks of Tarren Hendre, Tarren y gesail and Tarren Cadian, which soar above the village, invite walkers and climbers to explore their crags and valleys.

Continue on the A493, later joining the shores of the Dyfi estuary to reach Aberdyfi.

ABERDYFI, Gwynedd
Seafaring and shipbuilding was the business of quiet and genteel Aberdyfi — formerly one of the most important ports along the Welsh coast; in the 16th century it accommodated both coastal and Continental shipping. The last boat was built here in 1880, so the scene today is a far cry from the days when at one time 180 ships loaded with coal, malt, flour and salt, which was traded for woollen cloth and slate from the Welsh hillsides, were recorded waiting for a berth outside the harbour. The seafaring tradition is continued by the Outward Bound Sea School, and by the town's sailing club, which first adopted the GP14 sailing dinghy as a club boat.

Follow the A493 behind sand-dunes then continue inland to Tywyn.

TYWYN, Gwynedd
Surrounded by the foothills of the Cader Idris range, the town lies in the plain of the Dysynni River. The older part of the town is about 1 mile from the sea, but over the years it has grown towards a sandy beach where safe bathing and a fine esplanade attract tourists. The church is 12th century, although it was extensively restored in the 1880s. Within is the 7th-century St Cadfan's Stone, 7ft high and inscribed with the earliest known Welsh writing. Three miles of sand and shingle beach stretch to Aberdyfi, and the river and sea afford excellent fishing, while Cader Idris offers beautiful scenery; but perhaps the greatest attraction to visitors is the Talyllyn Narrow Gauge Railway.

TALYLLYN NARROW GAUGE RAILWAY, Gwynedd
The Talyllyn Railway celebrated a centenary of unbroken passenger service in 1966. It was opened in 1866 to service the slate quarry above Abergynolwyn, but when the quarries declined in 1947 the 2ft 3in-gauge railway found itself having to rely solely on passenger service. It was taken over by the Talyllyn Railway Preservation Society in 1950, and through their efforts the run-down line has been refurbished and developed into the remarkable tourist attraction and museum it is today. The 7¼ mile-long track begins at Tywyn Wharf station and ends at Nant Gwernol.

Follow SP 'Dolgellau' and in 2¼ miles turn right on to the B4405. This road follows the attractive steep-sided Fathew valley, past Dolgoch and its well-known Falls, to Abergynolwyn station. In ½ mile reach Abergynolwyn village. Continue on the B4405 into the Dysynni valley and follow the river below high mountain ridges to its source at Tal-y-llyn Lake.

TAL-Y-LLYN LAKE, Gwynedd
Tal-y-llyn Lake lies at the foot of Cader Idris, which towers above to a height of 2,927ft — the second highest mountain outside the Snowdon range. These glittering waters, over 1 mile long, were formed during the last Ice Age.

A mile beyond the lake turn left on to the A487, gradually climbing to a 938ft summit, below the overhanging cliffs of Craig-y-Llam. Descend to the Cross Foxes Hotel and turn left on to the A470. A long, winding descent leads to Dolgellau. Turn left at the start of the bypass for Dolgellau town centre.

DOLGELLAU, Gwynedd
Dolgellau's ancient stone houses, narrow streets and austere beauty lies under the shadow of massive Cader Idris. Now a delightful touring centre, in the distant past the town was a more important place nationally, for here Owain Glyndwr held his last Parliament, and in 1199 Cymer Abbey was founded nearby; of which only the church and a few fragments survive. In Dolgellau itself perhaps the most outstanding feature is the 7-arched 17th-century bridge over the Afon Wnion which divides the town.

Leave Dolgellau on the A493 to follow the south shore of the Mawddach estuary. For a detour to the magnificently scenic Llynnau Cregennen (NT) below Cader Idris, turn left on to an unclassified road, SP 'Cader Idris', on leaving the town. This road climbs to Llyn Gwernan, with excellent views to the left. Continue, below Craig-Las (2,167ft), and later turn right, SP 'Llynnau Cregennen, Arthog', to reach the Llynnau Cregennen.

Looking towards the bulk of Cader Idris from the twin lakes of Llynnau Cregennen

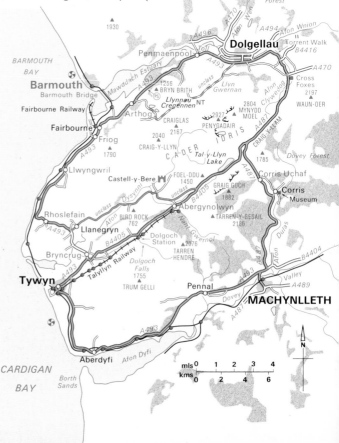

LLYNNAU CREGENNEN, Gwynedd

Situated at over 800ft, the Llynnau Cregennen are 2 small lakes at the foot of the main Cader Idris range, surrounded by 700 acres of National Trust property. Nearby, a marked footpath leads to the summit of the conical Bryn Brith (1,256ft). From here, and from near the car park, there are magnificent views of the Mawddach estuary.

Return to Dolgellau and turn left on to the A493 then follow the main road through Penmaenpool and Arthog to Fairbourne, with views on the right of the railway bridge.

FAIRBOURNE, Gwynedd

Here is one of the finest beaches in Wales and miles of golden sand and safe bathing make it a popular spot. Anti-tank blocks, a legacy of World War II, are scattered along the shoreline. This is the home of the Fairbourne Railway, first laid as a tramway to transport stone and materials for the construction of Barmouth Railway Bridge, before the road was built. However, it was soon realised that the locality and splendid sands were a potential tourist attraction, so the village of Fairbourne was created and developed on reclaimed land along the Mawddach estuary. Until 1916 the tramway was horse-drawn, but later became the Fairbourne Miniature Railway, devoted to passenger service, until its closure in 1940. Six years later it was bought by enthusiasts who were also business men, and has since been rebuilt and renovated.

Beyond Fairbourne the main road climbs high above the shore, with extensive views across Barmouth and Tremadoc Bays. Pass through Llwyngwril and later turn sharply inland. 1½ miles beyond Rhoslefain turn left, SP 'Llanegryn' for Llanegryn.

An engine in the dark Brunswick green of the Talyllyn Railway — one of the Great Little Trains of Wales — which operates in the Fathew valley

St Mary's Church, Dolgellau

LLANEGRYN, Gwynedd

Llanegryn stands at the mouth of the Dysynni valley, which, broad, flat and unspoilt, stretches away to the summits of the Cader Idris range. Three miles away, but clearly visible, is the extraordinary Bird Rock. This rises to 760ft above the valley floor and is the only inland nesting site of cormorants in Britain. The village itself lies in a hollow, gathered about a short main street which crosses a stream, near which stand 2 chapels joined by their vestries.

Keep forward across the river bridge and follow the Dysynni valley. Later, at the foot of the Bird Rock, turn left, SP 'Abergynolwyn'. In 2 miles turn right to follow the river though a narrow gap. For Castell-y-bere (AM) 1 mile away, turn left at this point.

CASTELL-Y-BERE, Gwynedd

Hidden by trees lies Castell-y-bere (OACT), ruined fortress of the Dysynni valley and once the most important castle in Wales. Great expense was lavished on this castle by the independent Welsh, and here Dafydd, Llewelyn the Last's brother, held out against Edward 1 and the English. The castle, however, eventually surrendered, and Dafydd fled. Victorious Edward took over the castle and gave it borough status, but a town never developed here, as around other castles, and the scant ruins remain lonely, and beautifully unspoilt.

The main tour continues alongside the river through a narrow gap in the hills, then turns left, SP 'Tal-y-llyn'. Shortly rejoin the B4405, again passing Tal-y-llyn Lake. In 1 mile turn right on to the A487. Shortly enter Corris Uchaf (Upper Corris) before descending past Corris village (left) in the valley.

CORRIS, Gwynedd

The village is surrounded by fir-clad slopes, almost the southern boundary of Snowdonia National Park, and consists of a tortuous main street, old solid stone houses and an old stone bridge over the River Dulas. In the village is a small museum of the Corris Railway (closed in 1948) which ran alongside the main road to Machynlleth.

Continue down the winding and thickly wooded Dulas valley to rejoin the Dyfi valley. Turn left and shortly re-enter Machynlleth.

THE ISLE OF ANGLESEY, Gwynedd

Isolated Anglesey, in which this tour is contained, is separated from the rest of Wales by the Menai Strait and presents a landscape of low, undulating hills unlike anywhere else in the Principality. First impressions are deceptive, however, for much of the coast is as wild and rugged as any to be found in the British Isles. The family holidaymaker will find good facilities and amenities here, and the lone wanderer can find all the solitude he desires. In prehistoric times the island was *Mona*, 'The Mother of Wales', and visible remains of the cultures that flourished here are everywhere.

MENAI BRIDGE, Gwynedd

This largely Victorian town, named after Thomas Telford's superb bridge, is clustered round the Anglesey end of the crossing. Places of interest here include the Tegfryn Art Gallery and a fascinating Museum of Childhood, in which many rare and valuable exhibits illustrate the interests of children over the last 150 years.

Leave Menai Bridge on the A545 'Beaumaris' road and drive alongside the Menai Strait.

MENAI STRAIT, Gwynedd

This 14-mile stretch of water, flowing from sea to sea between Anglesey's wooded shoreline and the sloping pastures of the mainland, might be considered the major geographical feature of North Wales. Its beauty matches the splendour of Snowdon, and its sheltered reaches provide a testing venue for the water-sports enthusiasts who flock here in the summer months. Both banks – island and mainland – offer superb walking country where seabirds and rabbits are more common than people. Above Port Dinorwic are the remains of Stephenson's amazing 19th-century tubular rail bridge; farther up is the graceful suspension bridge that has carried the A5 road since 1826.

Continue to Beaumaris

THE ISLE OF ANGLESEY

Today Anglesey is known for its quiet resorts and sandy beaches, its spectacular cliffs and a gentle interior threaded by narrow lanes. At one time it filled the bellies of North Wales with wheat and was known, almost reverently, as 'Mona', the Mother.

Beaumaris Castle is one of the best examples of concentric fortification in Britain.

BEAUMARIS, Gwynedd

The biggest attraction of Beaumaris is undoubtedly the castle (AM), an unfinished masterpiece that was the last in a chain built by Edward I to subjugate the Welsh people. A measure of the success with which this aim was achieved is the fact that the castle has never seen any military action and was never completed, the walls not being built to their intended height. The town contains much of interest, including the early 17th-century Court House and 15th-century Tudor Rose House, the Beaumaris Gaol and Exhibition, and the Museum of Childhood. Several excellent inns include the Bull's Head, which was visited by Dr Johnson and Charles Dickens. The church is of 14th-century origin.

Turn inland on the B5109 'Pentraeth' road and cross rolling countryside to pass through Pentraeth.

Turn right on to the A5025, and continue with fine views of attractive Red Wharf Bay.

RED WHARF BAY, Gwynedd

More than 10 square miles of sand are revealed here at low tide, so it is not particularly surprising that the bay was once famous for its cockles. During the last century a small local shipyard built boats for the Amlwch copper trade.

Continue to Benllech.

BENLLECH, Gwynedd

Perhaps the most popular seaside resort on the island, Benllech offers 2 miles of golden sand and safe bathing.

Continue with the Amlwch road and in 2 miles at a roundabout take the 1st exit. A detour from the main route can be made by keeping forward on to an unclassified road for Din Lligwy.

DIN LLIGWY BURIAL CHAMBER, Gwynedd

This important Bronze-Age tomb (AM) consists of a huge capstone resting on a number of uprights and horizontals. Much of the chamber is cunningly hidden in a rock-cut pit.

DIN LLIGWY ANCIENT VILLAGE, Gwynedd

Some of the ancient enclosed dwellings on this remarkable site (AM) still stand to a height of 6ft, and date from around the early Roman period. The surrounding wall was built in the late 4th century. Near by is the beautiful ruin of a 14th-century chapel.

Continue on the main drive to Amlwch, with Parys Mountain rising to the left.

One of engineer Thomas Telford's finest works, this suspension bridge carries the London to Holyhead road over the Menai Strait and has a central span of 579ft.

PARYS MOUNTAIN, Gwynedd
Now desolate and scarred, 419ft-high Parys Mountain was exploited for its copper in a small way by the Romans, but in 1768 came a boom. Fortunes were made and for a while Anglesey was the copper centre of the world, but by 1820 it was all over. Falling prices and the exhaustion of the ore forced the industry into collapse.

AMLWCH, Gwynedd
At the height of the copper boom Amlwch was a major port and shipbuilding centre. Now an oil terminal and chemical industries provide the town's employment.

Continue on the Cemaes road to Bull Bay.

BULL BAY, Gwynedd
Sheltered rocky coves and a good beach are the main attractions of this little holiday resort.

Continue to Cemaes Bay.

The Marquess of Anglesey's tall statue overlooks the Menai Strait.

CEMAES BAY, Gwynedd
Cottages cluster round a small harbour in this quaint little fishing village. Spectacular cliff walks lead in both directions from the bay, and on the headland to the west is Wylfa nuclear power station (open).

Continue with signs for Valley to Llanrhyddlad.

LLANRHYDDLAD, Gwynedd
Llyn Llygeirian and a large number of prehistoric sites are situated north of this hamlet.

Continue to Llanfaethlu.

LLANFAETHLU, Gwynedd
Distant views of Snowdonia can be enjoyed from this village, and secluded bays and rocky headlands are features of the nearby coast.

Continue through Llanfachraeth and Llanynghenedl to Valley.

VALLEY, Gwynedd
Plane spotting enthusiasts can see RAF jet trainer aircraft and the occasional rescue helicopter operating from the base near here.

Meet traffic signals, turn right on to the A5, and cross the Stanley Embankment to Holy Island.

HOLY ISLAND, Gwynedd
The silhouette of a giant aluminium plant dominates the approach across the Stanley Embankment these days, but 720ft Holyhead Mountain still exercises a compulsive attraction as the highest point on the island. Many prehistoric monuments survive here.

Continue to Holyhead.

HOLYHEAD, Gwynedd
This, the largest town in Anglesey, is a major ferry terminal for Ireland and is constantly busy with the jostling of travellers, seamen, and holidaymakers. The old parish church of St Cybi is built within the walls of a Roman fort, and the flank of Holyhead Mountain – which towers over the town – is scattered with the remains of prehistoric huts. Beyond the mountain a yawning chasm separates South Stack Lighthouse from the rest of the island.

Return along the A5 and shortly branch right on to the B4545 to reach Trearddur Bay.

TREARDDUR BAY, Gywnedd
This fashionable Anglesey resort has fine sandy beaches broken up by occasional rocky outcrops.

Cross Four Mile Bridge and return to Valley. Meet traffic signals and turn right on to the A5. Pass through Bryngwran, and in 1 mile at crossroads turn right on to the A4080 SP 'Rhosneigr'. Continue through open country, and at Llanfaelog turn right for Rhosneigr.

RHOSNEIGR, Gwynedd
Cheerfully unpretentious, Rhosneigr is an ideal spot for holidaymakers who like the quiet life.

Continue on the A4080 and in 1¼ miles turn right 'SP 'Aberffraw' to reach Barclodiad-y-Gawres.

BARCLODIAD-Y-GAWRES, Gwynedd
The carved stones of this megalithic passage grave (AM) are among the finest of their kind in Britain.

Continue to Aberffraw.

ABERFFRAW, Gwynedd
Aberffraw is a grey, somnolent village which has little to show of its historic past. Between the 7th and 13th centuries it was the capital of the Kingdom of Gwynedd, but no trace of the palace or associated buildings survives. A rocky islet to the south-west features an ancient church which is accessible at low tide.

Proceed for 3 miles to Malltraeth.

MALLTRAETH, Gwynedd
In c1800 a high embankment was built here to stop the incursion of the sea. Before this the estuary of the Cefni penetrated far inland, nearly cutting Anglesey in two. The village is well known for its fine sands and bird-haunted salt marshes.

Skirt Malltraeth Sands and continue through Newborough Forest to reach Newborough.

Holyhead Mountain's 720ft height offers superb views over the island.

NEWBOROUGH, Gwynedd
Former inhabitants of Llanfaes, ousted by Edward I, founded this English-sounding village in 1303. A national nature reserve covers 1,566 acres of duneland and rocky coast to the south of the village, and Newborough Forest is constantly being extended to fix the dunes in the north part of the sanctuary. Three nature trails enable casual visitors to see much of the natural beauty of the area, but access to unmarked parts of the reserve is by permit only. Nearby Llanddwyn Island is accessible except at times of very high tide.

In ½ mile at a roundabout turn left and 2 miles beyond Bryn-Siencyn reach a road on the left which leads to Bryn-celli-ddu.

BRYN-CELLI-DDU, Gwynedd
This is a magnificent Bronze Age passage grave (AM) of a type more usually found in Ireland. It consists of a passage leading to a polygonal chamber beneath a large mound.

Continue on the A4080 and shortly reach the entrance to Plas Newydd.

Llanfair PG's full name contains 59 letters and is the longest in Britain.

PLAS NEWYDD, Gwynedd
Rebuilt by architect James Wyatt in the 18th century, this fine mansion (NT) overlooks the Menai Strait and is famous for the Rex Whistler mural in its dining room.

At the edge of Llanfair PG turn right.

LLANFAIR PG, Gwynedd
The full name of this village, Llanfairpwllgwyngyllgogerychwyrndrobwyllllantysiliogogogoch means 'Church of St Mary in a hollow of white hazel near to a rapid whirlpool and to St Tysilio's Church, near to a red cave' and was invented by a tailor who combined the business of tourism with this wry joke against the tourists. George Stephenson's famous tubular railway bridge over the Menai Strait has been replaced by steel arches and road deck after being damaged by fire in 1970, and an unassuming tin hut in the village was where the Women's Institute formed its first branch in the early 20th century. Overlooking the bridge, the village, and the Strait the splendid Marquess of Anglesey Column affords remarkable views for anybody with the stomach to climb it.

Return to Menai Bridge on the A5080.

LLANFAIRPWLLGWYNGYLLGOGERYCHWYRNDROBWYLL-LLANTYSILIOGOGOGOCH
RAILWAY STATION

THE LLEYN PENINSULA, Gwynedd

In many respects the Lleyn is similar to the other western peninsulas of St David's in South Wales and Cornwall in England. All three were settled by Iberian peoples in prehistoric times, and their cultures are still strongly Celtic in character. Their coastlines are rugged and invariably magnificent, and their inland hills are scored by numerous small river valleys. The great mountain barrier at the eastern end of Lleyn has enabled the peninsula to preserve more of its own special character than was possible for the others.

PWLLHELI, Gwynedd

Seaside resort and market town, Pwllheli is the unofficial capital of the Lleyn Peninsula and has an old harbour that was once busy with sea-going craft. Even now it provides a safe haven for small boats, but is frequented more by holiday-makers than ancient mariners. Butlins Holiday Camp lies 3 miles east.

Leave Pwllheli on the A497 'Criccieth' road and continue to Llanystumdwy.

LLANYSTUMDWY, Gwynedd

This village is assured of a permanent place in history because of its association with David Lloyd George, the small-town solicitor who became Prime Minister. His childhood was spent in a roadside cottage here (open), and his body was brought back to lie beside the River Dwyfor. Interesting items are displayed in the Lloyd George Museum.

Continue to Criccieth

CRICCIETH, Gwynedd

Waves break constantly on the rocks beneath the ruins (AM) of a fortress built here by the princes of North Wales in the 13th century. The castle was enlarged by Edward I after he had occupied the region. Victorian charm and a relaxed atmosphere supplement the obvious amenity of the resort's excellent sun and sea-bathing beach.

Leave by the B4411 SP 'Caernarfon' and in 4½ miles turn left on to the A487 for Bryncir.

AN ARM IN THE OCEAN

The coast of the lovely Lleyn Peninsula is a confusion of wide sands and massive cliffs. Vagrant lanes run through fields cut from the flanks of mountains, and ancient churches mark a pilgrim's way to Bardsey – burial place of a thousand saints.

The eastern peak of Yr Eifl, a forked mountain on the north coast of the Lleyn Peninsula, is crowned by a magnificent hillfort called Tre'r Ceiri.

BRYNCIR, Gwynedd

Good-quality cloth is sold from the working woollen mill in this Dwyfach Valley village. A 6th-century tombstone stands at Llystyngwyn Farm.

Continue to Llanllyfni.

LLANLLYFNI, Gwynedd

The Afon Llyfni flows north of this Victorian quarryman's village from its source at Llyn Nantlle Uchaf, among disturbingly derelict slate workings. Of the several old chapels in Llanllyfni, only Ebenezer has retained its 19th-century interior.

Continue to Penygroes.

PENYGROES, Gwynedd

This colourful quarryman's town grew from its sister community of Llanllyfni with the development of the slate industry during the 19th century.

From Penygroes turn left on to an unclassified road SP 'Clynnog and

Porth Dinllaen was considered as a possible rail terminus for Ireland in the 19th century.

Pwllheli'; After 2 miles meet a T-junction and turn left on to the A499. Drive through Pontllyfni and enter Clynnog-fawr.

CLYNNOG FAWR, Gwynedd

St Beuno founded a monastery here in AD 616, and is buried in a chapel connected to the local church by a passage. His tomb was once reputed to hold great curative value. The church itself, a magnificent structure with a massive tower, was an important stopping place for pilgrims to the monastery on Bardsey Island. Between the main road and the sea is a well-preserved prehistoric tomb called Bachwen.

Continue for 3¼ miles and turn right on the B4417, SP 'Nefyn', and pass a lay-by under the slopes of Yr Eifl.

Welsh architect Clough Williams-Ellis designed David Lloyd George's memorial at Llanystumdwy.

YR EIFL, Gwynedd

Englishmen know the triple peaks of this 1,849ft mountain as 'The Rivals', but a more accurate translation of the Welsh name is rendered 'The Fork'. Footpaths lead to the summits. The mountain is the haunt of

cuckoos in spring, and its rock-strewn and heather-clad peaks afford stunning views in the crystal conditions that often prevail at that time of year. One of the finest iron-age hillforts (AM) in Wales, with mighty stone walls defending an interior crowded with hut circles, is sited on the eastern peak. It is possible that the complex was inhabited until cAD 400.

Descend through Llithfaen to Nefyn.

NEFYN, Gwynedd
At one time it was claimed that Nefyn sent more of its men to sea than almost any other British town. In 1284 Edward I celebrated his conquest over the Welsh here, and in 1353 the Black Prince made the town one of the 10 royal boroughs of North Wales. Today Nefyn enjoys a genteel retirement from politics and makes the most of the resort possibilities offered by its fine sands.

Turn right on to the 'Aberdaron' road and enter Morfa Nefyn.

MORFA NEFYN, Gwynedd
Rugged headlands shelter a long sweep of sandy beach at Morfa Nefyn, and an unclassified road leads right from the tour route to the picturesque hamlet of Porth Dinllaen. This small community was once considered as a rail terminus point for Ireland; some might think it had a lucky escape.

Continue on the B4417 and pass through Edern to reach Tudweiliog.

TUDWEILIOG, Gwynedd
The coast near this village is indented by many small sandy coves, backed by formidable cliffs pocked with caves. Architect Sir Gilbert Scott designed the simple but effective local church in 1850.

Continue and in 4¼ miles turn right on to the B4413. After ¼ mile the route allows a possible detour to Porth Oer:, turn right on to an unclassified road.

PORTH OER, Gwynedd
Famous for its Whistling Sands, which really do whistle when trodden on, Porth Oer is a sheltered little bay offering cliff walks and fine seascapes.

Continue to Aberdaron on the B4413.

ABERDARON, Gwynedd
Last stop on the old route for Bardsey Island, Aberdaron is an attractive village with a café reputed to have been a pilgrim's halt. The name of the café, Gegin Fawr, means Big Kitchen. A large church on the site of a foundation established by St Hywyn in the 6th century probably sheltered pilgrims as they waited for a boat to take them across to the island, the burial ground of saints.

BRAICH-Y-PWLL, Gwynedd
A spectacular 500ft cliff dramatically ends the Lleyn here. Views inland extend along the whole peninsula to Snowdonia, and a little over a mile out to sea is the holy island of Bardsey, destination of pilgrims since

Abersoch is a popular holiday resort with a sheltered harbour.

the 6th century. Most of this magnificent coastline is protected by the National Trust.

Continue from Aberdaron on an unclassified road to Rhiw.

RHIW, Gwynedd
The scattered cottages and 18th-century church of this village do little to obstruct views of the magnificent South Lleyn coast (NT). The village itself is windswept and exposed, but 1,000ft Mynydd Rhiw shelters the house and gardens of nearby Plas-yn-Rhiw from the Atlantic weather.

PLAS-YN-RHIW, Gwynedd
This charming house, built in the 16th century and modernized in Regency times, is surrounded by nearly 60 acres of woodland and garden. The whole property and large areas of beautiful coastline were given to the National Trust in 1952 by the Misses Keating. Views from the house embrace an incomparable panorama extending across Hell's Mouth and Cardigan Bay to the enigmatic mountain of Cader Idris.

Keep forward on the 'Abersoch' road to reach Llangian.

LLANGIAN, Gwynedd
Neat cottages with well-tended gardens full of flowers have helped this lovely place win the coveted Best-kept Village in Wales Award.

Turn left, then ascend and turn right to descend to Abersoch.

ABERSOCH, Gwynedd
Smart villas, expensive-looking yachts, and plush hotels are the typical signs of fashionable affluence displayed by this resort. Its popularity can be mostly attributed to its sandy beaches, mild climate, and safe bathing, but lanes leading to the windswept headland of Trwyn Cilan are also a major attraction.

ST TUDWAL'S ISLANDS, Gwynedd
Seen from the coast at Abersoch, these two grass-covered islands are named after a saint who came to live on one of them in the 6th century. They are privately owned, but trips can be made round their coasts by hired boats from Abersoch.

Follow the Pwllheli road A499 along the coast to Llanbedrog.

LLANBEDROG, Gwynedd
Excellent sandy beaches and attractive cliff walks have assured Llanbedrog's popularity as a resort. The parish church is embowered in trees and preserves a medieval screen. Fragments of ancient glass can be seen in the east window. Above the village is a hill which features a ruined mill (NT) and affords good views.

Continue through low-lying countryside and in 3 miles join the A497 to re-enter Pwllheli.

Clynnog Fawr's magnificent church dates from the 16th century, and is the burial place of St Beuno.

THE WELSH LAKES

At one time the valleys of the Elan and its tributaries were noted for their beauty, but now they lie under the surface of a massive water storage scheme that has turned the area into the Lake District of Wales. Down-stream on the Afon Rheidol are the stupendous falls of Devil's Bridge.

RHAYADER, Powys
This little market town retains a 19th-century atmosphere even though many of its shops have been modernized. Its old inns include The Triangle, a partly weather-boarded building across the Wye in the Cwmdeuddwr district, and, on the town side of the bridge the Cwmdeuddwr Arms. Both are grand old institutions with histories that stretch back several centuries. All that remains of Rhayader's castle is a large mound between Church Street and West Street, high above a reach where the river flows over boulders and rocky platforms to dash under the bridge in pretty falls. Rhayader was one of the centres of the Rebecca Riots in the first half of the 19th century, when men dressed as women and calling themselves Rebecca's Daughters smashed turnpike gates as a protest against heavy tolls. Some light industry has been introduced into Rhayader in an attempt to curb the depopulation which has bedevilled the region in recent decades.

Leave Rhayader on the B4518 'Elan Valley' road and continue to the edge of Elan village where there is a new visitor centre. Keep forward on to an Caban Coch Dam and Reservoir.

ELAN VALLEY & CABAN COCH RESERVOIR, Powys
Late in the 19th century the Corporation of Birmingham constructed a reservoir system in an area now unofficially known as The Lakeland of Wales. The new landscape is very beautiful and highly popular, but the scheme called for the drowning of a whole valley complete with attractive waterfalls, meadows, farms, houses and a church. Beneath the placid surface of the new lake is a house in which the poet Shelley lived for some time. He wrote appreciatively about the splendid local scenery in a letter to his friend Hogg, suggesting that it had impressed him even though his mind was on higher, less substantial things.

Continue to the Garreg-Ddu viaduct and turn left to cross it. Proceed through pleasant woodland, with the remains of the Dol-y-Mynach Dam on the left, and enter the attractive Claerwen Valley. At an AA telephone box turn right to reach Claerwen Dam.

CLAERWEN RESERVOIR, Powys
The Claerwen project, officially opened by Queen Elizabeth II on 23rd October 1952, is a vast 600-acre lake held back by a massive dam. The Afon Teifi rises in the high moorlands to the west of the reservoir, and the route of an ancient road used by monks travelling from Strata Florida Abbey to Abbey Cwmhir runs through the area.

Return across Garreg-Ddu viaduct and turn left. Follow the wooded shores of Garreg-Ddu Reservoir.

GARREG-DDU RESERVOIR, Powys
A unique submerged dam separates this reservoir from Caban Coch Reservoir. The entire Elan Valley complex supplies Birmingham with an amazing 75 million gallons of water a day and provides a haven for many forms of aquatic and marginal wildlife, including various plants.

From the end of Garreg-Ddu Reservoir ascend a short winding stretch of road to Penygarreg Dam and Reservoir.

PENYGARREG RESERVOIR, Powys
Some 124 acres of lake, unbroken except where a tiny fir-covered islet rises at the centre, backs up the Elan Valley from yet another of the project's great dams. This and the other reservoirs can be fished for trout by permit holders.

Continue alongside Craig Goch Reservoir.

CRAIG GOCH RESERVOIR, Powys
Topmost of the Elan Valley dam and reservoir complex, Craig Goch has a surface area of about 200 acres and may be extended. Plans were prepared to increase the capacity of the lake by allowing it to back up the valley close to the source of the Afon Elan.

At the end of the reservoir cross a bridge and ascend then turn left on to the 'Aberystwyth' road. Continue along the wide moorland valley of the Afon Elan to a road summit of 1,320ft. Descend into the deep and wild Ystwyth Valley, and within 4 miles reach Cwmystwyth.

CWMYSTWYTH, Dyfed
Ruins of mine workings, buildings and cottages in the neighbourhood of this village illustrate the 19th-century's insatiable desire for mineral wealth, but the village itself – no longer a centre of the mining industry – has settled into attractive retirement. Beyond Cwmystwyth, off the Pontrhydygroes road, is a pile of rubble that once stood as the proud mansion of Hafod, built by one Thomas Johnes in the late 18th century. The building was twice burnt down, and each blaze destroyed many priceless works of art and irreplaceable manuscripts. Johnes improved the estate by planting over 2 million trees and introducing new farming techniques, but the fires and the death of his beloved daughter Marianne in 1811 turned the innovator into a broken old man. A charred monument to Marianne in Hafod Church testifies to a final irony – the gutting of the church by fire in 1932.

Beyond Cwmystwyth bear right to join the B4574 'Devil's Bridge' road. Ascend a wooded slope and reach The Arch Picnic Site.

THE ARCH PICNIC SITE, Dyfed
Thomas Johnes of Hafod erected an arch over the road here in 1810 to commemorate the Golden Jubilee of George III. Three Forestry Commission trails lead from the picnic site.

Descend with the Mynach Valley on the right and enter Devil's Bridge.

DEVIL'S BRIDGE, Dyfed
Cwm Rheidol narrows to form a spectacular 500ft-deep wooded gorge at Devil's Bridge, where Afon Mynach adds its own 300ft of impressive waterfalls to the grandeur of the Afon Rheidol's Gyfarllwyd Falls. Excellent views into the gorge can be enjoyed from the road bridge, but the full scenic splendour of the area can only be fully appreciated by a descent into the valley bottom. A flight of 91 steps known as Jacob's Ladder zig-zags down to river level, where a small bridge and platform afford views of five separate waterfalls which make up a superb 300ft cascade. Water erosion has resulted in the formation of curious cavities known as punchbowls at the bottom of the

Penygarreg Reservoir is one of a series created to supply Birmingham with water.

The spectacular 300ft Mynach Falls are set amid trees festooned with moisture-loving ferns and mosses.

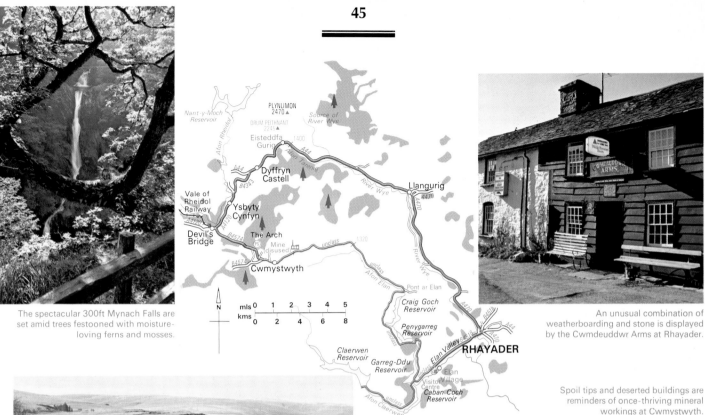

An unusual combination of weatherboarding and stone is displayed by the Cwmdeuddwr Arms at Rhayader.

The elegant dam which separates Craig Goch Reservoir from Penygarreg Reservoir.

Spoil tips and deserted buildings are reminders of once-thriving mineral workings at Cwmystwyth.

series. Similarly magnificent views are available from a terrace in front of the Hafod Arms Hotel, which was rebuilt in the 1830s. Of the three bridges stacked on top of each other at Devil's Bridge the oldest is – naturally – the lowest, and is thought to have been built in the 12th century by monks from Strata Florida Abbey. Legend has it that the Devil built it as a complex trick to win a soul, and abandoned it after he failed. The second bridge was built in 1753, and an iron bridge was built above the other two much later in the early part of this century.

VALE OF RHEIDOL LIGHT RAILWAY, Dyfed

British Rail's only narrow-gauge line uses steam locomotives and is an unfailing tourist attraction. Its Devil's Bridge terminus is a charming miniature, attractively laid out and set amid dense rhododendron thickets.

Leave Devil's Bridge village by crossing the Devil's Bridge on the A4120 'Ponterwyd' road. Continue high above the Rheidol Valley and after a short distance reach Ysbyty Cynfyn.

YSBYTY CYNFYN, Dyfed

Several stones of the prehistoric circle in which this immaculate, evergreen-shrouded church stands have survived in place. Many gravestones in the churchyard bear Cornish names and are reminders of the days when West Country miners came to Wales in search of better opportunities. A path leads from the church to a wooded gorge featuring a waterfall and the 'Parsons Bridge', so called because it was built for the convenience of a travelling parson who held services both here and at Llanbadarn Fawr.

Continue and shortly in ½ mile turn right on to the B4343 'Dyffryn Castell' road. In 1¾ miles turn right SP 'Llangurig' on to the A44 and reach Dyffryn Castell.

DYFFRYN CASTELL & PLYNLIMON, Dyfed

A path leads from here to the slopes of Plynlimon, a 2,470ft mountain. The views afforded by its summit are spectacular enough to make the ascent easily worth the effort involved. On a clear day the view encompasses much of Wales, from Cader Idris in the north to the Brecon Beacons in the south-east.

Plynlimon, famous for its wetness, is the source of the mighty Severn, the lovely Wye, and several lesser but equally vigorous rivers. Ascents to the summit can also be made from Eisteddfa Gurig (a little north of Dyffryn Castell) and from Nant-y-Moch Reservoir, which is on the west side of the mountain. The banks of the reservoir afford views of low crags that give Plynlimon a more mountainous aspect than is obvious from other vantage points. It should be stressed that although the ascent of Plynlimon is not difficult, the would-be explorer should wear sensible clothing and beware of the mountain's mercurial moods.

Ascend to Eisteddfa Gurig and a 1,400ft road summit. Continue alongside the Afon Tarenig and reach its confluence with the River Wye. In 5 miles enter Llangurig.

LLANGURIG, Powys

Small and beautiful Llangurig is delightfully set in the upper valley of the River Wye, amid hill ranges. The church of St Gurig owes much of its appearance to J W Lloyd of Llandinam, who commissioned Sir Gilbert Scott to restore the building. Lloyd, famous for his inconstancy, began his career as a curate in Llangurig but later became a Catholic and eventually aspired to become a Knight of St Gregory. In later life he returned to the Anglican faith. Stained-glass windows show scenes from the life of St Gurig, relate incidents associated with the royal families of Wales, and depict members of the Lloyd family.

Leave Llangurig on the A470 SP 'Rhayader' and drive down the attractive Wye Valley, accompanying the river itself for part of the way, and return to Rhayader.

SWANSEA, W Glam

Almost three centuries of intensive industrialization have left scars upon the Swansea landscape. The lower Swansea Valley once presented a view of unparalleled devastation, but intensive land reclamation and landscaping is restoring the greenery. Not all of Swansea is built over or barren; over 900 acres of tended parkland bring the country into the city. Bombing during World War II flattened the town's centre and destroyed much of Swansea's tangible history, but scant remains of a 14th-century fortified manor house (AM) can be seen in Wind Street, and 15th-century St Mary's Church was rebuilt in 1955. In 1919 the former Technical College became a university which has since expanded to occupy several buildings in the town. There is a fine Civic Centre, a new Leisure Centre, and a Maritime Museum and Marina.

THE GOWER PENINSULA, W Glam

This small 18- by 5-mile peninsula contains some of the most unspoilt and beautiful scenery in South Wales. Cliffs fringing excellent beaches on the southern coast are considered to be among the finest in Britain, and the soft agricultural landsdcape of the interior is scored by numerous thickly-wooded valleys. Ancient remains point to the Gower's one-time colonization by the Celts and Romans, and reminders of later times are everywhere in the shapes of ruined castles.

Leave Swansea on the A4067 SP 'Mumbles'. Pass the university, and after 1¼ miles follow SP ahead for 'Mumbles'. After 1½ miles reach Oystermouth.

OYSTERMOUTH, W Glam

Picturesque Oystermouth Castle is a 13th-century ruin which occupies the summit of a small hill above a holiday and residential area.

Detour straight ahead on the B4433 to reach The Mumbles seaside resort.

THE MUMBLES, W Glam

In 1807 a horse-drawn tramway was opened between Swansea and The Mumbles as the first passenger-carrying railway in the world. The line was closed in 1960, but The Mumbles remains a popular resort offering a good beach, a pier, and the facilities for a variety of water-based leisure activities. Mumbles Head overlooking Bracelet Bay is a starting point for delightful coastal walks.

From Oystermouth turn right on to the B4593 SP 'Langland'. In ¼ mile reach the church and turn left, then in ½ mile meet crossroads and keep forward along an unclassified road. Descend to Langland Bay.

LANGLAND BAY, W Glam

A sandy beach and views which extend across the Bristol Channel to Somerset are the main features of this popular little bay.

SWANSEA AND THE GOLDEN GOWER

The counties of Glamorgan form an area of contrasts, where astonishing scenes of industrial dereliction rub shoulders with the rural and coastal beauty of the Gower Peninsula, the green lung of Swansea.

Drive to the carpark at Langland Bay and turn right into Brynfield Road. After ½ mile go forward on to the B4593 then turn left. Descend to pass Caswell Bay, then continue forward along an unclassified road and ascend inland. After ¾ mile meet a T-junction and turn left. Follow the road as it turns right to reach Bishopston.

BISHOPSTON, W Glam

An interesting old church survives in this village, but the main attraction here is the local scenery. Lovely

Bishopston Valley leads down to Pwil-du Bay and Head, and marvellous cliff ranges extend along the coast (NT) to the west.

Leave Bishopston, and at the T-junction turn left on to the B4436 SP 'Port Eynon'. Drive through Kittle and after ½ mile turn right. After ¾ mile turn left on to the A4118 SP 'Parkmill and Port Eynon'. Continue to Parkmill.

Swansea Docks have their origin in the 14th century, when a charter confirmed the town's right to build ships.

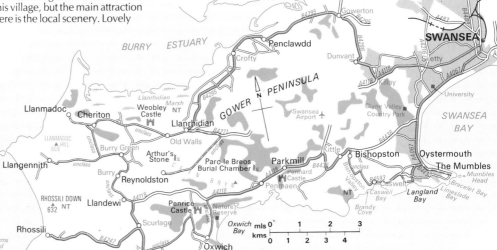

Pennard Castle stands on a rocky outcrop amongst sand dunes near Parkmill.

PARKMILL, W Glam
Ilston Stream flows through Parkmill and continues past the ruins of Pennard Castle to its outlet at beautiful Threecliff Bay (NT). Extensive wind-sculpted sand-dunes hereabouts are known to have buried two churches and threatened to engulf the castle. Near by is the prehistoric Parc Le Breos tomb.

PARC LE BREOS BURIAL CHAMBER, W Glam
This fine example of megalithic tomb architecture (AM) can be reached on foot along a path from Parkmill.

Continue through Penmaen and pass the ridge of 609ft Cefn Bryn on the right. Several paths afford access to this eminence, which makes a fine viewpoint. After 1¾ miles reach the gatehouse of Penrice Castle.

PENRICE CASTLE, W Glam
Open only by written application, ruined Penrice Castle dates from the 13th century and was built to replacve an earlier structure which occupied the mound near Penrice Church.

Turn left here on to the unclassified Oxwich road. Descend through pleasant woods to marshland behind Oxwich Bay.

OXWICH BAY, W Glam
Sand-dunes and marshlands behind Oxwich Bay comprise a large National Nature Reserve which protects a wide variety of flora and fauna. Access is restricted to permit holders, but Oxwich Bay itself has superb sands and excellent scenery that can be enjoyed by anyone.

Continue into Oxwich.

OXWICH, W Glam
Thatched and whitewashed cottages more suggestive of England than South Wales are a feature of Oxwich, and the pleasant local church stands shaded by sycamores at the village edge. Inside the church is the lovely de la Mare tomb, installed by the Norman rooted family who once owned Oxwich Castle (AM). The castle was rebuilt as a Tudor manor house in 1541, but still incorporates relics from the original 14th-century stronghold. At time of publication the structure was closed for repairs.

Drive to the crossroads in Oxwich and turn right. After ½ mile reach a T-junction and turn right SP 'Horton'. After ¾ mile reach another T-junction and turn left SP 'Horton'. After 1½ miles meet crossroads and continue straight across. In ¾ mile turn left on oto the A4118 and descend to Port Eynon.

PORT EYNON, W Glam
Situated at the bottom of a steep hill and noted as a surfing centre, Port Eynon preserves several thatched cottages and lies east of breathtaking cliff scenery (NT). The churchyard has a fine memorial statue of a lifeboatman.

Return along the A4118 from Port Eynon and after 1¾ miles reach Scurlage. Turn left on to the B4247 and continue to Rhossili, below Rhossili Down.

RHOSSILI AND RHOSSILI DOWN, W Glam
Golden sand stretches round the whole 3-mile arc of Rhossili Bay from spectacular Worm's Head (NT), where there is a large sea-bird colony. Behind the village is Rhossili Down (NT), which rises to 632ft and is known for its distinctive flora.

Return along the B4247 to Scurlage and turn left on to the A4118. After 1 mile go forward along an unclassified road SP 'Burry' and reach Llanddewi.

LLANDDEWI, W Glam
Features of this tiny village are the Gower Farm Museum, a primitive little church which preserves an ancient font and slight remains of a Tudor castle.

Continue, passing through Burry to reach Burry Green. Here turn left for Llangennith.

LLANGENNITH, W Glam
During the 6th century St Cenydd founded a monastery here. This was adopted by Norman monks in the 12th century, and today a few remains of its buildings are preserved in the structures of College Farm. The nearby church is sited on a sloping green and displays the best example of a saddle back-roofed tower in the Gower Peninsula. Llanmadoc Hill, affords excellent views.

Return along the 'Burry Green' road. After 1½ miles turn left SP 'Llanmadoc'. In 1½ miles, just beyond the right turn for Cheriton and slightly off the route, is Llanmadoc village.

LLANMADOC, W Glam
Situated below an Iron-Age fort on the slopes of Llanmadoc Hill this small village has a medieval church displaying many interesting features, not the least of which is a triangular door. Nearby are the wild and wind-haunted expanses of Whiteford Burrows (NT).

On the main route turn right into Cheriton.

CHERITON, W. Glam
David Davis, a former rector, executed much of the woodwork displayed in the local church. Many ancient features are preserved in the structure of the tiny 13th-century building itself.

From Cheriton continue east to Weobley Castle.

WEOBLEY CASTLE W Glam
Medieval Weobley Castle (AM) overlooks Llanrhidian Marsh from a

Planned additions to 14th-century Weobley Castle were never built because of financial difficulties.

lovely setting that belies its war-like function. It was built during the 13th and 14th centuries, and later rebuilt as a fortified manor house.

Continue through Old Walls and enter Llanrhidian.

LLANRHIDIAN, W Glam
A mysteriously-carved stone stands in the church porch here, and near by are two ancient upright stones of equally enigmatic purpose. Llanrhidian Marshes (NT), more typical of East Anglia than Wales, are rich in wildlife.

At the end of the village a detour to Reynoldston can be made by turning right on to the B4271 SP 'Swansea'. After 1¼ miles turn right on to an unclassified road and climb over Cefn Bryn to Reynoldston.

REYNOLDSTON AND ARTHUR'S STONE, W Glam
Reynoldston's Victorian church stands on the west flank of the Cefn Bryn ridge and contains various 17th- and 18th-century monuments. Arthur's Stone, on the ridge of Cefn Bryn, is a prehistoric tomb covered by an enormous capstone.

Return to Llanrhidian and turn right on to the B4295. Pass through Crofty to enter Penclawdd.

PENCLAWDD, W Glam
Cockle gathering on the nearby sands is a traditional occupation of the Penclawdd women, but the famous pony-drawn carts on which they carried their spoils are not as much in evidence as they were before the last war.

Continue to Gowerton. Meet crossroads and go forward, then bear right on to the B4296. Reach Dunvant and turn left into the suburbs of Swansea. Follow SP 'Swansea' to Killay and turn left on to the A4118. Continue through Sketty to Swansea town centre.

The outline of Worm's Head resembles a recumbent dragon.

ALONG THE DYFED COAST

From the ancient borough of Pembroke with its magnificent castle, through picturesque inland villages, to the rugged red sandstone cliffs and mysterious caves of the coast that abound with mystery and superstition.

TENBY, Dyfed
One of the most popular resorts in South Wales, Tenby is a charming old port with many holiday facilities. See page 19.

Leave Tenby on the A4139 Pembroke road, with glimpses of the coastline and Caldy Island, to reach Lydstep.

The neat and colourful resort of Tenby offers all the attractions of the seaside, including deep-sea fishing, boating, water-skiing and aqua-diving

LYDSTEP, Dyfed
Lying in the centre of the small village of Lydstep are the ruins of the Palace of Arms. This is said to have been a hunting lodge of Bishop Gower of St David's. The coastal views around Lydstep Point (NT) to the east are breathtaking, and Lydstep Caverns beneath are well worth exploring when accessible at low tide.

Continue on the A4139 and in ½ mile turn left on to the B4585, SP 'Manorbier', to reach Manorbier.

MANORBIER, Dyfed
An imposing stone castle (OACT) perches above the sandy beach of Manorbier Bay with its tidal pools and rocks of red sandstone. The de Barri family, Norman barons, built Manorbier Castle and it was always more a baronial residence than a fortress. Medieval castles were practically self-sufficient and had their own mills, orchards and fields: the stream below powered the castle's corn mills. Giraldus Cambrensis, 'Gerald the Welshman', was born here in 1146, and he claimed it was the 'pleasantest spot in Wales'. A wax model of him can be seen inside the castle.

Keep left (one-way) then turn right, SP 'Pembroke'. In ½ mile turn left on to the A4139 and pass through Jameston and Hodgeston to Lamphey.

LAMPHEY, Dyfed
Just north-east of Lamphey lie the remains of a 13th-century Bishop's Palace. The romantic ruins (AM) — originally set amid elegant gardens, orchards and fishponds — represent one of 7 medieval manors built as country retreats for the Bishops of St David's. Still visible are the arcaded parapets signifying the hand of Bishop Henry Gower, who also contributed to the design of Swansea Castle and the palace at St David's. The Earl of Essex, greatly favoured by Elizabeth I, lived here as a boy.

Turn sharp left on to the B4584 to Freshwater East, then turn right on to the unclassified Stackpole road. Descend (1 in 5) and follow a high banked road for 2¼ miles. A road to the left leads to Stackpole Quay.

STACKPOLE QUAY, Dyfed
Stackpole Quay (NT) is an extremely picturesque feature of this stretch of beautiful coastline. The stone jetty was used for the shipping of limestone when the nearby quarry was in use. The beach here is very rocky but a charming cliff path to the south leads to the peaceful sandy beach of Barafundle Bay, behind which lie the dunes of Stackpole Warren.

The main tour continues to Stackpole. Remain on the unclassified road, then turn left on to the B4319, SP 'Bosherton'. In ½ mile turn right, SP 'Castlemartin'. Alternatively, turn left on to an unclassified road for Bosherton.

BOSHERTON AND ST GOVAN'S CHAPEL, Dyfed
Bosherton is a peaceful village and its group of pools known as Bosherton Lakes make an enchanting picture when the hundreds of water lilies covering them burst into flower. The road through the village leads on to St Govan's Head and, by the steep steps leading down to the sea, lies St Govan's Chapel. The minute building, just 17ft by 12ft, wedged in to a crack in the cliffs, is shrouded with mystery and legend. Who Govan was is uncertain: suppositions vary between King Arthur's knight Sir Gawaine; Coren, wife of a 6th-century prince, or the Irish saint Gobham. Outside the chapel a boulder known as Bell Rock is said to contain a silver bell, which was in the bell tower, but was stolen by pirates; angels brought the bell back and hid it in the rock.

Another legend says the water from a well inside was able to cure skin and eye complaints and a second well below the chapel could cure cripples. Nearby there is a deep narrow ravine called Huntsman's Leap. The story behind the name is that a brave man jumped his horse over it and, having safely landed, died of fright when he realised the great risk he had taken.

The main tour continues to Castlemartin.

CASTLEMARTIN, Dyfed
The once flourishing village of Castlemartin is now a windswept place in the middle of a tank and artillery range. A breed of black cattle, called Castlemartin, was one of the 2 strains which were interbred to become the Welsh Black. The local Norman church contains an organ which belonged to the German composer Mendelssohn.

Turn left, SP 'Angle' and 'Freshwater West'. In 2 miles pass through the sand dunes of Freshwater West with views of St Ann's Head and Skokholm Island. In 1 mile turn left on to the B4320 with glimpses of Angle Bay and Milford Haven. In 1½ miles turn right on to an unclassified road, then descend and turn left into Angle.

ANGLE, Dyfed
A single main street of colour-washed cottages, dominated by the grand colonnaded front of the Globe Hotel, links Angle's 2 tiny harbours which face Milford Haven. Within the boundaries of the churchyard is a small Fisherman's Chapel — dating from 1447 — that has outside steps leading to its upper storey. North of the churchyard is an ancient dovecot: probably dating from

medieval days when doves were an important source of meat.

Pass the church and in ½ mile turn left (forward for West Angle Bay) to leave on the B4320 Pembroke road. In ½ mile turn sharp left and later pass through Hundleton and continue to Pembroke.

PEMBROKE, Dyfed
The ancient borough of Pembroke was built around the great 12th-century fortress of Pembroke Castle (OACT). Beside the sea on a rocky spur above the town, the castle, one of the finest in the country, was once the hub of a complex medieval defence system. Restoration work was started on the castle in 1880 and has been continued at intervals ever since. Beneath the castle lies a huge natural limestone cavern called the 'Wogan', which was linked to the main structure by a winding staircase and has an opening to the river. Pembroke's long main street, running east from the castle, is the scene in October of a centuries-old fair. In many places, notably the Park and the Mill Bridge, the old town walls are still visible. In Commons Road is the National Museum of Gypsy Caravans. It contains a fine collection of caravans, carts and other artefacts related to Romany life.

PEMBROKE DOCK, Dyfed
About 2 miles north of Pembroke town stands this stately dock, built on a grid-iron system with grey buildings lining its straight streets. Until the 1920s it was one of the chief Naval dockyards, but it is now used mainly by ship repairers and chandlers. An obelisk commemorating the launching of the *Valorius* and the *Ariadne* c1814, the first 2 ships made here, stands in Albion Square. It was here too that the first steam ship

There has been a mill at Carew on the tidal Cleddau River since 1560

man-of-war — *The Tartar;* the first Royal yacht — *The Victoria and Albert;* and the first iron-clad warship — *The Warrior* were made. The latter is moored at Portsmouth.

From Pembroke join the one-way system and pass Pembroke Castle. Keep forward along the main street, SP 'Tenby', and at the end of town turn left on to the A4075, SP 'Carmarthen'. In 2¼ miles, at the T-junction, turn right on to the A477 to reach edge of Milton. Keep forward, and in ½ mile turn left on to the A4075 for Carew.

CAREW, Dyfed
An ivy-clad ruin stands on the banks of the Cleddau River with only seagulls wheeling overhead for company. Just below the castle is a tidal corn mill and although a mill has stood here since the mid-16th century, the existing 'French' mill (OACT) — 3-storeyed and rectangular — dates from the late 18th century. It is open now as a working museum and utilises the tides by damming the water, then using it as required. A third feature of interest in the village is Carew Cross (AM). It was built during the 11th century and was a great technical achievement in those days. Standing 14ft high, its shaft is inscribed with several traditional Welsh patterns.

Return to the edge of Milton and turn left on to an unclassified road, SP 'Lamphey' and 'Manorbier'. Gradually ascend, and at the T-junction turn left. This road, known as 'The Ridgeway', has occasional all-round panoramic views. Continue following SP 'Tenby' and at the A4139, turn left for the return to Tenby.

CASTLES ON THE BORDER

South from one of the tortuous meanders carved by the River Severn runs the border between England and Wales – a contentious division guarded by medieval fortresses at Powis, Montgomery, and Clun.

WELSHPOOL, Powys

Prior to the 19th century this 'English town in Wales' was known simply as Pool, a name derived from the marshy nature of the area in which it stood. The 'Welsh' prefix, ironic in the light of the town's hotly disputed position in the borderlands between England and Wales, was added in 1835 to distinguish it from Poole in Dorset. Opposite the town hall is a half-timbered building with a Jacobean staircase, one of several such examples in the town. Severn Road leads to a splendid railway station incorporating many gables, end towers, and a platform canopy resplendent with wrought-iron arcading. Powysland Museum stands in Salop Road and was started in 1874 by Morris Jones, who had previously founded the Powysland Club – claimed to be the oldest archaeological society in Wales.

Also of interest are a restored 18th-century cockpit, the Montgomery Canal Exhibition Centre with narrowboat trips, and the Oriel Gallery.

POWIS CASTLE, Powys

Approached from Welshpool through a magnificently-wooded park, Powis Castle dates originally from the 13th century. Subsequent alterations which continued right up until the end of the last century have changed the building beyond all past recognition, and it now appears as a vast mansion. As an historic treasure Powis is very special because it has been continuously occupied, its present form having gradually evolved through the centuries in response to the tastes of various owners. The 18th-century terraced gardens that complement the building are especially noteworthy, and the interior of the castle is rich with curios including mementos of Clive of India. In 1952 the castle and park were passed over into the protection of the National Trust.

Leave Welshpool on the A483 'Newtown' road and follow the Shropshire Union Canal past the grounds of Powis Castle. After 4 miles turn right on to the B4390 to reach Berriew.

BERRIEW, Powys

Recipient of an award for the best-kept village in Wales, Berriew is a picturesque combination of black-and-white cottages and a few more recent buildings interspersed with trim flower gardens. Pretty falls can be seen near by on the Afon Rhiw, which joins the Severn 1½ miles east.

Leave Berriew by turning left on to the B4385 and cross the Rhiw. Shortly turn left again. Later meet a T-junction and turn right to rejoin the A483 'Newtown' road. Continue to Garthmyl and turn left on to the B4385 SP 'Montgomery'. Cross the Severn and continue to Montgomery.

MONTGOMERY, Powys

Montgomery's superficially Georgian character is shown in the red-brick town hall that dominates Broad Street, a thoroughfare almost as wide as it is long. Elsewhere fine examples of Tudor and Jacobean architecture make surprise appearances round secretive corners or at the tops of quaint slopes and steps. The parish Church of St Nicholas was built just before Henry III granted Montgomery's Royal Charter in 1227. Its best features include 15th-century nave roofs, a double screen, and monuments to the Herbert family. Poet George Herbert was born in the now-ruined castle (AM), built by Henry III to replace a Norman stronghold at Hendomen to the north-west. Also of interest is the Historical Exhibition Centre.

Continue on the B4385 SP 'Bishop's Castle', with views across the River Camlad valley – the only river to flow from England into Wales. Enter Bishop's Castle.

BISHOP'S CASTLE, Salop

This hillside market town stands on the edge of Clun Forest and preserves a number of interesting old buildings, the most picturesque of which is the 16th-century House on Crutches. Its Victorian church retains a Norman tower, and the 18th-century town hall stands over a medieval lock-up.

At the end turn left and in ½ mile at crossroads turn right on to the A488 SP 'Clun'. Continue through wooded hill country to Clun.

CLUN, Salop

Thousands of flint implements displayed in the museum at Clun's 18th-century town hall demonstrate that man has lived in this area for a very long time. Attractive almshouses of 1618 enliven the somewhat stolid appearance of the village. Remains of a Norman castle overlook the River Clun from a small hill, and the large expanse of Clun Forest stretches west as a patchwork of treeless uplands and recent afforestation.

Leave Clun on the A488 'Knighton' road and ascend Clun Hill to a summit of 1,150ft. Slowly descend and cross the River Redlake, then ascend again before skirting Kinsley Wood to reach Knighton.

KNIGHTON, Powys

The Offa's Dyke long-distance footpath was officially opened here in 1971. The dyke itself, built by a king of Mercia in the 8th century, runs through the town. Built largely of local stone, Knighton occupies a delightful hillside position in the Teme Valley and has scant remains of a Norman motte-and-bailey castle. Knighton Railway Station stands on the Central Wales line and is a little gem of Victorian-gothic railway architecture. The town's livestock sales are famous.

Leave Knighton on the A488 SP 'Newtown'. After ¼ mile turn right on to the B4355 to follow the River Teme. Continue to Knucklas.

KNUCKLAS, Powys

Crowning the hill above Knucklas are the remains of a 13th-century castle which is connected in legend with Gwynhwyfar (or Guinevere), whom the heroic folk figure King Arthur married. A beautiful 75ft-high railway viaduct which can also be seen here is of Victorian date and carries crenellated towers.

Continue through pleasant valley scenery to Beguildy.

A ruined keep and two 13th-century towers are the most outstanding features of Clun's impressively sited castle.

Elegant ironwork surrounds the grave of social reformer Robert Owen at Newtown.

Victorian romanticism is reflected in the crenellated towers of the railway viaduct at Knucklas.

BEGUILDY, Powys
Some years ago a would-be benefactor offered to donate a large sum of money to the local school on condition that the village should revert to its correct Welsh spelling of Bugail-dy meaning the 'Shepherd's House'. The offer was declined. Features of the local church include a rood screen with fine tracery and a Jacobean pulpit and altar.

Drive on through Felindre and later ascend on to open moorland; to the right below 1,732ft Cilfaesty Hill is the source of the Teme. Descend into Dolfor.

DOLFOR, Powys
Dolfor stands at an altitude of 1,000ft and affords extensive mountain views to the north west. Views south to the Brecon Beacons range can be enjoyed from the 1,565ft summit of nearby Kerry Hill. The rivers Teme, Ithon, and Mule all rise in the area.

In Dolfor turn right on to the A483, then right again (no SP) on to a narrow unclassified road. Beyond the local church keep forward to a 1,200ft road summit, offering splendid views north over Newtown and the Severn Valley. Continue down a long descent and turn left on to the A489. Enter Newtown and turn right for the town centre.

NEWTOWN, Powys
Robert Owen, a social reformer who became known as the father of trade unionism, was born in Newtown and is buried in the churchyard of the old parish church. Some of the reasons why Owen was such an assiduous campaigner for workers' rights can be understood by a visit to the Newtown Textile Museum, and a museum dedicated to his memory is situated over the Midland Bank. The 15th-century rood screen from the old church has been preserved in a handsome 19th-century successor. Newtown was originally established in 1279, but the 20th century has incorporated it in a designated development area and made it into a new town all over again. Extensive new building has given the community two new bridges over the River Severn plus a theatre and various civic buildings.

Leave Newtown on the B4568, cross the River Severn, and at a roundabout, take the 3rd exit SP 'Bettws Cedewain'. After 2½ miles turn left on to the B4389 'Llanfair Caereinion' road. Proceed to Bettws Cedewain.

BETTWS CEDEWAIN, Powys
Close-knit round a stone bridge spanning the little River Bechan, this attractive village has an interesting 14th-century church which carries a timbered and louvred tower typical of the area. A barrel organ and a pre-Reformation brass, depicting a priest vested for mass, can be seen inside.

Continue for 2 miles and turn right to enter Tregynon. After 1½ miles cross the Afon Rhiw and enter New Mills. Turn left and make a winding ascent to a road summit of 980ft. Descend into Llanfair Caereinion.

LLANFAIR CAEREINION, Powys
The river at the foot of the hillside on which this quiet little greystone town is built has two names – Banwy and Einion. In the local church, which was rebuilt in 1868, is the 14th-century stone figure of a knight. The ancient doorway of the church is a good example of medieval building.

The charming House on Crutches in Bishop's Castle straddles a passage between the High Street and Market Place.

To leave Llanfair turn right, bear left and cross the Banwy-Einion, then turn right on to the A458 'Welshpool' road. After ¼ mile note the terminus of the Welshpool and Llanfair Railway on the right.

WELSHPOOL AND LLANFAIR LIGHT RAILWAY, Powys
Opened in 1903, this narrow-gauge railway was the only line of its type built in Wales to carry general goods. Passenger services ceased in 1931, but the railway continued to fulfil its original function until it was completely closed down in 1956. Four years later in 1960 the Welshpool and Llanfair Railway Preservation Co was formed, and by 1973 was large enough to purchase the line outright. The line has been restored and progressively re-opened, reaching a new terminus on the west side of Welshpool in 1981. A wide variety of locomotives and rolling stock is used to operate the railway.

Continue through pleasant scenery, with the railway to the right, and return to Welshpool.

WELSH CASTLES

Wales is a land of castles. A dramatic remnant of her turbulent past they now grace the landscape they once threatened. Many crown hilltop sites or overlook the sea, evoking reminders of the age of warfare, chivalry and romance.

Wales has more castles to the square mile than any other country in the world and the following colourful section of the book illustrates in alphabetical sequence a small selection of these mighty structures.

Some of the castles listed, by nature of their remains and locations, are freely accessible at all times. Many are governed by a convenient system of standard opening hours. However, it is recommended that in most cases inquiries are made beforehand to avoid disappointment as all opening arrangements may change.

The gaunt remains of the tower of Aberystwyth's castle still stands firm despite the storms that over the centuries have taken their toll

BEAUMARIS

Beaumaris, begun in 1295, was the last and largest castle to be built in Wales by Edward I. Here, his architect Master James of St George has perfected the ultimate in symmetrical concentric design, surrounded by a water-filled moat with its own protected access to the sea. Though planned to have lavish accommodation, the money dried up before it could be completed and it never reached its full height. However, Beaumaris remains the best example of a concentric castle in Britain with fine views across the Menai Strait.

The 'Gate next the Sea' of Beaumaris Castle, and the medieval dock where ships of 40 tons could be moored

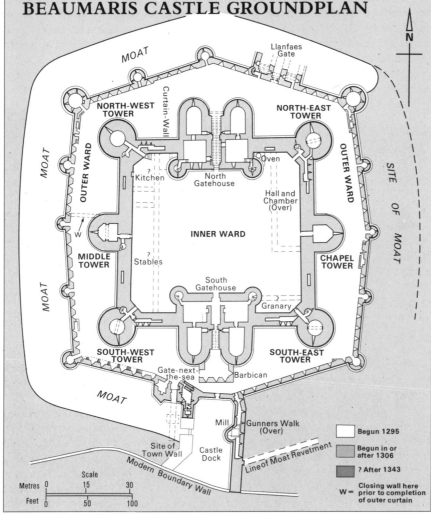

BEAUMARIS CASTLE GROUNDPLAN

N

MOAT

Llanfaes Gate

NORTH-WEST TOWER

NORTH-EAST TOWER

Curtain Wall

OUTER WARD

MOAT

OUTER WARD

SITE OF MOAT

?Kitchen

North Gatehouse

Oven

Hall and Chamber (Over)

INNER WARD

MOAT

W

MIDDLE TOWER

?Stables

CHAPEL TOWER

South Gatehouse

Granary

SOUTH-WEST TOWER

SOUTH-EAST TOWER

Gate-next-the-sea

Barbican

MOAT

Mill

Gunners Walk (Over)

Site of Town Wall

Castle Dock

Modern Boundary Wall

Line of Moat Revetment

	Begun 1295
	Begun in or after 1306
	? After 1343

W = Closing wall here prior to completion of outer curtain

Scale

Metres 0 15 30

Feet 0 50 100

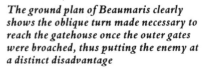
The ground plan of Beaumaris clearly shows the oblique turn made necessary to reach the gatehouse once the outer gates were broached, thus putting the enemy at a distinct disadvantage

A drawbridge gave access to the 'Gate next the Sea', one of the 14 obstacles an attacker had to negotiate before reaching the inner ward

Although King Edward I of England might well have considered Beaumaris to be his finest creation after Caernarfon, today this castle is perhaps the least known and least visited of that mighty group of fortresses constructed after his second campaign against Wales in 1282. Those other castles, at Conwy, Caernarfon and Harlech, seem to clamour stridently for attention, each advancing its own undeniable claim of power, dominance or location. Beaumaris, on the other hand, has an altogether lower profile. It is not blessed with the impact of situation which the others all possess. Neither has it been, in recent times, along any major route, so it has not received the recognition that it unquestionably deserves.

The coast road running north east from Menai Bridge passes under an umbrella of trees on its way to Beaumaris, an unexpectedly English looking town with its clustered Georgian façades lining the seafront. Only at the far end of the main street does the castle, quite unannounced, come suddenly into view, its low, squat walls and close-set drum towers neatly reflected in the waters of its moat. Even at this distance it belies its proportions. But in walking around the moat, or entering through the outer gate into the inner ward, the sheer size of the immense castle soon becomes apparent. An enormous square of open, grass-covered courtyard unrolls beyond the narrow confines of the gatehouse. Here, inside its walls until not so many years ago, lay four good-size tennis courts, with plenty of room to spare.

MADOG'S REVOLT

It is across the water of the Menai Strait, to Caernarfon, that we must look first for events that were directly responsible for the creation of Beaumaris. At the end of September 1294, the Welsh in the north rose unexpectedly, under their leader Madog ap Llywelyn, spurred on by the threat of compulsory enlistment for a war in Gascony. They directed their main efforts at the unfinished defences of Caernarfon, which they took, killing

The castle as seen by an 18th-century engraver

its governor. The revolt spread quickly throughout Wales, forcing Edward to conduct another difficult winter campaign in order to quell it. Some time during the course of the fighting, a decision was taken to build a new castle at Beaumaris. The plan was not new. The king had been here, to the Welsh town of Llanfaes, in 1283, when he appointed Roger de Pulesdon as Sheriff of Anglesey. It was a natural place to build any such fortification, for Llanfaes was the commercial centre of the island, its principal trading port and the ferrying point for traffic to the mainland. Quite probably, the king had intended to build a castle here then but, with resources stretched so thinly elsewhere, its construction was postponed until a more appropriate time.

On 10 April 1295, that time arrived. The English pioneer corps threw a pontoon bridge across the Menai Strait near Bangor and the whole army, together with a huge labour force, crossed over to the island and set up headquarters at Llanfaes. The entire Welsh population of the town was summarily evicted some twelve miles away to Newborough. Near to the old town was a 'fair marsh,' far more extensive than now and covered in bulrushes. On this unpromising ground building of the new castle of Beaumaris was begun.

ARCHITECT AND PLAN

In sole charge of the work was that very experienced master, James of St George. He was probably then in his sixties and already had to his credit seven major castles in North Wales. The structure which he designed and built on the marshes of Beaumaris is counted today as the high point of military engineering in the Middle Ages, for here, on this somewhat uninspiring site, sits the ultimate in concentric castle plans.

The idea of the concentric castle, with one high ring of defence inside a lower one, had gradually been growing since the late 1260's, when it was first perfected at Caerphilly in South Wales. It had great advantages of economy, unity and compactness over the older keep and bailey system, but its major asset was the tremendous increase in firepower which it provided. Defenders on the great inner walls could fire their missiles with ease over the heads of their fellows on the outside. Wherever possible, this approach had been adopted, in one form or another, at most of Edward I's Welsh castles. But only at the last of them, here in Beaumaris, does the system demonstrate its advantages with such force and yet such elegance.

In modern terminology, Beaumaris was a greenfield site. Unlike so many other places, it did not have an earlier existing fortification upon which to build. Nor was there any convenient natural feature of geography that could be exploited. With only the flat marsh and the sea at its disposal, the new castle would have to rely exclusively upon its own man-made defences.

Their first line is a wet moat of 18ft width which once encircled the whole castle but today it is no longer quite complete. At its southern end there stood a tidal dock for shipping, connected by a short channel to the sea. Here, ships of 40 tons laden weight could sail right up to the castle, tie up at the iron ring which still projects from its walls and unload their cargo straight into the outer ward through the door in its northern side. The dock was protected by the shooting deck on Gunners' Walk and here too lay the sluice gates, to control water levels, and a corn mill, which utilized the flow.

ACCESS DIFFICULTIES

Immediately across the moat is the low, eight-sided curtain wall of the outer ward. The battlements have nearly gone, but the circuit is complete enough to see that this curtain, together with its 16 towers, must have provided something like 300 firing positions at two or three levels. To enter the castle in the 13th century, one would have had to negotiate no less than 14 separate obstacles. Across the moat, a drawbridge gave access to the outer ward, through the Gate Next the Sea, with its murder holes and its stout wooden doors. Once through here, a cunningly devised oblique right turn gives access to the barbican and its gate while, inside the main inner gatehouse passage, there were two sets of wooden doors, an arrangement of spyholes, three portcullises and three groups of murder holes to negotiate before the inner ward was gained.

The medieval advantages of Beaumaris's concentric plan can still be appreciated for this castle approaches the ultimate goal of defence: it would have been virtually impossible to take by storm and, with its protected dock giving access to the sea, could not have been starved into surrender. The elegance of Master James's design can best be appreciated from the air, for Beaumaris is quite regular and symmetrical, combining with great skill and virtuosity the twin requirements of defence and accommodation.

An engraving showing the north entrance to Beaumaris

LAVISH ACCOMMODATION

It is to that accommodation we turn next, for here the intention seems to have been particularly generous. Both gatehouses of the inner ward were to have had grand suites of state rooms at their rear, much as at Harlech. The north gate, on the far side of the inner ward, was only completed as far as the Great Hall to its first floor level and the projected second storey was never built. Even as it stands today, with its five blank and gaping windows, it dominates the courtyard. Had it been finished, it would have towered to twice its present height. Another block of equal size was planned for the south gate, but this was never to rise further than its footings. The courtyard itself was originally lined, to east and west, by building ranges – stables and kitchens on one side, a further vast hall block on the other leading to the chapel – although here again we cannot be sure that they were ever built to full height. The six towers of the inner ward also had their chambers and all were interconnected by wall passages, so familiar to visitors to Caernarfon.

As at Caernarfon, one is left wondering who all this lavish accommodation was designed for. The answer may simply be that, in 1295, such luxury was thought to be a necessary requirement for the twin households of a king and, if he should marry again, his queen. At this time, the Prince of Wales was fast approaching marriageable age and, when that day arrived, might also need to put up at Beaumaris. There were also various royal officers to consider, from the constable and sheriff downwards, who would occupy the less grand quarters.

Master James of St George's great castle at Beaumaris was never finished. Events outside of Wales were to overtake its construction. The enormous injection of £6,736, which had supported 2,600 labourers in that first year of 1295, dwindled all too soon, with campaign demands from Gascony and Scotland. By 1298, the money dried up altogether. Despite minor building works in later times, it was never completed as originally intended and so it sits to this day, the proud blueprint never quite realized.

IN CARE OF Welsh Office

OPEN all reasonable times (standard hours)

ADMISSION some charge

LOCATION eastern end of town

COUNTY Gwynedd

THE ORIGIN OF THE CASTLE

Man has needed protection ever since he made his first enemy. But early fortifications were for the protection of large communities – Iron Age hillforts, Roman camps, Anglo-Saxon burghs. By contrast, the castle is a private fortification, the fortified residence of a lord.

The idea seems to have arisen in 9th-century western Europe, with the break-up of the Western Roman Empire after the death of Charlemagne. New local lords, struggling to survive, needed to fortify their bases either by making their homes out of strong towers or by putting separate defences around their places of residence. Stone defensive towers built about AD 1000 can still be seen in the Loire valley, France.

THE CASTLE COMES TO WALES

The Normans' success in expanding their influence in Europe is due mainly to their use of cavalry operating from such fortified bases. When Edward the Confessor returned to England in 1051 after his temporary exile, he brought with him some Norman supporters, who settled around Hereford and built three or four castles (including Hereford itself) in the next few years before their expulsion.

Soon after the Norman Conquest of England, these Herefordshire castles were rebuilt and many others were built on the Welsh March. The Norman penetration of Wales along the coastal plains and up the Severn valley is marked by a series of earthwork castles reaching as far as Anglesey in the north-east and St David's in the west by the 1080s. Naturally enough, the Welsh themselves built castles in response, and the fluctuating fortunes of war meant that some lords, both English and Welsh, found it necessary to rebuild their castle elsewhere from time to time.

THE CASTLES OF WALES – THEIR IMPORTANCE

The majority of the Norman castles in Wales were built of timber and have long-since rotted away. There are no great stone keeps like the Tower of London, although at Chepstow there is the earliest complete stone castle hall in Britain.

The 13th-century castles of Wales, on the other hand, are quite superb. This is especially true of the remarkable, unparalleled series built by King Edward I, each different yet part of one overall grand design. Although the Edwardian castles tend to dominate, the stone castles built by the Welsh themselves must not be overlooked (Edward found they had little need for improvement when they fell into his hands). The same can be said of those built by the English baronage, which often contained ideas well ahead of their time. Caerphilly and Pembroke, for example, must appear on any list of the world's great castles.

To end on a less military note, no traveller in the peaceful Usk valley should fail to visit the complete fortified manor-house at Tretower and the palatial (but wrecked) Raglan Castle, to understand how the low and the high Welsh lords lived in the later Middle Ages.

This detail from the Bayeux Tapestry, created in the 11th century, shows the building of a castle

CAERNARFON

Last great castle of King Edward I's second Welsh campaign of 1282–83, Caernarfon is both fortress and palace. Designed as the new seat of government for North Wales, it was the birthplace, in 1284, of its new English Prince, the ill-fated Edward II. Though sacked by the Welsh in 1294, it withstood all assaults by Owain Glyndwr and was never again surrendered until the Civil War. Extensively restored in Victorian and later times, it has, this century, seen two ceremonial Investitures of latter-day Princes of Wales. One of Britain's best known historic sites.

'If it be well manned, victualled and ammunitioned, it is invincible.'

So wrote John Taylor of Caernarfon Castle in the middle of the 17th century. It is easy enough for us, following in his footsteps today, to echo these sentiments on entering this great castle for the very first time. Climb the modern stone steps up from the road towards the King's Gate and look carefully about. Then, with the help of a little imagination, try to visualize the daunting task facing a would-be 13th- or 14th-century intruder.

The obstacles would have begun with a drawbridge, spanning the deep outer ditch which was twice as wide as now, taking up the whole width of the modern roadway. Whilst negotiating the bridge, our intruder might be prey to unseen archers, hidden behind the arrow-loops that pierce the gatehouse walls – two or even three times as many of them as he would expect, for these loops are cunningly designed with multiple embrasures on the inner face which more than doubled their firepower. (Firepower, in the end was what the castles of Edward I were all about.) Having, for the moment, overcome this hurdle, he would then be faced with an impenetrable series of stout wooden doors and iron-shod portcullises, five of the one and no less than six of the other, each and every stage flanked by yet more arrowloops whilst, all the time, danger lurked overhead from the aptly-named murder holes in the roof of the gate-passage. Small wonder, then, that the King's Gate at Caernarfon has been described as the mightiest in the land.

Although the castle has undergone successive alterations and repairs throughout its life, evidence of long-vanished features of defence still exists: the carved stone bearings that took the pivots for the drawbridge, the rebates and drawbar holes which show the position and thickness of the doors, and also the grooves down which once slid the weighty portcullis grilles. Two of these portcullises would have had to rise right through the floor of a chapel located directly above the gate passage – not an uncommon arrangement in a medieval castle where religion may have had its place, but was often tempered by rules of the sternest practicality and common sense.

Exhibits from the Royal Welch Fusiliers Museum in Queen's Tower

A PALATIAL RESIDENCE

Caernarfon Castle was designed to fulfil two functions. Self-evident is its role as a fortress, but it was also intended to be a great official residence and seat of government for King Edward's newly-created shire counties of North Wales. Indeed, it is the nearest building Wales has to a royal palace, having been owned continuously by the Crown ever since Edward I founded it in the summer of 1283. Its planning is unusual, being shaped rather like an hour glass which was originally divided by a cross wall, at the narrowest point, into two wards. Occupying most of the upper ward was the great earthen mound of an earlier Norman motte and bailey castle, thrown up around 1090 by Earl Hugh of Chester, during an early successful foray into North Wales. More recently, this has been levelled, but it still accounts for the difference in heights between the two wards.

In the 14th century, the lower ward would have been lined by timber-framed buildings though only foundations remain. To the south was a 100ft long Great Hall. Halls were often the most important single building

Floodlit Caernarfon Castle, one of Britain's finest medieval fortresses

in a medieval castle. Visitors were received and daily business transacted in them, and all the occupants of the castle would eat there.

Normally, they had a service end, with pantry for dry goods and buttery for drink hidden by an elaborate carved wooden screen. The kitchen was usually located in a separate building, often some distance away, because of the high fire risk from the open cooking hearths, an eminently sensible arrangement which unfortunately resulted in the serving of luke-warm food. In Caernarfon's case, the kitchens were on the opposite side of the courtyard to the hall. One or two of their fixtures survive, such as the stone trough for the piped water supply.

Well-endowed though the public and service areas of the castle are, Caernarfon's private accommodation is outstanding. Most imposing, and commanding attention from everywhere within the enclosure, is the solid mass of the Eagle Tower, crowned by its triple cluster of turrets. Here, in the 13th century, lay the quarters of the castle's constable or governor, the King's lieutenant and first Justiciar of North Wales, Sir Otto de Grandson. Everything about it is on the grand scale, from its basement access to the water gate (more recently used by Her Majesty the Queen to enter the castle, when she invested her eldest son Prince of Wales in July 1969) to its imposing upper rooms and even the carved eagles, one of which originally crested each turret. Next in order of merit comes the Queen's Tower, almost as spacious, but having only three floors and, like all the other towers, one turret. The accommodation did not stop here: there was plentiful, if slightly less grand, space in the Chamberlain, Black, Cistern, North East and Granary Towers, to say nothing of what must have been meticulously planned and yet never built over the Queen's Gate and of a second Great Hall.

Why was there a need for all these private quarters when the castle's permanent garrison was normally a mere 30 men? The answer must be sought in its role in the newly created and annexed Principality of Wales. Not only was Caernarfon the official residence of the King's chief administrator and legal officer; it was also the birthplace of the country's new prince whom, so tradition has it, was presented to the Welsh nobles as a babe in arms. Caernarfon, with its capacity to take an entire royal household, council and guests, was undoubtedly designed as a base from which this Prince of Wales could rule his new dominion.

The groundplan of Caernarfon Castle

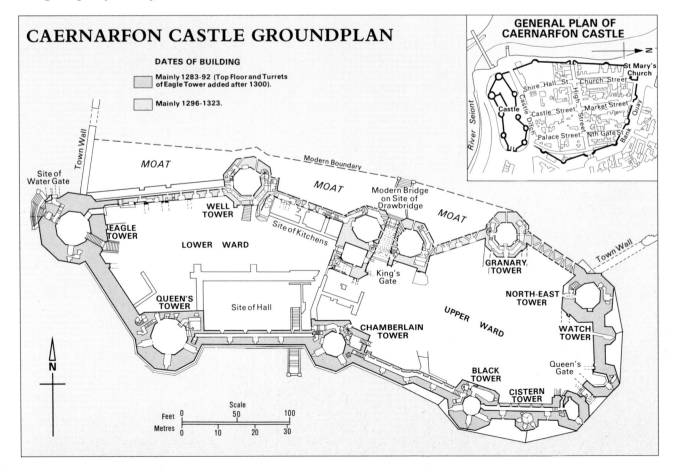

AN IMPERIAL TOUCH

Though built at a time when the concentric idea of walls within walls prevailed, Caernarfon, as we have seen, had but a single curtain wall, albeit a massively powerful one. To make up for its lack of outer defences, the curtain was honeycombed by continuous defended wall passages at two separate levels. It is, however, the angular towers that lend that touch of architectural distinction not found to the same extent at Edward I's other castles. The majestic aspect is further enhanced by the many bands of coloured red sandstone that embellish its outward façade. To find a parallel to this, we must travel to the very gateway of Asia and Istanbul, once the great imperial city of Constantinople. Edward must have drawn inspiration from Constantinople's massive 5th-century walls – among the wonders of the Middle Ages – with their angular towers and alternating bands of Roman tile and masonry.

Caernarfon had its own links with the Roman Empire. Its Roman fort of Segontium, just above the modern town, was inseparably linked, in legend at least, with the emperors Constantine and Magnus Maximus. The latter, in particular, caught the imagination of the ancient Welsh story-tellers, becoming the central figure in one of the tales of the *Mabinogion*, a group of early Welsh romances. When Edward came to build at Caernarfon his own fortress palace, he seems to have made a deliberate attempt to recreate in stone some of the *Mabinogion's* spectacular descriptions of a great city with towers of many colours and eagles fashioned out of gold. Where better to turn, when casting around for a model, than to the fabled walls of Constantinople itself?

POMP AND CEREMONY

Throughout the Middle Ages, history largely passed Caernarfon by, the castle never fulfilling the role Edward I had evidently envisaged. The timber-framed apartments, so hurriedly rushed up in the spring of 1284 to accommodate the king and queen while awaiting the birth of their new son, lasted barely ten years. They were swept away in the Madog rebellion of 1294, when both castle and fortified town were captured and sacked. Prince Edward, indeed, never again set foot in Caernarfon. Created Prince of Wales in 1301, at a great ceremony farther down the coast at Nefyn, he spent the remainder of his life in England or France, only rarely visiting his lands of Wales.

A century later Caernarfon saw almost its last action, when its 28-strong garrison managed successfully to fend off the spirited assaults of Owain Glyndwr in 1403 and 1404. Surrendered finally in the Civil War to the Parliamentary forces under General Mytton, Caernarfon then suffered the fate of most of the castles in Wales. Neglect and cruel weather soon took their toll and within a short space of time the place was roofless.

An engraving made in about 1770 shows how little the castle has changed

The view across the outer and inner wards from the castle's ramparts

IN CARE OF Welsh Office

OPEN all reasonable times (standard hours)

ADMISSION some charge

LOCATION western end of town

COUNTY Gwynedd

SPECIAL FEATURES Eagle Tower – exhibition and audio visual programme, Queen's Tower – Royal Welch Fusiliers Museum; North East Tower – 'Princes of Wales' exhibition; Chamberlain Tower – arms exhibition

The great revival in Caernarfon's fortune came in the 1840's when the eminent architect, Anthony Salvin, was commissioned to restore the ruined stonework. This renovation was carried on throughout the century, later under the direction of the castle's deputy constable, Sir Llewellyn Turner. So it was that by the early years of the present century David Lloyd George was able to suggest that the young Edward should be invested as Prince of Wales in an open-air ceremony at Caernarfon Castle. It was the first time that a Prince of Wales had been invested in his principality since those far off days of 1301 and no effort was spared to ensure the success of the event. Finishing touches were made to defective battlements, many of the towers were given new roofs and floors of Quebec oak, and decorative wrought ironwork was used to complete the fixtures and fittings.

Since Edward's investiture in July 1911, Caernarfon Castle has become an almost obligatory venue for any Royal Tour of Wales. Over the years, it has received King George VI and Queen Elizabeth (the present Queen Mother) after the Coronation in 1937, Her Majesty Queen Elizabeth II in 1953, after her own Coronation, and, more recently, the Prince and Princess of Wales on their first joint tour in 1981.

Caernarfon is probably best known though as the majestic setting for the last ceremonial Investiture of Prince Charles as Prince of Wales in July 1969. Watched by an estimated worldwide television audience of 500 million, the Prince swore fealty to his Sovereign. Caernarfon Castle had at last come into its own.

CAERPHILLY

'Giant Caerffili' as a medieval Welsh poet termed it, its towers and curtain walls rising from the waters of its lakes, is one of the great surviving fortresses of the medieval western world. This huge, 30-acre site in Mid Glamorgan is equalled in size among British castles only at Dover and perhaps Windsor. With its massive gatehouse, water defences and concentric lines of defence, Caerphilly represents a high point of medieval military architecture. Only recently has its stature as one of Britain's great castles been generally recognized.

The site chosen in 1267 by the Norman lord Gilbert de Clare for his castle had been, 1,200 years earlier, occupied by a Roman fort whose remains were found unexpectedly during excavation in 1963. It would have held a battalion of 500 infantry, stationed here to pacify the surrounding hill country. The Romans arrived in the time of the Emperor Vespasian (about AD 75) but about 50 years later conditions were sufficently peaceful for them to be moved to northern Britain by Hadrian.

When the Normans conquered South Wales, they concentrated on the fertile coastal plains. The mountain uplands, devoid of good ploughland, difficult to capture and hard to retain, were left to the Welsh. So, from the initial conquest of Glamorgan by FitzHamon to the time of Gilbert de Clare 200 years later, the boundary between Normans and Welsh hereabouts lay on Caerphilly mountain, a moorland massif that is still a geographical barrier between Cardiff and Caerphilly.

THE EARLY CASTLE

This period of virtual truce ended when, due to the embroilments of national politics, the minor Welsh lords of upland Glamorgan found themselves caught between the ambitions of the last native Prince of Wales, Llywelyn ap Gruffudd, in the north and Gilbert de Clare to the

Caerphilly Castle boasts a tower that out-leans Pisa and has fine defences

Line drawing of Caerphilly c1770

south. Llywelyn wanted to unite all Welsh-controlled territory under his rule and in 1262 he seized Breconshire. Only the small Welsh lordships in areas close to Caerphilly such as the Rhondda, Machen and Senghenydd stood between the two mighty opposites.

Five years later, when Llywelyn had been politically weakened by the defeat of his English ally Simon de Montfort, Gilbert de Clare struck. He strengthened his northern frontier by seizing Gruffudd ap Rhys, ruler of Senghenydd and imprisoning him in Kilkenny in Ireland. He then began building his new castle, probably initially a rapidly-built wooden structure of palisades and towers which could gradually be replaced in stone.

In the previous year, Gilbert had been present at the siege of Kenilworth Castle, where the surviving supporters of Simon de Montfort had been starved out after a long and bitter struggle. Kenilworth was surrounded by wide lakes which had greatly helped the defenders, and memories of these water defences must have been very much in Gilbert de Clare's mind as he planned Caerphilly. It is doubtful, however, that he had any conception of how large and elaborate the finished work would be when he began building here on 11 April 1268.

SITING AND STRENGTH

The strategic importance of the site is best appreciated by approaching Caerphilly on the A469 north from Cardiff. As the road crests Caerphilly mountain, there is a panoramic view of the town below.

The castle itself was built to a concentric design with successive lines of defence set one inside the other, so that when the attacker stormed one line he would then find himself face to face with a second; moreover, this second wall would usually stand higher than the first, the unfortunate attacker becoming a nicely-positioned target for the archers on the wall top. This is the system of defence which is also seen at its fullest development in Edward I's great North Wales castles.

WATER AND STONE

Although the moat is obviously wide and wet enough, and the walls intimidating enough, the defensive principles applied at Caerphilly can only be understood, in their totality, from the air. A seemingly impregnable series of concentric stone and water defences radiates, in a succession of larger and larger circles, from a central inner ward.

The first line of defence against any attack consisted of the outer moat spanned by two drawbridges backed by a huge curtain wall and gatehouse (through which one enters the castle today). The lakes made it almost impossible to use many of the normal methods of siege warfare. Stone-firing catapults could not be brought within range of most of the perimeter; siege ladders were useless (save from boats) and it was impossible to tunnel under the waters of the lake to undermine the walls. In addition, a large number of besiegers would be needed to picket the perimeter of the lakes to prevent supplies reaching the garrison.

The inner moat and the gatehouses of the outer ward were the second line of defence. Finally, there stands the very core of the castle, its inner ward. This is a large quadrangle enclosed by four curtain walls, with massive round towers at each corner (one of them is the celebrated leaning tower which out-leans even Pisa) and yet more gatehouses on the east and west sides. These gatehouses protect the points of entry and could be shut off and held separately should the rest of the castle fall.

DE CLARE AND DESPENSER

Work on these formidable defences had scarcely begun before they were seized by Llywelyn in October 1270. King Henry arranged for them to be held by a neutral force pending negotiation, but in the following February, de Clare's constable of Cardiff Castle arrived at the gates and asked to be allowed to check the armoury. Once inside, he let in armed men who recaptured Caerphilly for de Clare, who was never again parted from his castle. Building probably continued until his death in 1295 and his son, another Gilbert de Clare, may have completed his father's work before his death in battle at Bannockburn in 1314, the last of his line.

Caerphilly passed to his sister Eleanor and her husband Hugh le Despenser the younger, the beloved favourite of Edward II. Despenser earned the hatred of the Welsh by putting to death in 1318, the native chieftain Llywelyn Bran, who had been imprisoned after leading a rising against the harsh rule of the royal administrator of Glamorgan after de Clare's death. As was the style of medieval politics, within a few years Despenser, along with his king, suffered the same fate.

THE GREAT HALL

Before his demise, however, Despenser rebuilt the Great Hall of Caerphilly in magnificent style. The timbers of its roof rested on carved capitals with portrait busts which probably represent King Edward II, his Queen Isabella and the young Prince, the future Edward III. The tall windows are decorated with the fashionable 'Ball-flower' ornament of the period and two of the king's leading craftsmen, the carpenter William Hurley and the mason Thomas of Battle were employed on the work. This cavernous hall, now used frequently for banquets and other social functions, is one of the most striking features within the castle. The present roof dates from about 1870 and the windows have recently been re-glazed and partly restored.

DECAY AND RESTORATION

With the threat of an independent Wales removed, and with the main seat of the lordship of Glamorgan over the hill at Cardiff, Caerphilly Castle gradually fell into decay. In Elizabethan times, its stone was robbed to build a house for a local family of gentry. It may have been then that the leaning tower shifted, perhaps as a result of the marshy soil, for the wall of the north platform also leans, though not so dramatically.

In the 19th century, the ruins were restored, and in places rebuilt, by Lord Bute. The extent of his work can be seen from photographs of the castle before and after restoration in the exhibition in the outer gatehouse. This tells the story of Caerphilly Castle and the surrounding area in detail. Models, many illustrations and an audio visual programme on the tragedies of Llywelyn Bran and Edward II are also included.

Caerphilly is an unexpected site, standing as it does in the middle of an unpretentious South Wales valley town. Possibly because of the prejudice surrounding its location, only now is the castle's true stature as a fortress of tremendous power and dignity becoming generally appreciated. Experts may quibble about Caerphilly's precise placing in the ranking order of medieval castles. Indisputably, it is near the top.

This 14th-century bronze tankard was found at Caerphilly Castle

IN CARE OF Welsh Office

OPEN all reasonable times (standard hours)

ADMISSION some charge

LOCATION in town centre

COUNTY Mid Glamorgan

SPECIAL FEATURE exhibition in outer gatehouse

Caerphilly's groundplan shows its concentric design and water defences

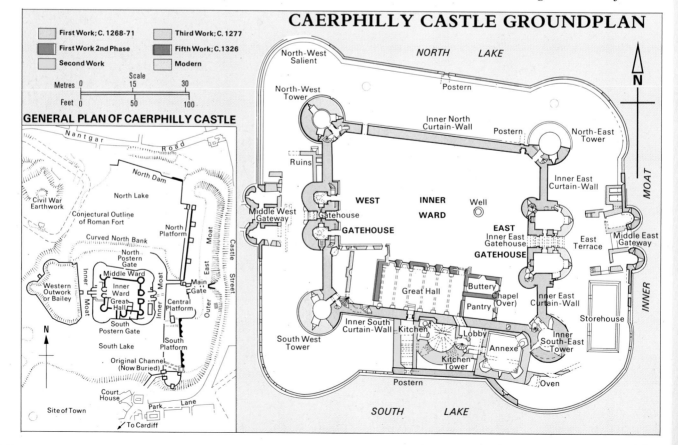

CAERPHILLY CASTLE GROUNDPLAN

First Work; C. 1268-71
First Work 2nd Phase
Second Work
Third Work; C. 1277
Fifth Work; C. 1326
Modern

Scale
Metres 0 — 15 — 30
Feet 0 — 50 — 100

GENERAL PLAN OF CAERPHILLY CASTLE

THE EARLY CASTLES

The early castles built by the Normans were, in comparison to the formidable stone structures of later times, rudimentary defences usually of earthwork and timber. Known as motte and bailey castles, they were primarily designed as cavalry bases. Such castles contained a hall and chapel, well and kitchen, sleeping quarters and stables, storerooms and workshops, all surrounded by a ditch with a bank on the inside, topped with a high wall. Entry would be by a bridge across the ditch to a gap in the bank. The enclosure was termed the bailey. A tower overlooked the bailey, both to control its operation and to act as a look-out point. Raising the tower on an earthen mound (the motte) gave it both extra security and a better view.

Most motte and bailey castles had only timber walls which have long since rotted away and allowed the earthworks to collapse. But large mottes are still visible all over Wales – for example inside the courtyard of Cardiff Castle, or between the Roman city of Caerleon and the River Usk. Practically every village in the old county of Montgomeryshire, Mid Wales, has a motte (or two), and a whole string of them can be spotted alongside the A5 between the towns of Llangollen and Betws-y-Coed.

BUILDING A MOTTE AND BAILEY

Although no Norman writer has described how castles were designed, painstaking excavation of some examples have given us the information. The actual layout depended on the site and resources available as well as on the needs of the lord and his men. Ditches would be dug to a V-shaped profile, unless they were to hold water, when the sides would be made as steep as possible.

The banks and mound might be faced with timber to make them unclimbable, or be finished with a crust of clay to prevent their erosion. Mottes often took advantage of a natural hill or rock or even an earlier man-made mound, such as the ancient tumulus in Rug Park, near Corwen. In some cases, the base of the tower might be incorporated into the motte as it rose.

Although timber was the building material of the time, the buildings themselves often stood on stone foundations to slow down rot. Owain Glyndwr's old-fashioned motte and bailey home at Sycharth (near Oswestry) illustrates this

Tomen y Rhodwydd, a few miles south east of Ruthin, is the site of an early motte and bailey castle

practice, even though it was built long after the early castle period. Excavation of the motte-top here revealed the base of Owain's medieval hall, burnt by Prince Henry in 1403.

VISITING THE EARLY CASTLES

Apart from a few in public parks, most motte and bailey castles are on private land. The owner's permission must be obtained before exploring them, although many can be easily seen from the road or a public footpath. Only a few can be mentioned here but hundreds exist; Tomen y Rhodwydd, in the Alun Valley near Ruthin; Pencader, near Carmarthen; Tomen y Mur near Trawsfynnyd; and Old and New Radnor.

At Bronllys, Llandovery, Skenfrith and Tretower Castles, the small motte carries a later round tower. In Powis Park, Welshpool, there are two motte castles as well as the stone one. Carew, Manorbier and Penhow Castles contain early defence towers built of stone. Other examples of early masonry include the Norman halls built by William the Conqueror's steward at Chepstow and Monmouth Castles, and a later example at Manorbier. All these are regularly open to visitors.

The grassy mound of Tomen y Mur, near Ffestiniog

CAREW CASTLE

Gerald of Windsor's private castle, Carew, has been altered several times. It contains unique medieval 'maisonettes' for the constable and chaplain of the garrison; also two successive Tudor wings of palatial grandeur, all standing two or three storeys high.

From the roadside, Carew is something of a disappointment, since this side was thrown down by a mine sprung underneath it at the time of the Civil War, and only the angle towers give a hint of the exciting remains. By the entrance gates is a Celtic cross erected about 1035 in memory of Mareddud who ruled Deheubarth (South West Wales). Nearby is a watermill of an unusual type, worked by the tide ebbing and flowing in Milford Haven.

This tidal creek determined the site of the castle, making it accessible to sea-going vessels. The ridge on which the castle stands was also of strategic importance near to the lowest point at which the creek could be forded at low tide. Unfortunately the ridge was waterless, and supplies had to be piped in from a distance away.

FROM RHYS AP TEWDWR TO ELIZABETH TUDOR

Tradition has it that Carew was founded by Gerald of Windsor, Constable of Pembroke Castle, who married Nest, daughter of Rhys ap Tewdwr. Nest, a figure of romance and intrigue, is said to have had a son by King Henry I whilst hostage. After Gerald's death, she married the Constable of Cardigan Castle and had a third family. All three families took part in the Norman conquest of Ireland. In Wales, Nest is best remembered as the grandmother of Giraldus Cambrensis.

Nothing remains of Gerald's original castle, but the 'Old Tower' (see below) may have been part of the 'house of Carrio' which King John seized in 1210 whilst passing through Pembroke on his way to Ireland.

Most of the medieval parts of the castle were built between about 1280 and 1310 for Sir Nicholas de Carew, a monumental effigy to whom can still be seen in the Carew Parish Church.

Renowned for its beautiful setting, Carew Castle towers above the tidal waters of the Carew River

Sir Nicholas's grandson sold Carew to Sir Rhys ap Thomas, who joined Henry of Richmond (Harri Tudur) immediately upon his landing at Dale nearby, and accompanied him to the Battle of Bosworth (1485) where Henry defeated King Richard III, thus becoming Henry VII, first of the Tudor monarchs.

Rhys turned Carew into a comfortable residence; with Pembroke so near, he had little need of major defence. In 1507 he held a great tournament here in celebration of the Tudors, but 25 years later his grandson was beheaded and the castle seized by King Henry VIII. First Queen Mary, and later Queen Elizabeth I, gave Carew to Sir John Perrott, who was said to have been a natural son of Henry VIII. Perrott built a new wing on to the castle but he in turn fell from favour and died in the Tower of London, before he could be beheaded.

AFTER THE TUDORS

According to a bizarre local legend, Sir Roland Rhys, a tenant of the castle in Jacobean days, set his tame ape on a local Flemish merchant whose daughter had eloped with his son. Later, this unreliable animal attacked its owner, and the castle was set on fire. But most of the damage seems to have been caused by a mineshaft dug under one side of the castle at the time of the Civil War in order to make such a strong place untenable.

DEFENCES AND FORTIFICATIONS

As you approach the castle along the ridge, look out for the ruined wall on each side of the path running back in the form of a V, with a platform for guns on the left. This is a ravelin, a cheap and common form of defence during the Civil War, designed to break up a frontal assault on a stronghold.

The next line of defence, on this one side only, is a plain wall enclosing the original castle ditch. The original doorway is concealed behind a Tudor gate. Notice the size of the holes on each side, nearly a foot square, for the bars which closed the door (there are similar barholes on the inner door). This middle ward between the two doors was protected by the large tower on the left, which seems to have been the lavatory block for the whole castle, and is perfect right up to its battlements. To the right is the half-octagonal tower containing the chapel (see below).

The original entrance to the inner ward was through the 'Old Tower' of King John's time, just to the right of the present entrance, but this passage was blocked up in the 13th century. Notice the murder holes in the vault above the present passage, and the vertical grooves at the far end to take the portcullis. Boiling oil was far too expensive to pour through murder holes: rocks, wastewater and rubbish made far better and more cost-effective missiles.

A MEDIEVAL STRONGHOLD AND TUDOR PALACE

Carew is interesting not only for its fortifications. Architecturally, it bridges the gulf between the primarily military castles of the late 13th century and the more comfortable fortified manor houses of the 15th century. The 13th-century Great Hall in the inner ward is flanked by large round towers (on the far side) which rise from square bases. Sir Rhys ap Thomas altered all the medieval windows into a 'Tudor Gothic' style, adding an oriel window and a new staircase to the hall. The stair was housed in a three-storey porch, with heraldic shields carved below the upper windows – the coats of arms are Henry VII's, flanked by those of Arthur, Prince of Wales and of Catherine of Aragon. Taken together, this dates the porch to 1501 or 1502, just before the time of the great tournament.

The range on the right with rows of large rectangular windows, was built by Sir John Perrott later in the 16th century. Notice the great half-round oriels on the outside toward the water. This range consists of only five rooms, the top floor forming an Elizabethan 'long gallery' aptly named at over 50yd in length.

At the corner between the Elizabethan range and the entrance passageway is the residential block, a complicated set of buildings containing the unique medieval 'maisonettes'. The large rooms near the courtyard form another hall (over vaulted storage), backed by a separate suite of rooms adjoining the vaulted chapel, running up through three storeys. Sir Rhys altered these too, and put in the grand staircase.

IN CARE OF private owner

OPEN summer months, check in advance

ADMISSION some charge

LOCATION On A4075, 3m E of Pembroke

COUNTY Dyfed

CARMARTHEN CASTLE

The Earl Marshal's 13th-century keep and gatehouse stand beside the site of the most westerly Roman fort and town in Wales.

William FitzBaldwin came by sea from Devon on the orders of King William II (Rufus) and built a castle at Carmarthen, probably on a site further down river, in 1093. It was soon abandoned, periodically being rebuilt and destroyed. It is not certain when the move was made to the present site, on the edge of the derelict Roman fort, but the position was probably chosen as overlooking a good crossing point of the River Tywi. In 1215 it took Llywelyn ab Iorwerth ('the Great') only four days to capture the castle and raze its defences to the ground.

Seized by the Earl Marshal from Llywelyn, the castle was rebuilt so strongly that it withstood a three-month siege. A detailed survey of the time mentions the great gate and keep with its five clustered turrets which can still be seen, together with a hall, stable, chapel and kitchen. Buildings for the royal administrators of South West Wales were

Carmarthen Castle's most significant remains are the motte and gatehouse flanked by impressive twin towers

added in the 14th century, and the whole castle was regularly repaired and whitewashed to protect the stonework. This whitening, a common practice in medieval times, is the source of the familiar names of White Castle (near Abergavenny) and the White Tower of London.

The castle had to be considerably repaired after being sacked by Owain Glyndwr, supported by a French force of 800 men-at-arms, 600 crossbowmen and 1,200 infantry. Amongst the new fittings was a Flemish painting of St Mary and St John, on a wooden panel, for the reconsecrated castle chapel.

IN CARE OF local authority

OPEN at all times

ADMISSION free

LOCATION town centre

COUNTY Dyfed

CARREG CENNEN CASTLE

An 'eagle's nest' on a spectacular site near Llandeilo, the castle is still much as it was when built 700 years ago, with complicated defences including a genuine underground passage. A romantic, beautiful site.

Alan Sorrell captured the timeless atmosphere of Carreg Cennen Castle in his romantic reconstruction

Roman coins have been found on the summit of this lofty castle crag, which rises 300ft above the Tywi valley. Such a site must have been used as a fortress from early times, but it first appears in written history in the 13th century. Captured from the Welsh by Payn de Chaworth, Lord of Kidwelly, it was surprised and retaken by Llywelyn ap Gruffud's brother and dismantled in 1282. Patched up by the Earl of Gloucester, the castle held out even though its garrison had been badly cut up in a Welsh ambush. A local Welsh rising took place in 1287, when Rhys ap Maredudd captured both Carreg Cennen and Dryslwyn in one day. The existing castle was built about this

time by John Giffard, Lord of Brimpsfield in Gloucestershire.

A century later, John Skidmore held the castle against Owain Glyndwr for over a year, but eventually surrendered it. Some of the walls were demolished then, but the castle was finally garrisoned by Sir Richard Herbert of Raglan and Sir Roger Vaughan of Tretower to prevent it from falling into the hands of brigands and robbers. Eventually 500 men with picks and crowbars were dispatched to make Carreg Cennen unin-

habitable. It was repaired in the 19th century, though it still retains the air of a romantic ruin.

A NATURAL STRONGHOLD

The fortifications do not cover the whole hilltop, but they do block access from the only easy approach. The rest of the site is well protected by formidable natural defences in the shape of sheer limestone cliffs and steep-sided slopes. Entry is through the outer ward, whose wall has small solid round watchtowers at the corners as well as on each side of the gate. To the left is the base of a large medieval limekiln, burning material dug from the limestone quarry ditch alongside.

A long, stepped ramp formed the approach to the inner ward. It had three gates, each with a pair of deep pits crossed by wooden bridges which could be removed in time of danger. The inner ward was protected by a ditch cut in the rock, a defensive structure which also served as a medieval reservoir, for part of it was lined with clay to collect rainwater. The decorated holes draining the castle roofs into the reservoir can still be seen in the curtain wall.

INNER WARD

The corner towers now rise only a little above the curtain walls, giving the castle a very squat – and solid – appearance. Some of the towers are square in plan (with the corners cut off) but the oldest is the round tower to the right of the gatehouse. The evolution of weaponry has left its mark here, where an arrowslit has been opened up to make it suitable for the insertion of an early musket. Above the entrance are traces of an open arch for a murder hole, and the grooves for a portcullis can be seen at each end of the passage – so the gatehouse, with its arrowslits at all levels, could be held against attack whether from within or without the inner ward; there are even watercisterns attached to the towers. Galleries at first-floor level lead into the curtain walls on each side, with upper doorways giving access to the battlements.

A magnificent vista across the Brecon Beacons National Park and the Black Mountain from Carreg Cennen Castle

Acres of picturesque farmland surround the limestone crag where Carreg Cennen Castle sits, above the Tywi Valley

To the left of the gatehouse is the main residential block. Notice the size of the kitchen fireplaces and the remains of the Great Hall with its chapel in a projecting tower.

UNDERGROUND PASSAGES

One of the castle's most interesting and dramatic features can be found in the far left-hand corner of the inner ward. Here, steps lead down to a postern (or sallyport) from which a narrow vaulted passage runs along the edge of the cliff to the entrance to a cave. The cave itself runs back from the cliff under the outer ward. We know that it was occupied in prehistoric times, since four skeletons were found here under a stalagmite layer, one with a pendant made from a horse's tooth.

The entrance to the cave is partly walled up (the pigeonholes in it suggest that it served as a dovecot to improve the food supply). At the far end is a natural basin into which water percolating through the rock drips slowly. This supply would have been quite insufficient for any sizeable garrison, so we can assume that the passageway and wall were constructed simply to prevent attackers from establishing themselves here under cover.

IN CARE OF Welsh Office

OPEN all reasonable times (standard hours)

ADMISSION some charge

LOCATION 4½m SE of Llandeilo on minor road. Access by 2–300yd uphill footpath from car park

COUNTY Dyfed

CASTELL COCH

Castell Coch is a Victorian fantasy and pure fairytale. Its grey needle-sharp spires and rosy-brown towers rising out of green beech-woods on a hill slope north of Cardiff are one of the most unexpected sights in Wales. It was the creation of Lord Bute and the architect William Burges. Their love of the Middle Ages was matched with erudite knowledge and the result is unique; like something from a Hans Christian Andersen fairy story.

Driving north on the A470 out of Cardiff, past the suburbs, golf courses and motorway flyovers, the first-time visitor often blinks twice at what seems a medieval mirage amongst the modern predictability at the fringes of the city. Above the dual carriageway, on a rocky slope in thick woods, stands a vision of Camelot, a Sleeping Beauty's castle, a refugee from Disneyland. Castell Coch, a few miles north of the city centre, is no phantom. It is real enough, though without the historic pedigree of a genuine medieval fortress. Inevitably, Castell Coch is another of architect William Burges's 19th-century romantic, fantastic re-creations.

Its Welsh name means 'The Red Castle', a reference to the unfaced red sandstone used in the construction of a much earlier stronghold here: Castell Coch, for all its Victorian whimsy, is a site of great antiquity. In the late 13th century, the new Lord of Glamorgan, Gilbert de Clare, built a castle here in the Taff gorge, protecting Cardiff from the north. Its small circular ward and projecting round towers, perhaps on the site of an earlier earthwork castle, recall Neath. By the 19th century it was a picturesque ruin, half buried in its own debris. Castell Coch's rebirth as a Victorian phoenix was due to the two men, Burges and Bute, who were concurrently performing a similar rescue mission at Cardiff Castle.

BURGES'S PLAN

In 1871, the Marquess of Bute asked his architect, William Burges, to report on what should be done with Castell Coch. Burges prepared a richly-illustrated report, a work of art in its own right, recommending reconstruction. Work began in August 1875 and the structure of the castle was complete by the end of 1879. Burges died suddenly in April 1881 and the interior decoration and fittings were completed over the next ten years from Burges's drawings and models. J S Chappell's furniture in the style of Burges is a worthy tribute, but often the hand of the master is missing. Camelot remains a dream.

William Burges was a small, bearded man with an almost adolescent delight in dogs, parrots, practical jokes and medieval fantasies. He was also a highly professional architect, the son of a successful Victorian civil engineer. Burges's respect for sound construction and for the use of durable materials of good quality gave even his wildest dreams a structural integrity, keeping them firmly based in reality.

MEDIEVAL INFLUENCES

Burges also had a profound knowledge of medieval architecture, gained not only from books and from a formidable amount of travel in Europe and beyond, but from many cold and wet days, often spent perched upon scaffolding, measuring and drawing medieval buildings. Yet he was no mere antiquarian, faithfully reproducing the past. His variations on medieval themes are highly original compositions.

Medieval architecture had a powerful appeal for many Victorians, who had seen England change from a land of villages ruled by landowning squires to one where wealth and influence came from smoke-grimed cities full of cotton mills, blast furnaces and cholera-ridden slums. Reaction against this took many forms. One was a craving for the medieval Catholic Church and its architecture (Lord Bute's own conversion to the Roman faith caused no little stir). This hankering after a medieval, feudal past is a thread that runs through much Victorian art and literature, from Tennyson's idylls of King Arthur to the Gothic splendours of the Houses of Parliament. Ironically, Lord Bute's evocation of his idealised past was created from iron and coal royalties as an industrial magnate.

The visitor approaches Castell Coch through beech-woods scented with wild garlic. Lord Bute had vineyards here, but the product never caught on, save as communion wine. At the top of the drive the towers and spires of the castle suddenly come into view. The lower parts of its walls are medieval, but all above is Victorian. Outstanding are the striking conical tower-tops, which taper to needle sharpness and lend the castle its romantic, fairytale air.

Across the bridge (which is a real working drawbridge) and under a gate with a portcullis, the visitor passes through into a small circular cobbled courtyard with a staircase up to an encircling gallery.

INSIDE THE CASTLE

The first of the decorated rooms is the banqueting hall, the most restrained of the rooms and something of a dry aperitif to the rich feast that is to follow. It has a religious theme. King Lucius, the mythical bringer of Christianity to Roman Wales, stands over the chimney piece and the walls are decorated with themes from some illustrated book of legends of saints and martyrs. This decoration, like the furniture, was carried out after Burges's death.

The drawing room next door is undiluted Burges, with rich colours, lofty ribbed dome and galleries to astonish the visitor. Burges originally intended this as two rooms, one above the other, but he later threw the two into one with magnificent effect. The lower part of the walls have wood panelling in dark green and gold inset with flower paintings. Above are murals of scenes from Aesop's fables, full of typical Burges touches. A frog holds a bottle of medicine for the frog in his throat and a monkey has Victorian side whiskers.

Portraits of members of the Bute family hang from painted ribbons with a background of cranes, foxes, cats, monkeys and flocks of wild birds set among golden apples and green foliage. Even the door surrounds have moulded caterpillars and snails. Over

John Patrick Crichton Stuart, 3rd Marquess of Bute, was responsible for Castell Coch, a Victorian extravagance

Fantastic murals depicting Aesop's fables decorate the walls and ceiling

(above) The conical turrets of Castell Coch in true fairytale style

the fireplace the three Fates measure and divide the span of life in painted statues not to everyone's taste. Above is the gallery and the ribbed vault where Burges's beloved parrots and exotic birds fly amid the starry vault of heaven. The theme is the whole world of nature, and time, like an ever rolling stream, bearing all its sons away.

THE BEDROOMS

At another level, the room is something of an anthology of aspects of late Victorian romanticism. Its form appears to be a copy of the interior of a medieval castle in the south of France (the Tour de Constance at Aigues Mortes near Arles). In contrast to this opulence, Lord Bute's bedroom up the spiral staircase is of spartan austerity, with an uncomfortable-looking bed, a hip bath and sparse stencilled decoration. Even the delightful sculptured rabbits, hedgehogs and guinea pigs on the fireplace mantel have an air of the Victorian schoolboy.

Lady Bute's bedroom is at the top of the tower, with wide views over the landscape of the Taff valley. Its colours are deep reds, greens and golds, silhouetted against white. In the panels of the domed ceiling, monkeys and squirrels cavort among bunches of grapes and foliage. Around the room is an arcade of Gothic arches, on the capitals of which are birds with their nests and young.

In the centre of the room stands Lady Bute's bed flanked by two splendid but uncomfortable looking chairs. Burges once made it plain that he regarded medieval authenticity as far more important than mere comfort. The medieval-style painted cupboard and the celebrated castellated hand basin also add to the splendour, but all the furniture dates from after Burges's death and is really a tribute to his memory by his associates.

A READY-MADE FILM SET

Back in the open air, the gallery leads to the kitchen, equipped with furniture for formidable Victorian dinners and a baby's high chair – a suitable haunt for Alice in Wonderland's Cook/Duchess. Further on, past authentically recreated shutters to the battlements, and down a long and narrow flight of steps, is the dungeon. The only prisoner ever recorded to have languished here in chains was the film star Alan Ladd (not surprisingly, the castle is a favourite location for many film-makers). A small square opening high in the wall projects a suitably-dramatic pencil of light on the centre of the dungeon floor.

Castell Coch is a decorative extravaganza. As with Burges's work at Cardiff, words are ultimately not enough. His architecture, more than most, is a visual experience. It demands to be seen. The rooms within the castle draw the visitor into a closer and closer focus of attention, an initial jumble of shape and colour narrowing down to a

Close attention to detail for which William Burges was famous, extends even to the courtyard of Castell Coch

multitude of beautifully-executed points of individual detail. Always, there is something else to look at; usually, it is surprising, humorous or stimulating.

An exhibition in a room off the courtyard tells more of Lord Bute, of Burges and of other buildings created by him. Some of Burges's original drawings for Castell Coch are particularly worth seeing.

Castell Coch was never intended as a permanent habitation, but rather as a pleasure dome 'for occasional occupation in the summer', as Burges put it. The intended chapel was never completed. The castle's last brief occupant was King Edward VIII on a tour in the 1930s of the depressed industrial valleys, his last function before abdication.

IN CARE OF Welsh Office

OPEN all reasonable times (standard hours)

ADMISSION some charge

LOCATION Just off A470 at Tongwynlais, 5m NW of Cardiff

COUNTY South Glamorgan

CASTLES OF THE WELSH PRINCES

Although about 14 earthwork castles are known to have been built in the early 12th century by Welsh princely rulers, they are totally indistinguishable in the landscape from their Norman counterparts. Built largely because of internal family squabbles that were so common, they can be identified only by the careful linking of records to ground features.

The later stone castles of the two Llywelyns ('the Great' and 'the Last') in the north are more easily recognized. They are to be found in naturally strong, isolated positions, away from the older centres of government. Perched high on the sides of landlocked valleys, they were built to guard the natural routeways around the borders of Gwynedd and through the mountains of Snowdonia.

CHARACTERISTIC FEATURES

Several common architectural features distinguish these native Welsh castles from contemporary English sites, making them almost instantly identifiable. All tend to have curtain walls that are low and comparatively insubstantial. They enclose areas of irregular shape and are often confined merely to a keep and a single ward. Normally, the gatehouses are not strong (Criccieth is the spectacular exception to this rule); indeed there is often no gatehouse at all to protect the entrance. Towers are rarely over two storeys high and do not usually include circular stairwells, although Dolbadarn is an exception on both counts.

Perhaps the most characteristic feature, however, are the apsidal ('D' shaped) and rectangular towers. These sometimes stand keep-like and alone, as at Ewloe, but are more often joined haphazardly to the curtain wall, as at Caergwrle, Dinas Brân, Castell-y-Bere, Criccieth, Dolbadarn and elsewhere. Where towers of any sort do join the curtain wall, though, rarely are they sited in such a way as to cover its outer face with a field of fire, as on an English castle.

EXPLAINING THE DIFFERENCE

As there are practically no records of the building of any of these Welsh princely foundations, we can only advance suggestions to account for the difference in their basic design. In the first place, the typical fighting man of North Wales, we are told, was a spearman and not an archer, as in the south. If this were so then the whole basis of castle defence – normally

Llywelyn the Great's coffin in Gwydyr Chapel, Llanrwst

so dependent upon the bow and arrow – would have been quite different. It would certainly account for what, to English eyes at least, must have seemed the totally ineffective siting of the wall towers.

Then, too, there would undoubtedly have been a marked difference in the monetary resources of a Welsh prince, compared to those at the command of a wealthy English lord. Partly because of this, but also because there was little tradition of stone building within Wales at this date, the quality and numbers of available, skilled craftsmen would have been that much less. Perhaps this explains why Castell-y-Bere is the only native site where any quantity of high-quality carving has come to light.

We must also consider the possibility that, in the planning of these castles, there may have been an almost unspoken reluctance to embark upon an ambitious programme of fortification for fear of provoking a hostile reaction from the other side (this happened in the end at Dolforwyn). Above all of these considerations, however, there was the over-riding difference in the two cultures. In Wales, the bonds between a lord and his followers were essentially those of kinship; in England authority was very largely maintained by fear and force of arms.

The ruin of Castell-y-Bere, Welsh native fortress, is dramatically set in the shadow of Cader Idris

CONWY

Built by Edward I as part of his master plan to subdue the Welsh, Conwy was both fortress and garrison town. It still retains a complete ¾ mile circuit of town walls, much of it open to the public. The castle, dating from 1282, is one of Wales's finest, with eight massive round towers and barbicans at either end. Originally approached up an enormous stone ramp, which no longer survives, it is divided into two wards. Though now roofless, the great hall and royal apartments are still impressive. Fine views from the battlements.

The first view of Conwy Castle, on crossing the estuary from the Llandudno side, is almost guaranteed to quicken the pulse. In the distance, its towers rise majestically, even menacingly, as if standing guard over the trio of latter-day bridges which now speed the crossing from the gentler landscape of North East Wales into the foothills of Snowdonia.

The river crossing was once made only by ferry. Then came the great era of highway improvement and with it, in 1826, Thomas Telford's new suspension bridge, its castellated towers echoing those of the medieval fortress above it. Two decades later came the railway, forging across the Conwy river on its way towards Holyhead and the boat to Ireland; so, in 1848, the engineer Robert Stephenson built his own castellated bridge, its single span of tubular grey metal running side by side with Telford's elegant suspension cables. Stephenson's bridge still carries the railway but time and progress have overtaken its neighbour, for Telford's road bridge, now an historic monument in its own right, can be crossed only on foot. Today, the highway is carried across on a third bridge, built in 1958 to a functional design devoid of any mock battlements.

THE TOWN

From Telford's bridge, the skyline is dominated by towering castle walls. It soon becomes apparent, however, that here is not just a castle but a whole fortified town, protected by walls and regularly-spaced towers. From the castle, they run along the front of the little quay, then climb steadily up to a rocky brow above the town before descending, once again, to the castle on the other side. Of all King Edward I's foundations in North Wales, Conwy retains most authentically its historic status as a garrison town. Its complete circuit of town walls is still intact, over ¾ mile in length, with 22 towers and three original gateways. Walls and castle were all built during a frenzied period of activity between 1283 and 1287, a tremendous achievement which only amounted to about 36 months of continuous work all told. The final cost of the project to the Crown was around £15,000, equivalent today to something like £10 million.

Conwy's town walls may be the finest in North Wales, but they were by no means unique. All but three out of the 17 Edwardian castles here were built with defended town boroughs into which English merchants and traders were encouraged to come and settle, promoting their new way of life. Most of these boroughs had little more than earthworks to surround them, but Conwy and also Caernarfon were given elaborate fortified walls where, 700 years later, visitors can still walk along the battlements or wander the medieval streets. For all their grandeur, one of the most endearing features of the walls at Conwy is the neat row of 12 garderobes, latrines for the garrison, which project over the outside of the section beside the Mill Gate. Here, one can still catch a brief glimpse, across the centuries, of the stark yet ordered day to day life of a 13th-

(above left) Alan Sorrell's interpretation of the castle in its prime shows how little time has changed it

Conwy's groundplan (right) illustrates the architectural genius put to use in its building

century garrison soldier – not so different, in many respects, to that of his modern counterpart.

THE CASTLE

No visitor to Conwy should leave without walking at least part of the walls. The castle, by virtue of its pre-eminence, speaks for itself. First impressions are of tremendous military strength, dominating position and a unity and compactness of design. Its eight almost identical towers seem to spring from the living rock as if they had sprouted there; indeed it was the very formation of that rocky site which dictated the castle's eventual layout.

Unlike most of King Edward's other new fortresses in Wales, Conwy was built not to a concentric, but to a linear plan (so too is Caernarfon). Instead of an outer circuit of walls, it has two lower barbican outworks at each end and, instead, it was divided by a cross wall into two quite separate wards, so that either could hold out independently if the other should fall. In the Middle Ages, both the castle and the town walls would have looked startlingly different to our eyes for, instead of bare grey stonework, they would have had an overall white rendering, quite common in those days.

FORCING AN ENTRY

Today's way in, up the sloping concrete path that leads into the castle, imparts a mild sense of disappointment. Could this really have been the way the entrance looked in the 13th century? Where were all the gates and portcullises and where was the drawbridge? It is not, of course, the original arrangement, for the opening in the side of the gate passage is entirely modern. Once, a huge stepped ramp of masonry would have led up, from the site of the present day roadway, towards the entry. A drawbridge, guarded by a portcullis, would have dropped down onto it, crossing what must have been a very deep chasm. The grooves for the portcullis are still there, as are the pivot holes for the drawbridge axle and, in the far wall, the remains of the steps that led up to a room above the gate containing the winches and pulleys that controlled them. The outer gate passage was probably roofed over and would have led up towards the west barbican, where a stout wooden door barred the way. The barbican itself was quite open, so that any attackers who might reach it could be picked off with ease from the walltops of the castle above. In short, entry was no easy matter, whatever the modern arrangements might imply.

INSIDE THE WALLS

Once inside the inner ward, there is an impression of openness. But look at the foundations on the ground and you will see that, in fact, it would

Telford's graceful bridge, spanning the estuary, leads to Conwy's gatehouse

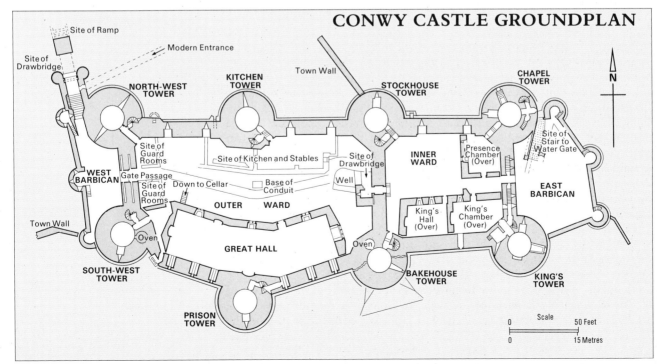

CONWY CASTLE GROUNDPLAN

Site of Ramp
Modern Entrance
Site of Drawbridge
Town Wall
NORTH-WEST TOWER
KITCHEN TOWER
STOCKHOUSE TOWER
CHAPEL TOWER
N
Site of Guard Rooms
Site of Kitchen and Stables
Site of Drawbridge
INNER WARD
Presence Chamber (Over)
Site of Stair to Water Gate
WEST BARBICAN
Gate Passage
Site of Guard Rooms
Down to Cellar
Base of Conduit
Well
EAST BARBICAN
OUTER WARD
King's Hall (Over)
King's Chamber (Over)
Town Wall
Oven
GREAT HALL
Oven
SOUTH-WEST TOWER
BAKEHOUSE TOWER
KING'S TOWER
PRISON TOWER
Scale
0   50 Feet
0   15 Metres

View over the Castle's ramparts and surrounding area from the Bakehouse Tower at Conwy Castle

originally have been rather cramped for space. Here, just inside the gate passage, would have stood the guardrooms, the stables and also the kitchens serving the Great Hall opposite. The Great Hall dominates the outer ward, 125ft in length and built to an unusual bowed plan to adapt to its rocky foundation. Though some of the tracery in the windows still survives to give an impression of its former grandeur, the uninitiated visitor might find the place bewildering, for it is now split longitudinally into two separate levels. Not surprisingly, it would never have looked like this; formerly there was a basement for storage and a grand first floor (the level one now comes in at). For the first few days in the year when the king, or some other important guest was in residence, Conwy's hall no doubt looked a fine sight – bustling with activity, its walls hung, perhaps, with fine tapestries and its tables glittering with silver plate. The rest of the time, it would have been quite a different story because, for most of the year, the castle would have been half empty, its occupants reduced to a governor and small resident garrison.

Leaving the hall, one passes beside the castle well and, over the site of a further drawbridge, through to the inner ward. Here lay the private quarters of the king and queen, installed at a cost of approximately £320 in 1283. When they were in residence, royal standards would have billowed from the tops of the turrets, which crown each tower of the inner ward. Sadly, these once sumptuous apartments have been reduced now to bare shells. One tower, however, still retains its beautiful little chapel which, even now, displays a quality of decoration in a state of preservation that is quite unmatched at any other Edwardian castle. This chapel has been re-floored and re-roofed to protect it from exposure.

A veritable armada of small boats bob lazily on the tide of the River Conwy's wide estuary

IN CARE OF Welsh Office

OPEN all reasonable times (standard hours)

ADMISSION some charge

LOCATION eastern part of town

COUNTY Gwynedd

THE QUEEN'S GARDEN

In the east barbican, just outside the inner ward, there was originally a small garden. It was probably planted at the request of Edward I's wife, Queen Eleanor, who seems to have been a keen gardener. She had one outside Caernarfon Castle and another was planted outside her temporary quarters in Conwy town, during July 1283. Turf for the lawn was shipped specially from further up river and the plot was fenced with the staves from an empty barrel. Records tell us that on a warm evening in July, her squire, Roger le Fykeys, was paid three pence for attending to its first watering.

The east barbican had its own access to the river, through a small water gate in the gap beside the Chapel Tower, but the stepped ramp that once curved around and down to the river below has long since vanished. Despite this additional means of escape, King Edward I was actually besieged in Conwy by the rebel forces of Madog ap Llywelyn, during January 1295. Though food and drink were running dangerously low, the chroniclers of the time reported with astonishment that the king resolutely refused to take for himself the last remaining cask of wine but, instead, chose to drink the water and honey mixture with his men.

Afterwards, Conwy subsides almost into obscurity, a magnificent, forgotten relic. Its greatest battle proved to be the one against decay and, only a generation after its completion, it was in need of substantial repair. By 1627, a survey reported it dangerous to enter, 'the leads being decayed and broken above and almost all the floares fallen down'. It saw some action during the Civil War, but afterwards was left to the elements. Today, Conwy is one of Wales' most atmospheric sites, its jumble of walls, towers and masonry evoking an authentic medieval air.

CRICCIETH CASTLE

Standing high upon its rock, dominating the little seaside town, Criccieth is mainly a native Welsh castle of the two Llywelyns. Taken by Edward I in 1283 and refortified, it was eventually destroyed by Owain Glyndwr in 1404. The castle commands superb views over Tremadog Bay.

Most visitors go to Criccieth for the sea, not realizing that it has a castle at all until, on rounding the brow in the road from Porthmadog, the fortress comes into view, perched high above the town. With its pleasant seaside air, the resort of Criccieth is largely sheltered from severer forms of weather, tucked up safe beneath the crook of that long finger of land, the Lleyn Peninsula. Criccieth's benign location is best appreciated from the top of the castle hill. Here, on a fine day, the views are truly panoramic – westwards, out to the tip of Lleyn, north and east towards Snowdonia and southwards over the broad, majestic sweep of Cardigan Bay. A more splendid situation would be hard to imagine and its value as a military lookout is immediately evident.

OBSCURE ORIGINS

In origin, Criccieth is a native Welsh castle. It seems to be of three main building periods, none of them directly recorded and, unfortunately, scholars now disagree about who built what, so that it is impossible to be certain about its history. What we do know is that part was built by Llywelyn ab Iorwerth ('the Great'), part by his grandson, Llywelyn ap Gruffudd ('the Last') and part by King Edward I.

The castle is nearly concentric in plan, having an inner ring, with twin-towered

Criccieth Castle crowns a rocky promontory and commands sweeping views over Tremadog Bay (top left)

The crumbling north west side of Criccieth Castle (bottom left)

Good examples of arrow-slits can be seen within the walls of Criccieth (below)

gatehouse, curtain walls and a rectangular tower. To the north, east and south, there is the outer curtain wall with two further rectangular towers at either end and a small outer gateway.

THE GREAT GATEHOUSE

The inner ward, most likely the earliest part of the castle, is all of one build. It was probably built around 1220–30 by Llywelyn the Great. Most impressive today is the high, twin-towered gatehouse, with three outward facing arrow-loops to each tower and its lofty, defended gateway. Standing over twice the height of any other surviving parts, it is the main feature of the castle. Although ruined on the inner side, it still presents an imposing spectacle from without. This Great Gatehouse has no parallel at any of Llywelyn's other castles. Indeed, apart from Castell-y-Bere, most of them have no gatehouses at all. Interestingly, both gatehouse and the whole inner ward are close in style to the inner ward of Montgomery Castle, built by the young King Henry III, between 1223 and 1227.

On the outside of the gatehouse, at low level, are traces of the rendering which once covered all the rougher masonry of the castle. The entrance itself was protected by a portcullis and barred gate, with murder slots above while, from the battlements, regularly-spaced square holes indicate that there was provision for a timber fighting platform to overhang the gate. Later in its history, probably during the time of Edward II, the top stage of the gatehouse was heightened, as one can see from the tell-tale lines of the filled-in crenellations.

The next part of the castle to be built was probably the south western part of the outer ward, with its simple gateway and large,

rectangular tower. This most likely dates from the 1250s or '60s, during the time of Llywelyn the Last and may, at one stage, have joined the western angle of the inner ward, making an outer bailey extension.

THE ENGINE TOWER

Almost certainly, the latest addition is the Engine Tower at the north end of the castle. From recent research, we know that Edward I spent £353 on refortifying Criccieth in 1283 and most of it went, no doubt, on building this tower and its adjacent lengths of curtain walling. Two pairs of garderobe, or latrine shafts, on its seaward side show that it had at least two floors. The tower can be seen with siege engine installed, in the foreground of the painting by Alan Sorrell, depicting the castle as it would have looked in its prime.

During Madog's rebellion, both Criccieth and Harlech were victualled by ship from Ireland. Some of the supplies taken in were prodigious – 6,000 herrings, 24 salted pigs, 18 cheeses, 20 pounds of twine from crossbows, to say nothing of the 109 carcasses of mutton and 30 of beef already in store. Small wonder that the castle succeeded in holding out.

Under Edward the Black Prince, Criccieth had a distinguished Welsh constable, Sir Hywel ap Gruffydd ('Sir Howel of the Battle-axe') and, even well into the Elizabethan period, a daily dish of meat was served to the poor by the yeoman attendants in front of his axe.

Criccieth's end came abruptly in 1404, with its capture by Owain Glyndwr. The castle was sacked and burnt, never to rise again. The castle now houses an interesting exhibition on the theme of the native castles of the Welsh princes.

IN CARE OF Welsh Office

OPEN all reasonable times (standard hours)

ADMISSION some charge

LOCATION on hill overlooking town

COUNTY Gwynedd

HARLECH

Built in 1283, as part of King Edward I's iron ring of castles to contain the Welsh in Snowdonia, Harlech is perhaps the most impressive of them all today. It stands 200ft above the old sea level, astride a high outcrop of rock, its massive inner walls and towers still almost at full height. Noteworthy features are its dominant gatehouse and defended stairway to the sea. Harlech was captured in 1404 by Owain Glyndwr and held by the Welsh for five years before being lost. It stands in a wonderful location, with memorable views from its battlements.

Of all the overworked adjectives used by writers to describe the grander castles of North Wales 'spectacular' and 'dramatic' would no doubt top the list. Yet at Harlech they seem all too readily relevant. From the foot-worn boss of rock at the southern edge of the little town the view of castle, sea and mountain is breathtaking. The greystone bulk of the castle sits astride a rocky promontory, towering nearly 200ft above the green flatlands of Morfa and the sea, its backcloth the wide, distant panoply of Snowdonia.

Small wonder that this place has received the attentions of countless visitors, past and present. Small wonder too that, of all castles in Wales, Harlech is perhaps the most familiar to those who live elsewhere. Even after seven centuries, it still displays with clarity the genius of that architect, Master James of St George, who created it. The twin requirements of defence and accommodation have been perfectly adapted to suit a restricted, rocky crag and the whole structure possesses great elegance of line, an unmistakable sense of power and a position of strength.

THE IRON RING

Harlech was built during the second and final campaign of King Edward I in North Wales. It was the southern link in the iron ring of castles surrounding the coastal fringes of Snowdonia; a ring intended to prevent the region from becoming, ever again, a focal point of insurrection and a last bastion of resistance. Towards the end of Edward's campaign, the native stronghold of Castell-y-Bere finally fell in April 1283. This enabled the English army, under its commander, Sir Otto de Grandison, to march up through the mountains of Meirionnydd and establish a base at Harlech.

Work began on a new castle here almost immediately. Strangely, for a royal foundation such as this, the records of its first three years are surprisingly few, but one or two snippets of information here and there help to fill in the gaps. By the middle of June, we learn that 20 stonemasons and quarriers, together with a packhorse to carry their tools, had been dispatched from their base at Conwy to travel over the hills and report for duty at Harlech. The following month, they were followed by another 15 masons and a squad of carpenters, so things were evidently progressing.

Part of Harlech's stout defences, a portcullis groove

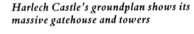

Harlech Castle's groundplan shows its massive gatehouse and towers

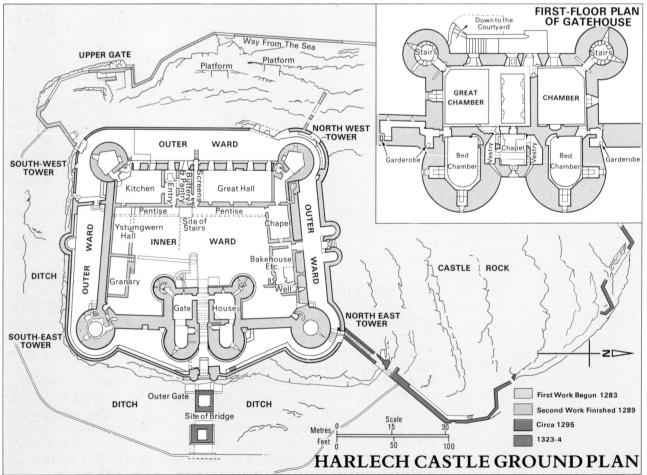

FIRST-FLOOR PLAN OF GATEHOUSE

HARLECH CASTLE GROUND PLAN

Alan Sorrell's impression of Harlech as it might have been

WORK IN PROGRESS

Not until the summer of 1286, when work here was at its height, do we manage to glean an overall picture of the building in progress. The labour force built up steadily that year, from only 60 in the slack winter months of January and February, to almost 950 by midsummer. Of these, we have a full breakdown by occupation – 227 masons, 115 quarriers, 30 smiths, 22 carpenters, 546 labourers and minor workmen. Materials for building, too, were being shipped in almost daily – limestone from Anglesey and Caernarfon, better quality freestone (for carving) from the quarries at Egryn, seven miles to the south, and iron and steel from Chester.

The bills and accounts for Harlech, as for most of the major Edwardian fortifications, are still preserved in the Public Record Office. They record in minute detail the amounts of money paid out, who received it, and what he had done in return for his payment. The records for 1289 are particularly comprehensive, the men being paid on a piecework basis. A certain Master William of Drogheda, in Ireland, was paid £111 7s 6d for his work on the 'north tower towards the sea' (ie the North West Tower) 49½ ft high @ 45s per foot. Two men, Robert of Frankby and Reginald of Turvey, built 18½ ft of the southern stair turret in the gatehouse and were paid £12 6s 8d, at the rate of 13s 4d per foot. Again, William of Thornton was paid the sum of eight shillings for making a fireplace in one of the upper rooms on the south side of the gatehouse.

THE CASTLE COMPLETED

By the end of 1289, after seven seasons of work, the castle of Harlech was virtually finished. It was the smallest of Edward's new works in North Wales and its final cost was over £8,000. Today, we should have to multiply this and all the other figures, by 600 or more, to arrive at an equivalent, so that Harlech's price would now be £5 million.

Harlech is very much a concentric castle. Its outer walls may seem low and insubstantial when compared with Beaumaris, but Harlech enjoys the ready-made natural advantage of a high rocky site and also, on the more level ground to the south and east, a deep rock-cut ditch. In most places, however, this outer wall is ruinous. Only on the north, with its postern gate, does it survive to anything like full height, so the effect today is not really comparable to what it would have been in the 13th century.

Harlech's gatehouse (left) gave a daunting display of power to would-be attackers

The castle's inner ward (above) shows foundations of domestic buildings

The vaulted ceiling of Harlech's gatehouse (below)

THE WAY IN – OLD AND NEW

Another false impression is given now by the approach. Today's visitor enters through a ticket office, carefully hidden at the outer edge of the ditch. From the inner side of the ditch, a veritable tower of solid-looking oak stairs then leads to the outer gate – an arrangement which, in original medieval terms, is all quite wrong. For a more authentic first impression, initially look at the castle from the children's playground. Even after all these years, that fortified east front still throws down its haughty challenge, the sense of might and power quite overwhelming. This, after all, was the only possible direction of attack. Once, a great bridge would have thrust across the ditch (its piers still visible) and straight up to the outer castle gate – at its ends, a drawbridge and beyond, inside the great inner gatehouse, three stout, barred doors and three more portcullises. After the dark of the gate passage came the inner courtyard. Instead of today's mown greensward and open aspect, it would once have presented a very different picture, its three now-blank and vacant walls surrounded by buildings which formed the castle's public areas – on the right, a Great Hall with a kitchen to its left, with a second hall, chapel and service areas to either side, all safe and protected by the massive curtain walls around.

PRIVATE QUARTERS

The main private accommodation at Harlech was above the guardchambers of its gatehouse. Within this imposing structure, standing defiantly astride the eastern curtain, lay two self-contained suites of grand residential quarters (just look at their fireplaces and the remains of those traceried windows). On the upper floor was probably a guest suite for visiting dignitaries – the king, perhaps, or the chamberlain.

The lower floor, with its controls for all three portcullises and direct access to the courtyard, must have been the lodgings of the constable, or castle governer, and his family. In 1290, and for the following three years,

Harlech's constable was none other than its own architect, Master James of St George. During this period, he received a salary of 100 marks a year (£66), which would have been enough to keep him in conditions of considerable comfort.

SEA AND SHIPS

The castle's other remarkable feature is the defended 'Way from the Sea', a gated and heavily-fortified stairway plunging almost 200ft down the castle rock on its west side. Today, one can drive down to the base of the cliff, then cross over the railway and enter the castle up these steps. But at one time, there could have been neither railway nor road, for the sandy flatlands at the foot of the castle would have been covered by sea. Like all King Edward's new castles in the north, Harlech was built so that it could be supplied and victualled by ship; this stairway provided the necessary link. Its purpose is no longer very evident today, because the sea has receded half a mile or more, leaving the castle isolated now upon its rock. The painting by Alan Sorrell of Harlech in its prime shows it as it might have looked.

In 1294, the 'Way from the Sea' fully justified its existence, when it enabled Harlech to be supplied by ship from Ireland and thus stand firm against the blockade of Madog and his rebels. Perhaps the most famous event in the castle's history was its taking, in the spring of 1404, by Owain Glyndwr. For nearly five years, it became the residence of his court and family. It was the meeting place for parliaments of his supporters and here, so it is said, he crowned himself Prince of Wales.

'MEN OF HARLECH'

Harlech saw action again during the Wars of the Roses, when it was held for the Lancastrian side by its Welsh constable. It was surrendered, at last, after a prolonged siege, forever immortalised in the song 'Men of Harlech'. The final curtain fell with the Civil War. Harlech was the last castle to fall to Parliament, ending forever its role as a place of defence.

So we find the place today, a Crown property still, its gates, its towers and curtain walls standing perpetual guard over the reclaimed Morfa dunelands, looking vainly out to sea for the ship that will never come.

ALAN SORRELL RWS

Devotees of ruined castles up and down the country will have become familiar, by now, with the reconstruction paintings which are often on display there, showing their likely appearance when first built. Often painted in sombre colours, with dramatic shafts of light breaking through the clouds, they are almost all the work of one remarkable artist – the late Alan Sorrell, member of the Royal Watercolour Society.

Born in London in 1904, the son of a master-jeweller, Sorrell spent his formative years and almost all of his subsequent life in remotest rural Essex. After training at the Royal School of Art, he won a scholarship to Rome and it was there that he met with the archaeological stimulus that was to dominate so much of his later work.

In the later 1930s, he formed a personal link with the National Museum of Wales, undertaking several reconstructive interpretations of the Roman and prehistoric sites which were then being excavated. This link continued and he soon formed a further, regular contact with the *Illustrated London News*. But it was not until 1956, when Sorrell carried out some reconstruction drawings of Hadrian's Wall for the then Ministry of Works, that his career as a reconstruction artist par excellence became firmly established.

Working in close collaboration with the Ministry's inspectors of ancient monuments, he produced what are generally reckoned to be the most carefully researched and artistically pure imaginative depictions of ancient monuments ever undertaken. Until his death in 1974, he produced 70 such paintings for the Ministry throughout the country. Fourteen were of historic sites in Wales, some of which are his castle views reproduced in this book.

PEMBROKE

First founded during the original Norman scramble for South West Wales, Pembroke Castle was completely rebuilt in stone by William Marshall, the greatest English knight of the Middle Ages. His magnificent castle, never captured by the Welsh, remains unaltered to this day. Birthplace of Harri Tudur, the Welshman who became the first Tudor monarch, it had otherwise an unexciting history until the Civil Wars, when it withstood a seven-week siege led by Oliver Cromwell himself, finally surrendering through lack of water.

Pen-fro, the 'land's end' in Welsh, is a suitable name for this area and, in a different way, for Pembroke town. For although the westernmost part of Wales is, to be geographically correct, away at St David's Head, Pembroke itself stands at the west of a peninsula on the Milford Haven. The tip of the peninsula is fringed by rocky cliffs above two parallel tidal creeks. Modern barrages, however, mean that they are tidal no longer.

On the death of the Welsh ruler in South West Wales in 1093, Earl Roger of Montgomery moved rapidly across the backbone of Wales and built a castle at Pembroke of stakes and turf, giving it to his son, who had made the journey by sea. This early castle must have been more than adequate, for alone of the Norman castles in Dyfed, Pembroke withstood the Welsh attacks in the following years. In 1105 Gerald of Windsor, Giraldus Cambrensis's grandfather, became the constable of the castle 'where he deposited all his riches, his wife and family and fortified it with a ditch and wall and a gate with a lock on it'. During one siege, Gerald indulged in a gory medieval ruse when he cut up his last four hogs and threw the pieces out. By this elaborate bluff he hoped to convince the Welsh that he was well supplied with food.

Pembroke's gatehouse had a complex barbican and three portcullises. This mighty defence was the work of William Marshall

WILLIAM MARSHALL'S CASTLE

Gilbert de Clare was made Earl of Pembroke by King Stephen. His son Richard ('Strongbow') took a leading part in the conquest of Ireland, so Pembroke from the first became the regular port of embarkation for those crossing the Irish Sea. King Henry II spent Easter 1172 here while on his way to assert his overlordship over Strongbow in Ireland. Strongbow's daughter married William Marshall in 1189. William had risen from

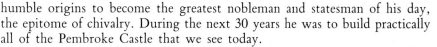

humble origins to become the greatest nobleman and statesman of his day, the epitome of chivalry. During the next 30 years he was to build practically all of the Pembroke Castle that we see today.

When the Marshall family died out in 1245, the castle passed to King Henry III's half-brother, William de Valence. During the next 50 years he improved the domestic buildings of the castle, but wisely left the enormously strong defences alone. During the invasion scare of 1377 the garrison was enlarged to three knights, 67 sergeants and 70 archers, but the castle thereafter was neglected to such an extent that, during the Glyndwr rising, the Constable had to ransom both himself and the castle!

HENRY VII AND OLIVER CROMWELL

Jasper Tewdwr was created Earl of Pembroke by his half-brother King Henry VI. In 1456, Jasper gave hospitality to his sister, the newly-widowed Lady Margaret Beaufort, who gave birth here in 1457 to Harri Tudur, first of the Tudors. Where this event took place is disputed. Most of the so-called Henry VII Tower is modern (as is the name) and a room over the gateway seems poor hospitality for one's sister!

Pembroke was the only town in South Wales to declare its support for Parliament at the beginning of the Civil Wars. Under its mayor, John Poyer, it remained a secure refuge despite Royalist threats. However, in 1648 Poyer, disappointed in his demands for reward for services rendered, threw in his lot with a band of Roundheads unwilling to be demobilized. Trounced by a regular Parliamentary army near St Fagans, Cardiff, they fell back on Pembroke, and Cromwell himself came up to besiege the town.

The siege dragged on for seven weeks, an attempt to scale the walls failed, but eventually the water supply was cut off and a train of siege cannons arrived to start a proper bombardment. The garrison surrendered on terms allowing the soldiers to go free, but the officers were to leave the country and the ringleaders were to be tried.

THE 'PEMBROKE FLOUNDER'

In plan Pembroke Castle is egg-shaped, with its apex cut off to form an inner ward containing the great round keep. The whole town and castle was compared by its Victorian owner to 'The skeleton of an ill-conditioned flounder, the Castle precinct being the head, the donjon (tower) the eye, the great south curtain its gills, the only street representing the vertebral bone and the various gardens its rays'.

THE GREAT GATEHOUSE

Approaching the castle from the town, do not be deceived by the apparently excellent state of preservation. Cromwell blew out the barbican walls in front of the gatehouse and the fronts of all the towers to prevent their future use after the surrender, and they were only restored early this century. One charge – that in the tower to the right of the gate – literally backfired and blew out the back instead of the front!

The gatehouse, with rooms on either side as well as above the passage, is one of the finest – as well as the earliest – of its kind. In the passage is a long series of successive defences: grooves for three portcullises, three murder holes in the vaulting and four arrow-slits in the side walls. One tower alongside has a prison cell in its basement, and there are two upper floors reached by stairs spiralling opposite ways. The rooms there have fireplaces and other domestic features, and lead on to wall passages forming fighting-galleries. In particular, those on the left (as seen from inside the castle) lead to and through a well-appointed round tower.

GATES AND GRAFFITI

The outer ward is completely bare of standing buildings, and the curtain wall on the left has been doubled in thickness, probably to resist cannon fire during the Civil Wars. To the right the bastion housing the modern toilets originally protected a narrow doorway reached by a steep path from the quayside below. The Monkton Tower on the opposite side of the outer ward is interesting, not only for the two postern passages at the different levels which it guards, but also because the plasterwork in the room on the other side still has medieval graffiti.

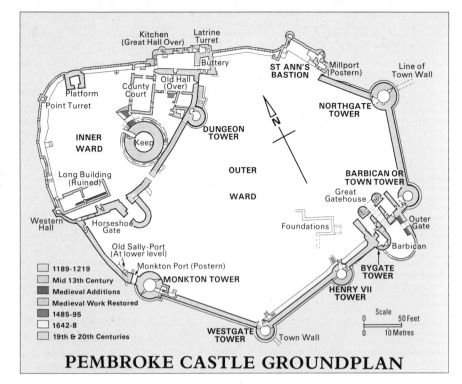

Kitchen (Great Hall Over) · Latrine Turret · Buttery · ST ANN'S BASTION · Millport (Postern) · Line of Town Wall · County Court · Old Hall (Over) · NORTHGATE TOWER · Platform · Point Turret · Keep · DUNGEON TOWER · INNER WARD · OUTER WARD · BARBICAN OR TOWN TOWER · Great Gatehouse · Long Building (Ruined) · Outer Gate · Western Hall · Horseshoe Gate · Foundations · Barbican · Old Sally-Port (At lower level) · Monkton Port (Postern) · MONKTON TOWER · BYGATE TOWER · HENRY VII TOWER · Scale · 0 50 Feet · 0 10 Metres

1189-1219 · Mid 13th Century · Medieval Additions · Medieval Work Restored · 1485-95 · 1642-8 · 19th & 20th Centuries

WESTGATE TOWER · Town Wall

PEMBROKE CASTLE GROUNDPLAN

Pembroke's groundplan shows its massive cylindrical tower

Pembroke's great dome as seen from the keep

THE HORSESHOE GATE

Between the Monkton Tower and the great round keep are the foundations of much of the inner curtain wall, pierced by a great U-shaped tower with its main entrance in one side and a very narrow postern in the other. This Horseshoe Gate and the Monkton Tower were sited so as to support each other in controlling all approach to the inner ward. This ward has only a low parapet wall around the cliff edge: no more was necessary. The long building to the left of the Horseshoe Gate seems to have been a minor hall, downgraded to stables. Across the inner ward, the large square platform supported a huge medieval catapult aimed at any attacking ships.

THE ROUND KEEP

The solid squat proportions of the round keep disguise both its height – 75ft – and its very slight lean. It had four floors under its domed top, reached by a single spiral staircase. Each floor was divided into two rooms with one arrow-slit or more, but only two of these rooms had a fireplace and window. Unfortunately, defensive considerations meant that the windows had to face northward, so they received no sunlight. An upper doorway gave an emergency exit on to the top of the curtain wall. There is a fine view from the top of the stone dome, where the details of the battlements are worth examining. But the large square holes below the battlements, designed to enable defenders to drop things on to attackers from a point of safety, can be best seen from the ground.

The other round tower (of lesser size) nearby is a grim fighting-deck over a prison, defending the other side of the keep and the hall buildings.

DOMESTIC BUILDINGS

In the corner behind the keep is a complex of buildings, one of which (the building nearest the stair leading up to the keep) housed the county court from at least the 14th century. Between it and the round tower just described was William Marshall's hall, later converted into the solar chamber of de Valence's hall which occupied the space beyond, with its service rooms at the right-hand end. The kitchen lay below the hall proper.

THE WOGAN

Pembroke is probably the only castle in Britain built over a natural cavern. A spiral stair leads down from the hall into a large cave known as the Wogan. The front of this cave can be seen from the quayside, blocked off by a wall with two rows of arrow-slits and a window (like those in the keep) nearly above a watergate. It must have been a boathouse, suitable for a ship on slender lines like a Viking galley.

The view from the top of Pembroke's Great Keep is magnificent

IN CARE OF a local trust

OPEN all reasonable times

ADMISSION some charge

LOCATION on NW edge of town

COUNTY Dyfed

TOWNS AND THEIR DEFENCES

On the top of the mountain north of Pwllheli are the foundations of 150 huts within a defensive wall, occupied by the native population both before and during the Roman period. The Romans themselves built only two fortified towns in Wales, at Caerleon and Carmarthen, both of which had been abandoned before the Normans constructed castles outside them. Rhuddlan, however, has been occupied as a town for over one thousand years, first as an Anglo-Saxon fortified burgh, next as a dependency of the Norman motte and bailey castle, and then as a bastide attached to the Edwardian stone castle.

NORMAN TOWNS

Giraldus Cambrensis states that town life was alien to the Welsh spirit, and that towns had no place in Welsh society. But in the Middle Ages the Welsh certainly engaged in trade, and moved into urban settlements when they could. The neighbourhood of a castle was an obvious place for a town to grow up. Traders were attracted by the wealthy customers living nearby (or at least passing through regularly), and the protection afforded against attack. Workmen discharged after building the castle might decide to settle nearby, together with other pioneers. Abergavenny, Brecon, Chepstow, Monmouth and Pembroke Castles all had towns at their gates soon after their foundation. The Bishops of Salisbury founded many a new town in England (including New Salisbury itself) and built an early one at Kidwelly. All had earthwork defences.

ORGANIZATION

The lord of the manor, particularly where he owned a castle, found it profitable to allow a community to develop nearby, both to provide for his needs and for those of each other. Settlers would be attracted by land grants, low rents and other privileges. An organized trading monopoly offered security in economic terms, and the rights of controlling one's own property within the town. Each freeholder had one or more long narrow plots of land in the town, with a house abutting on to the street acting as home, workshop and trading premises combined.

THE BASTIDES

Both King John and Henry III planted new towns in Wales. Montgomery is the best remaining example, even though it had only earth and timber defences at first. Henry's son, Edward, had seen and built new towns on a rectangular grid plan within stone walls during his campaign in Gascony, France, and brought the bastide idea back to Britain. Each of Edward I's new Welsh castles (with the exception of Harlech) was thus accompanied by a new bastide, the first being built in timber, but the later ones in stone. The fine betowered walls at Caernarfon and Conwy survive complete to this day, living examples of this French-influenced system of town defences. There were baronial new towns as well, at Denbigh and Ruthin. Tenby's town walls, probably built in the late 13th century and later refortified, will stand quite intact along certain sections. Historically, they protected the town far more effectively than its ruinous castle.

The economic importance of the town made it a prime target all over Wales during Owain Glyndwr's rising in the early 1400s. In these later medieval times, town records show a fairly heavy turnover of property ownership and the emergence of dominant groups, family oligarchies and the persistence of archaic legal institutions. Local taxes had to be raised to keep the walls in repair (sometimes the lord contributed out of self-interest). Sometimes a new market developed on a better site nearby, and the old fortified area was abandoned altogether, as at Denbigh, Flint and Kidwelly.

The defences of the town of Caernarfon, with its betowered walls and castle, are best seen from the air

Key to Town Plans

Holyhead

Llandudno   Rhyl
Conwy   Colwyn Bay

Wrexham

Aberystwyth

Carmarthen

Pembroke   Tenby

Swansea   Neath   Pontypool
Cwmbran

Port Talbot   Caerphilly   Newport

Cardiff

Barry

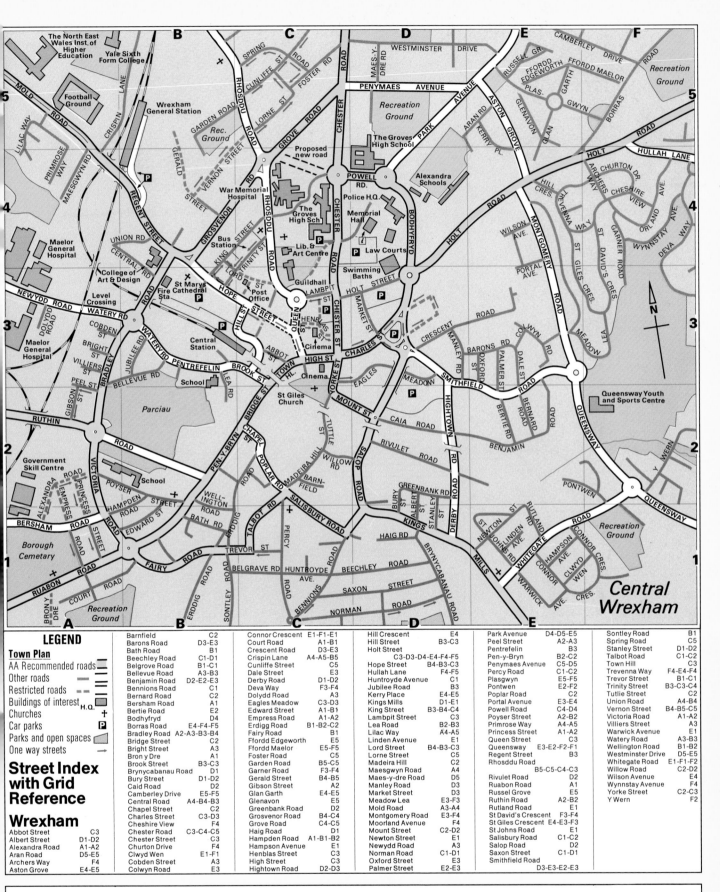

Central Wrexham

Wrexham

Gateway to North Wales, Wrexham has emerged from a turbulent past of medieval resistance to English rule and action during the Civil War to become a more peaceable — but still active — industrial and residential centre. Kelloggs and GKN (which owns the Brymbo Steel Works) are two of the large industrial concerns which have arrived to replace the coalmining and tanning industries which were previously prevalent, and modernisation has provided pedestrian shopping areas. The development in Regent Street includes a Methodist Church at first floor level above the shops; more traditional is the Parish Church of St Giles, with its 136ft 16th-century tower, a local landmark. The main body of the church dates from the 15th century, and its churchyard contains the grave of Elihn Yale, the local boy who founded Yale University in the USA.

Places of interest within the area include Bersham Industrial Heritage, dealing with the local iron industry, and Erdigg, a late 17th-century house containing most of its original furniture. On the sporting side, Wrexham has long been the home of Association Football in Wales: the Welsh FA has its headquarters here and the Racecourse ground is regularly used for international matches, as well as by Wrexham in the Canon League.

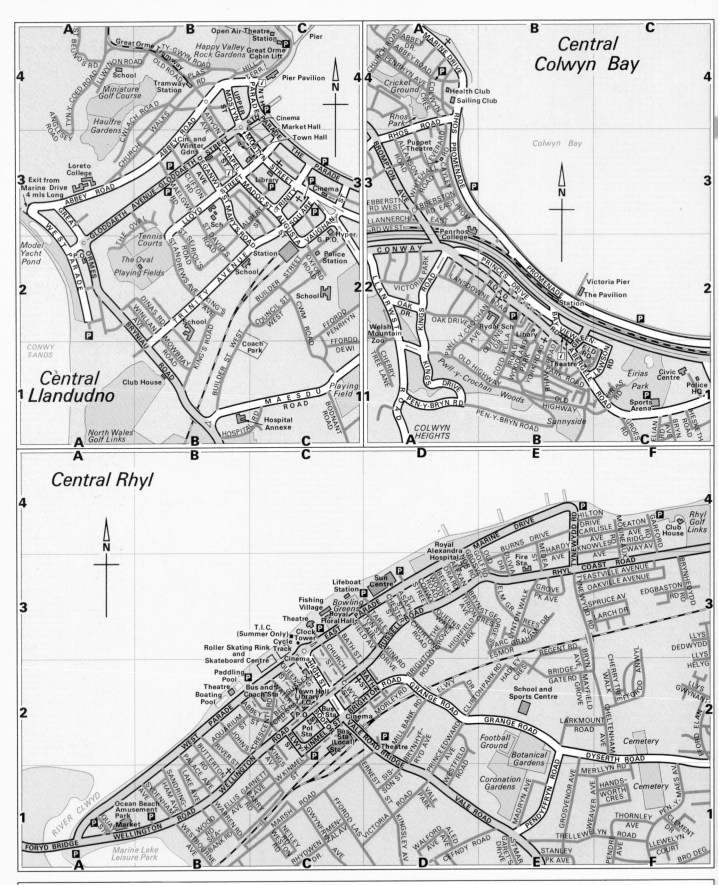

North Wales

Llandudno combines Victorian charm and elegance with the modern amenities of a popular holiday destination. Lying at the foot of Great Orme and Little Orme, its varied attractions include miles of sandy beaches, the Doll Museum, the Mostyn Art Gallery, and the Cabinlift (Britain's longest cable car run). St Tudno's Church is 6th-century.

Colwyn Bay Three miles of golden sand stretch between Rhos-on-Sea and Old Colwyn at Colwyn Bay. Notable in a host of activities for visitors are the Harlequin Puppet Theatre and the extensive facilities of 50-acre Eirias Park.

Rhyl has been a resort for over a century and now attracts more visitors than ever to the glittering attractions of Suncentre, Fishing Village, Skateworld, Cyclorama and Marine Lake. Part of the shoreline is bordered by an elegant promenade edged by flower beds and lawns.

Holyhead The ruins of an ancient settlement at the summit of Holyhead mountain provide a beautiful backdrop to Holyhead, which has become a busy port for car ferry traffic to Laoghaire. The Parish Church of St Cybi is medieval. Close by Trearddur Bay is excellent for watersports.

Conwy boasts Edward I's fine 13th-century castle and Telford's magnificent suspension bridge, built over 150 years ago. The smallest house in Britain stands on the Quay.

Central Holyhead (map)

A — Landing Stage — Slip — Lifeboat House — THE PRINCE OF WALES ROAD — NEWRY FAWR ST — PARK ROAD — BRYN GOLEU AVE — MARINE SQUARE — Town Hall — Library — Cinema — NEWRY ST — CYBI ST — BOSTON RD — STANLEY ST — QUEEN PK — Market Hall — Church & Roman Fort — HILL ST — WILLIAM ST — VICTORIA RD — CAMBRIAN SP — THOMAS'S ST — EDMUND STREET — LONGFORD ROAD — MAES HYFRYD RD — MORETON RD — HOLBORN RD — STATION ROAD — Station — Embank — Disembark — Car Ferry Loading Ramp Mail Boat Terminal — Container Berth — Freight Container Terminal — Freightliner Terminal — TURKEY SHORE ROAD — FFORD TUDUR — FFORD BEIBIO — MORAWELLON ROAD — LLANFAWR ROAD — Primary School

B — Slip — Commercial Vehicle Park — Lifeboat Station — Car Ferry Terminal — Control Barrier — Customs Shed — T.I.C. (Summer Only)

C — General Hospital — Reception & Customs Shed (Commercial Vehicles) — Customs House — Admiralty Arch — Admiralty Pier — Old Harbour — South Pier — Dock Yard

Central Holyhead

Central Conwy (map)

BANGOR ROAD — CADNANT PARK — BRYN CELYN — Council Offices — Harbour — RIVER CONWY — Tennis Courts — TOWN DITCH RD — LOWER GATE ST — Walls — P.O. — Plas Mawr — Pol. Sta. — Aber-conwy Hse — BERRY ST — CASTLE ST — QUAY — Town Hall & Library — Smallest House in Great Britain — CHAPEL STREET — HIGH STREET — Conwy Pottery — CHURCH — MOUNT PLEASANT — BRYN HYFRYD PARK — OLD ROAD — BANGOR ROAD — ROSEMARY LA — ROSEHILL ST — CASTLE SQUARE — NEW BRIDGE — Telford's Suspension Bridge — Stephenson's Tubular Bridge — Conwy Castle — SYCHANT PASS UPPERGATE ST — TY GWYN GARDENS — ST AGNES ROAD — MAES GWERYL — BRYN EITHIN — Cricket Ground — Cemetery — LLANRWST ROAD — BRYN CASTELL — BENARTH ROAD — Municipal Bowling Green

Central Conwy

N

LEGEND

Town Plan

AA Recommended roads

Other roads

Restricted roads

Buildings of interest — Hall

Churches — +

Car parks — P

Parks and open spaces

One way streets

Street Index with Grid Reference

Llandudno

Abbey Road	A3-B3-B4
Albert Street	B3-C3
Anglesey Road	A3-A4
Arvon Avenue	B3-B4
Augusta Street	C2-C3
Bodnant Road	C1
Brynian Road	A2-B2-B1
Builder Street	C2
Builder Street West	B1-B2
Chapel Street	B3
Church Walks	A3-B3-B4
Clifton Road	B3
Council Street West	C2
Cwlach Road	A3-B3-B4
Cwm Road	C1-C2
Deganny Avenue	B3
Dinas Road	B2
Ffordd Dewi	C1
Ffordd Penrhyn	C1-C2
Gloddaeth Avenue	A2-A3-B3
Gloddaeth Street	B3-B4
Great Ormes	A2-A3
Hill Terrace	B4-C4
Hospital Road	B1-C1
King's Avenue	B2
King's Road	B1-B2
Lloyd Street	B3-C3
Llwynon Road	A4-B4
Madoc Street	B3-C3
Maelgwn Road	B3
Maesdu Road	B1-C1
Mostyn Street	B3-C3
Mowbray Road	B1-B2
North Parade	C4
Old Road	B4
Oxford Road	C2
Plas Road	B4
St Andrews Avenue	B2
St Beuno's Road	A4
St David's Road	B2-B3
St Mary's Road	B3-B2-C2
St Seiriol's Road	B2-B3
South Parade	B4-C4-C3
The Oval	A2-A3-B3
The Parade	C3
Trinity Avenue	B1-B2-C2
Trinity Square	C3
Ty-Gwyn Road	B4
Tyn-y-Coed Road	A3-A4
Upper Mostyn Street	B4
Vaughan Street	C2-C3
West Parade	A2-A3
Winllan Avenue	A2-B2

Colwyn Bay

Abbey Drive	A4
Abbey Road	A4
Abergele Road	B2-B1-C1
Allanson Road	A3
Bay View Road	B2
Brompton Avenue	A2-A3-A4
Bryn Avenue	C1
Cayley Promenade	A3
Cherry Tree Lane	A1
Church Road	A4
Coed-Pella Road	B1-B2
Colwyn Crescent	A4
Conway Road	A2-B2
Ebberston Road East	A3
Ebberston Road West	A3
Eirias Road	C1
Elian Road	C1
Everard Road	A3-A4
Greenfield Road	B1-B2-C2-C1
Groes Road	C1
Hesketh Road	C1
Kings Drive	A1
Kings Road	A1-A2
Lansdowne Road	A2-B2
Lawson Road	B1-C1
Llannerch Road East	A3
Llannerch Road West	A3
Marine Drive	A4
Oak Drive	A2-B2
Old Highway	A1-B1-C1
Park Road	B1
Penrhyn Avenue	A4
Pen-y-Bryn Road	A1-B1
Princes Drive	A2-B2
Promenade	A3-B3-B2-C2-C1
Pwll-y-Crochan Avenue	A1-A2-B2
Queens Drive	A1-B1-B2
Rhiw Road	B1-B2
Rhos Promenade	A3-A4
Rhos Road	A3-A4
Victoria Park	A2
Whitehall Road	A3
Woodland Park	B1
York Road	B1

Rhyl

Abbey Street	B2-C2
Aled Avenue	D1
Alexandra Road	D3
Aquarium Street	B2
Barry Road	B1-C1
Bath Street	C3-C2-D2
Bedford Street	B3
Beechwood Road	D3
Bodfor Street	C2
Bridgegate Road	E2
Brighton Road	C2-D2-D3
Bro Deg	F1
Bryn Avenue	E2-E3
Brynhedydd Road	F3
Brynhyfryd Avenue	D2
Bryntirion Avenue	D3
Burns Drive	E3-E4
Butterton Road	B1-B2
Carlisle Avenue	E4-F4
Cefndy Road	D1-E1
Cheltenham Avenue	F2
Cherry Tree Walk	F2
Chester Street	D3
Church Street	C2-C3
Churton Road	D3
Clement Drive	F1
Clifton Park Road	D2-E2
Clwyd Street	C2
Conwy Street	D3
Crescent Road	C2
Dyserth Road	E2-F2-F1
East Parade	C3-D3
Eastville Avenue	E3-F3
Eaton Avenue	F4
Edgbaston Road	F3
Ellis Avenue	B1
Elm Grove	E3
Elwy Drive	D2
Elwy Street	C2
Ernest Street	C1-D1
Fairfield Avenue	C3-D3
Fford Anwyl	F2-F3
Ffordd Las	C1
Fford Elan	F2
Foryd Bridge	A1
Garford Road	F4
Garnett Avenue	B1-C1
Graham Drive	E3
Grange Road	D2-E2
Grosvenor Avenue	E1-E2
Grosvenor Road	D3
Grove Park Avenue	E3
Gwynfryn Avenue	C1
Hadley Crescent	E2
Handsworth Crescent	F1
Hardy Avenue	E3-E4
Highfield Park	D3-E3
High Street	C2
Hilton Drive	E4-F4
John Street	B2
Kinard Drive	D2-D3
Kings Avenue	C1-C2
Kingsley Avenue	D1
Kinmel Street	C2
Knowles Avenue	E3-E4-F4
Lake Avenue	B1
Larch Drive	F3
Larkmount Road	E2-F2
Llewelyn Court	F1
Llys Dedwydd	F3
Llys Gwynant	F2
Llys Helyg	F2
Lynton Walk	E3
Madryn Avenue	E1
Marine Drive	D3-D4-E4
Marsh Road	B1-C1-C2-D2
Mayfield Grove	E2
Medea Street	E3-E4
Mernal Avenue	C1
Merllyn Road	E1-F1
Mill Bank Road	D2
Molineaux Road	F3-F4
Morley Road	D2
Netley Road	C1
Oakville Avenue	E3-F3

Old Golf Road	E3-E4
Olivia Drive	E3
Palace Avenue	B1-B2
Parc Esmor	E3
Pendre Avenue	F1
Pendyffryn Road	E1-E2
Pen-y-Maes Avenue	F1
Prince Edward Avenue	D1-D2
Quay Street	A1
Queen Street	C2
Queens Walk	D3
Rees Avenue	E3
Regent Road	E3
Rhydwen Drive	C1
Rhyl Coast Road	E3-F3
Ridgway Avenue	F4
River Street	B1-B2
Russel Road	C2-D2-D3
St Asaph Street	D3
St George's Crescent	E3
St Margaret's Drive	E1
Sandringham Avenue	B1
Seabank Road	B1
Sisson Street	D1
Spruce Avenue	E3-F3
Stanley Park Avenue	E1
Sussex Street	C2
Sydenham Avenue	B1
Tarleton Street	D3
The Grove	D3
Thornley Avenue	F1
Trellewelyn Road	E1-F1
Tynewydd Road	E3-E4
Vale Park	D1
Vale Road	D1-E1
Vale Road Bridge	C2-D2-D1
Victoria Road	C1-D1
Walford Avenue	D1
Warren Road	B1
Water Street	C2
Weaver Avenue	E1
Wellington Road	A1-B1-B2-C2
Westbourne Avenue	B1
Westfield Road	D1-D2
West Kinmel Street	C1-C2
West Parade	A1-B1-B2-C2-C3
Weston Road	C1
Wood Road	B1

Holyhead

Boston Street	A3
Bryn Goleu Avenue	A4
Cambrian Street	A2-A3
Edmund Street	A2
Fford Beibio	C2
Fford Tudur	C2
Hill Street	A2
Holborn Road	A1
Llanfawr Road	B1
Longford Road	A1-A2
Maes Hyfryd Road	A1
Marine Square	B3
Market Street	A2
Morawellon Road	C1
Moreton Road	A1
Newry-Faws Street	A3-A4
Newry Street	A3
Park Road	A3-A4
Queen Park	A3
St Cybi Street	A3
Stanley Street	A2-A3
Station Road	A1
The Prince of Wales Road	A4-B4-B3
Thomas's Street	A2
Turkey Shore Road	B1-B2-C2-C3
Victoria Road	A2-A3-B3
William Street	A2
Wynne Street	A3

Conwy

Bangor Road	A4-A3-B3-B2
Benarth Road	C2
Berry Street	B3
Bryn Castell	B1
Bryn Celyn	A3
Bryn Eithin	B1
Bryn Hyfryd Park	A2
Cadnant Park	A3
Castle Square	C2
Castle Street	B2-B3
Chapel Street	B3
Church Street	B2
High Street	B2-B3
Llanrwst Road	A1-B1-B2
Lower Gate Street	B3
Maes Gweryl	A1
Mount Pleasant	A2-A3
New Bridge	C2
Old Road	A2
Quay	B3
Rosehill Street	B2
Rosemary Lane	A2-B2
St Agnes Road	A1-A2
Sychant Pass Road	A2
Town Ditch Road	B3
Ty Gwyn Gardens	A2
Uppergate Street	A2-B2

103

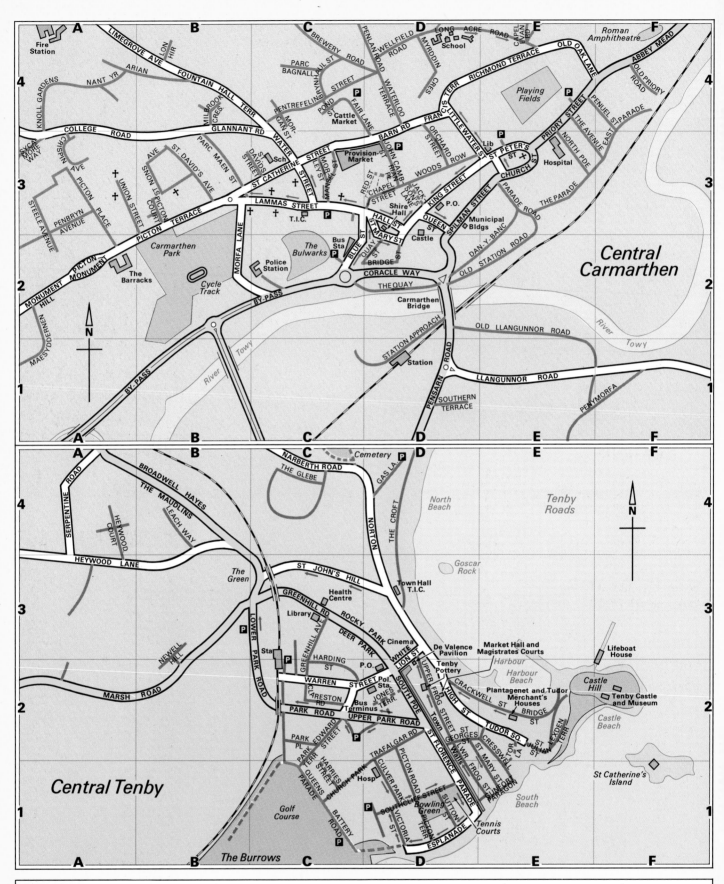

South Wales

Aberystwyth is both a picturesque seaside town and an important centre of learning. The National Library of Wales and several colleges and museums, are here, and by way of contrast, freshwater and sea fishing are also popular. Overlooking the southern seafront are the 1277 castle ruins; the Vale of Rheidol Steam Railway is nearby.

Carmarthen is a hive of activity of industries, colleges and schools. The River Towey offers boating and fishing; the Leisure Centre offers other sports, and St Peter's Church and the County Museum are full of interest. A Redevelopment Scheme has kept the town's old markets.

Tenby Surrounded by 13th-century walls and overlooked by medieval St Mary's church, this major resort boasts four beaches, a pretty harbour and interesting shops and streets. The Tudor Merchant's House and the Tenby Museum are worth seeing; across from Castle Beach stands St Catherine's Rock with its disused fort (closed to visitors). Three miles off the coast are the bird colonies and seals of Caldey Island, which is run by Cistercian monks skilled in producing goods such as perfume from wild flowers.

Pembroke is dominated by a magnificent Norman castle, and other attractions are Monkton Priory and the Mill Pond Walk. The town is a perfect touring centre for South Pembrokeshire.

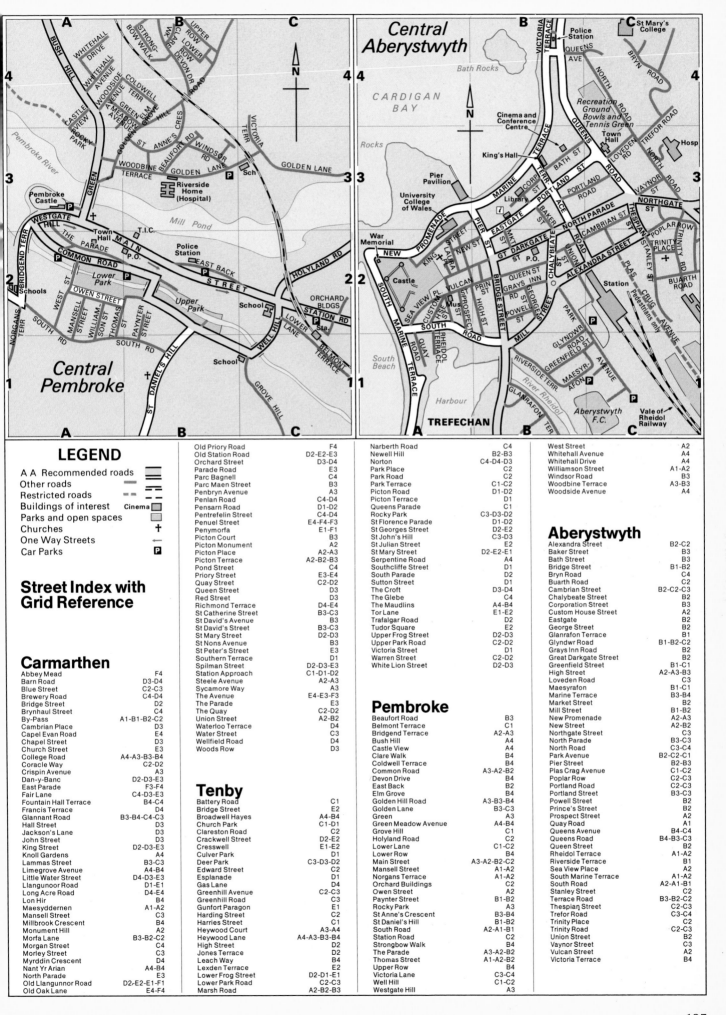

LEGEND

A A Recommended roads	▬▬
Other roads	▬▬
Restricted roads	---
Buildings of interest	Cinema ▪
Parks and open spaces	▪
Churches	†
One Way Streets	←
Car Parks	P

Street Index with Grid Reference

Carmarthen

Street	Grid
Abbey Mead	F4
Barn Road	D3-D4
Blue Street	C2-C3
Brewery Road	C4-D4
Bridge Street	D2
Brynhaul Street	C4
By-Pass	A1-B1-B2-C2
Cambrian Place	D3
Capel Evan Road	E4
Chapel Street	D3
Church Street	E3
College Road	A4-A3-B3-B4
Coracle Way	C2-D2
Crispin Avenue	A3
Dan-y-Banc	D2-D3-E3
East Parade	F3-F4
Fair Lane	C4-D3-E3
Fountain Hall Terrace	B4-C4
Francis Terrace	D4
Glannant Road	B3-B4-C4-C3
Hall Street	D3
Jackson's Lane	D3
John Street	D3
King Street	D2-D3-E3
Knoll Gardens	A4
Lammas Street	B3-C3
Limegrove Avenue	A4-B4
Little Water Street	D4-D3-E3
Llangunoor Road	D1-E1
Long Acre Road	D4-E4
Lon Hir	B4
Maesyddernen	A1-A2
Mansell Street	C3
Millbrook Crescent	B4
Monument Hill	A2
Morfa Lane	B3-B2-C2
Morgan Street	C4
Morley Street	C3
Myrddin Crescent	D4
Nant Yr Arian	A4-B4
North Parade	E3
Old Llangunnor Road	D2-E2-E1-F1
Old Oak Lane	E4-F4

Street	Grid
Old Priory Road	F4
Old Station Road	B2-E2-E3
Orchard Street	D3-D4
Parade Road	E3
Parc Bagnell	C4
Parc Maen Street	B3
Penbryn Avenue	A3
Penlan Road	C4-D4
Pensarn Road	D1-D2
Pentrefelin Street	C4-D4
Penuel Street	E4-F4-F3
Penymorfa	E1-F1
Picton Court	B3
Picton Monument	A2
Picton Place	A2-A3
Picton Terrace	A2-B2-B3
Pond Street	C4
Priory Street	E3-E4
Quay Street	C2-D2
Queen Street	D3
Red Street	D3
Richmond Terrace	D4-E4
St Catherine Street	B3-C3
St David's Avenue	B3
St David's Street	B3-C3
St Mary Street	D2-D3
St Nons Avenue	B3
St Peter's Street	E3
Southern Terrace	D1
Spilman Street	D2-D3-E3
Station Approach	C1-D1-D2
Steele Avenue	A2-A3
Sycamore Way	A3
The Avenue	E4-E3-F3
The Parade	E3
The Quay	C2-D2
Union Street	A2-B2
Waterloo Terrace	D4
Water Street	C3
Wellfield Road	D4
Woods Row	D3

Tenby

Street	Grid
Battery Road	C1
Bridge Street	E2
Broadwell Hayes	A4-B4
Church Park	C1-D1
Clareston Road	C2
Crackwell Street	D2-E2
Cresswell	E1-E2
Culver Park	D1
Deer Park	C3-D3-D2
Edward Street	C2
Esplanade	D1
Gas Lane	D4
Greenhill Avenue	C2-C3
Greenhill Road	B2
Gunfort Paragon	E1
Harding Street	C2
Harries Street	C1
Heywood Court	A3-A4
Heywood Lane	A4-A3-B3-B4
High Street	D2
Jones Terrace	D2
Leach Way	B4
Lexden Terrace	E2
Lower Frog Street	D2-D1-E1
Lower Park Road	C2-C3
Marsh Road	A2-B2-B3

Pembroke

Beaufort Road	B3
Belmont Terrace	C1
Bridgend Terrace	A2-A3
Bush Hill	A4
Castle View	A4
Clare Walk	B4
Coldwell Terrace	B4
Common Road	A3-B3-B4
Devon Drive	B4
East Back	B2
Elm Grove	B4
Golden Hill Road	A3-B3-B4
Golden Lane	B3-C3
Green	A3
Green Meadow Avenue	A4-B4
Grove Hill	C1
Holyland Road	C2
Lower Lane	C1-C2
Lower Row	B4
Main Street	A3-A2-B2-C2
Mansell Street	A1-A2
Norgans Terrace	A1-A2
Orchard Buildings	C2
Owen Street	A2
Paynter Street	B1-B2
Rocky Park	A3
St Anne's Crescent	B3-B4
St Daniel's Hill	B1-B2
South Road	A2-A1-B1
Station Road	C2
Strongbow Walk	B4
The Parade	A3-A2-B2
Thomas Street	A1-A2-B2
Upper Row	B4
Victoria Lane	C3-C4
Well Hill	C1-C2
Westgate Hill	A3

(Aberystwyth streets continued)

Street	Grid
Narberth Road	C4
Newell Hill	B2-B3
Norton	C4-D4-D3
Park Place	C2
Park Road	C2
Park Terrace	C1-C2
Picton Road	D1-D2
Picton Terrace	D1
Queens Parade	C1
Rocky Park	C3-D3-D2
St Florence Parade	D1-D2
St Georges Street	D2-E2
St John's Hill	C3-D3
St Julian Street	E2
St Mary Street	D2-E2-E1
Serpentine Road	A4
Southcliffe Street	D1
South Parade	D2
Sutton Street	D1
The Croft	D3-D4
The Glebe	C4
The Maudlins	A4-B4
Tor Lane	E1-E2
Trafalgar Road	D2
Tudor Square	E2
Upper Frog Street	D2-D3
Upper Park Road	C2-D2
Victoria Street	D1
Warren Street	C2-D2
White Lion Street	D2-D3

Street	Grid
West Street	A2
Whitehall Avenue	A4
Whitehall Drive	A4
Williamson Street	A1-A2
Windsor Road	B3
Woodbine Terrace	A3-B3
Woodside Avenue	A4

Aberystwyth

Street	Grid
Alexandra Street	B2-C2
Baker Street	B3
Bath Street	B3
Bridge Street	B1-B2
Bryn Road	C4
Buarth Road	C2
Cambrian Street	B2-C2-C3
Chalybeate Street	B2
Corporation Street	B3
Custom House Street	A2
Eastgate	B2
George Street	B2
Glanrafon Terrace	B1
Glyndwr Road	B1-B2-C2
Grays Inn Road	B2
Great Darkgate Street	B2
Greenfield Street	B1-C1
High Street	A2-A3-B3
Loveden Road	C3
Maesyrafon	B1-C1
Marine Terrace	B3-B4
Market Street	B2
Mill Street	B1-B2
New Promenade	A2-A3
New Street	A2-B2
Northgate Street	C3
North Parade	B3-C3
North Road	C3-C4
Park Avenue	B2-C2-C1
Pier Street	B2-B3
Plas Crag Avenue	C1-C2
Poplar Row	C2-C3
Portland Road	C2-C3
Portland Street	B3-C3
Powell Street	B2
Prince's Street	B2
Prospect Street	A2
Quay Road	A1
Queens Avenue	B4-C4
Queens Road	B4-B3-C3
Queen Street	B2
Rheidol Terrace	A1-A2
Riverside Terrace	B1
Sea View Place	A2
South Marine Terrace	A1-A2
South Road	A2-A1-B1
Stanley Street	C2
Terrace Road	B3-B2-C2
Thespian Street	C2-C3
Trefor Road	C3-C4
Trinity Place	C2
Trinity Road	C2-C3
Union Street	B2
Vaynor Street	C3
Vulcan Street	A2
Victoria Terrace	B4

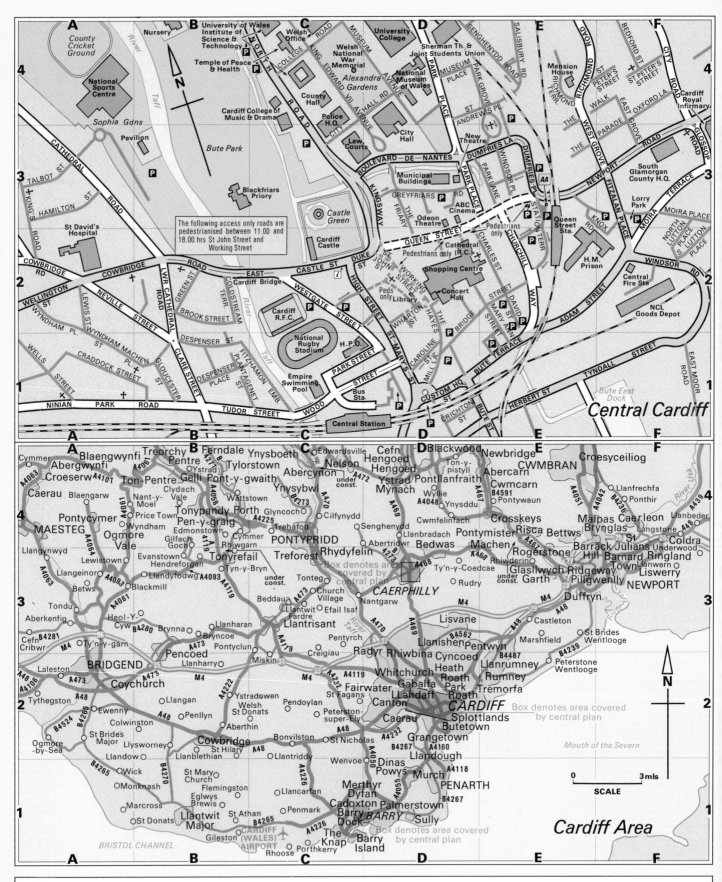

Central Cardiff

Cardiff Area

Cardiff

Strategically important to both the Romans and the Normans, Cardiff slipped from prominence in medieval times and remained a quiet market town in a remote area until it was transformed – almost overnight – by the effects of the Industrial Revolution. The valleys of South Wales were a principal source of iron and coal – raw materials which helped to change the shape and course of the 19th-century world. Cardiff became a teeming export centre; by the end of the 19th century it was the largest coal-exporting city in the world.

Close to the castle – an exciting place with features from Roman times to the 19th century – is the city's civic centre – a fine concourse of buildings dating largely from the early part of the 20th century. Among them is the National Museum of Wales – a superb collection of art and antiquities from Wales and around the world.

Barry has sandy beaches, landscaped gardens and parks, entertainment arcades and funfairs. Like Cardiff it grew as a result of the demand for coal and steel, but now its dock complex is involved in the petrochemical and oil industries.

Caerphilly is famous for two things – a castle and cheese. The cheese is no longer made here, but the 13th-century castle, slighted by Cromwell, still looms above its moat. No castle in Britain – except Windsor – is larger.

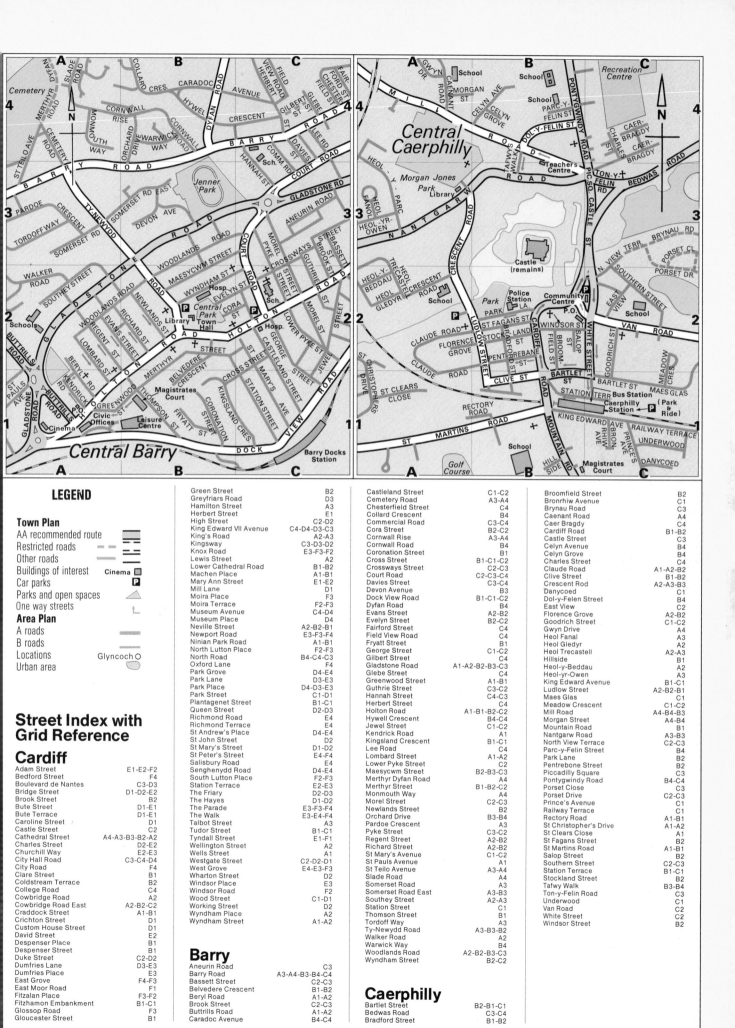

LEGEND

Town Plan

AA recommended route
Restricted roads
Other roads
Buildings of interest — Cinema 🔲
Car parks — 🅿
Parks and open spaces — ◭
One way streets — ⌐

Area Plan

A roads
B roads
Locations — Glyncoch ○
Urban area

Street Index with Grid Reference

Cardiff

Adam Street	E1-E2-F2
Bedford Street	F4
Boulevard de Nantes	C3-D3
Bridge Street	D1-D2-E2
Brook Street	B2
Bute Street	D1-E1
Bute Terrace	D1-E1
Caroline Street	D1
Castle Street	C2
Cathedral Street	A4-A3-B3-B2-A2
Charles Street	D2-E2
Churchill Way	E2-E3
City Hall Road	C3-C4-D4
City Road	F4
Clare Street	B1
Coldstream Terrace	B2
College Road	C4
Cowbridge Road	A2
Cowbridge Road East	A2-B2-C2
Craddock Street	A1-B1
Crichton Street	D1
Custom House Street	D1
David Street	E2
Despenser Place	B1
Despenser Street	B1
Duke Street	C2-D2
Dumfries Lane	D3-E3
Dumfries Place	E3
East Grove	F4-F3
East Moor Road	F1
Fitzalan Place	F3-F2
Fitzhamon Embankment	B1-C1
Glossop Road	F3
Gloucester Street	B1
Green Street	B2
Greyfriars Road	D3
Hamilton Street	A3
Herbert Street	E1
High Street	C2-D2
King Edward VII Avenue	C4-D4-D3-C3
King's Road	A2-A3
Kingsway	C3-D3-D2
Knox Road	E3-F3-F2
Lewis Street	A2
Lower Cathedral Road	B1-B2
Machen Place	A1-B1
Mary Ann Street	E1-E2
Mill Lane	D1
Moira Place	F3
Moira Terrace	F2-F3
Museum Avenue	C4-D4
Museum Place	D4
Neville Street	A2-B2-B1
Newport Road	E3-F3-F4
Ninian Park Road	A1-B1
North Lutton Place	F2-F3
North Road	B4-C4-C3
Oxford Lane	F4
Park Grove	D4-E4
Park Lane	D3-E3
Park Place	D4-D3-E3
Park Street	C1-D1
Plantagenet Street	B1-C1
Queen Street	D2-D3
Richmond Road	E4
Richmond Terrace	E4
St Andrew's Place	D4-E4
St John Street	D2
St Mary's Street	D1-D2
St Peter's Street	E4-F4
Salisbury Road	E4
Senghenydd Road	D4-E4
South Lutton Place	F2-F3
Station Terrace	E2-E3
Talbot Street	A3
The Friary	D2-D3
The Hayes	D1-D2
The Parade	E3-F3-F4
The Walk	E3-E4-F4
Tudor Street	B1-C1
Tyndall Street	E1-F1
Wellington Street	A2
Wells Street	A1
Westgate Street	C2-D2-D1
West Grove	E4-E3-F3
Wharton Street	D2
Windsor Place	E3
Windsor Road	F2
Wood Street	C1-D1
Working Street	D2
Wyndham Place	A2
Wyndham Street	A1-A2

Barry

Aneurin Road	C3
Barry Road	A3-A4-B3-B4-C4
Bassett Street	C2-C3
Belvedere Crescent	B1-B2
Beryl Road	A1-A2
Brook Street	C2-C3
Buttrills Road	A1-A2
Caradoc Avenue	B4-C4
Castleland Street	C1-C2
Cemetery Road	A3-A4
Chesterfield Street	C4
Collard Crescent	B4
Commercial Road	C3-C4
Cora Street	B2-C2
Cornwall Rise	A3-A4
Cornwall Road	B4
Coronation Street	B1
Cross Street	B1-C1-C2
Crossways Street	C2-C3
Court Road	C2-C3-C4
Davies Street	C3-C4
Devon Avenue	B3
Dock View Road	B1-C1-C2
Dyfan Road	B4
Evans Street	A2-B2
Evelyn Street	B2-C2
Fairford Street	C4
Field View Road	C4
Fryatt Street	B1
George Street	C1-C2
Gilbert Street	C4
Gladstone Road	A1-A2-B2-B3-C3
Glebe Street	C4
Greenwood Street	A1-B1
Guthrie Street	C3-C2
Hannah Street	C4-C3
Herbert Street	C4
Holton Road	A1-B1-B2-C2
Hywell Crescent	B4-C4
Jewel Street	C1-C2
Kendrick Road	A1
Kingsland Crescent	B1-C1
Lee Road	C4
Lombard Street	A1-A2
Lower Pyke Street	C2
Maesycwm Street	B2-B3-C3
Merthyr Dyfan Road	A4
Merthyr Street	B1-B2-C2
Monmouth Way	A4
Morel Street	C2-C3
Newlands Street	B2
Orchard Drive	B3-B4
Pardoe Crescent	A3
Pyke Street	C3-C2
Regent Street	A2-B2
Richard Street	A2-B2
St Mary's Avenue	C1-C2
St Pauls Avenue	A1
St Teilo Avenue	A3-A4
Slade Road	A4
Somerset Road	A3
Somerset Road East	A3-B3
Southey Street	A2-A3
Station Street	C1
Thomson Street	B1
Tordoff Way	A3
Ty-Newydd Road	A3-B3-B2
Walker Road	A2
Warwick Way	B4
Woodlands Road	A2-B2-B3-C3
Wyndham Street	B2-C2

Caerphilly

Bartlet Street	B2-B1-C1
Bedwas Road	C3-C4
Bradford Street	B1-B2
Broomfield Street	B2
Bronrhiw Avenue	C1
Brynau Road	C3
Caenant Road	A4
Caer Bragdy	C4
Cardiff Road	B1-B2
Castle Street	C3
Celyn Avenue	B4
Celyn Grove	B4
Charles Street	C4
Claude Road	A1-A2-B2
Clive Street	B1-B2
Crescent Rod	A2-A3-B3
Danycoed	C1
Dol-y-Felen Street	B4
East View	C2
Florence Grove	A2-B2
Goodrich Street	C1-C2
Gwyn Drive	A4
Heol Fanal	A3
Heol Gledyr	A2
Heol Trecastell	A2-A3
Hillside	B1
Heol-y-Beddau	A2
Heol-yr-Owen	A3
King Edward Avenue	B1-C1
Ludlow Street	A2-B2-B1
Maes Glas	C1
Meadow Crescent	C1-C2
Mill Road	A4-B4-B3
Morgan Street	A4-B4
Mountain Road	B1
Nantgarw Road	A3-B3
North View Terrace	C2-C3
Parc-y-Felin Street	B4
Park Lane	B2
Pentrebone Street	B2
Piccadilly Square	C3
Pontygwindy Road	B4-C4
Porset Close	C3
Porset Drive	C2-C3
Prince's Avenue	C1
Railway Terrace	C1
Rectory Road	A1-B1
St Christopher's Drive	A1-A2
St Clears Close	A1
St Fagans Street	B2
St Martins Road	A1-B1
Salop Street	B2
Southern Street	C2-C3
Station Terrace	B1-C1
Stockland Street	B2
Tafwy Walk	B3-B4
Ton-y-Felin Road	C3
Underwood	C1
Van Road	C2
White Street	C2
Windsor Street	B2

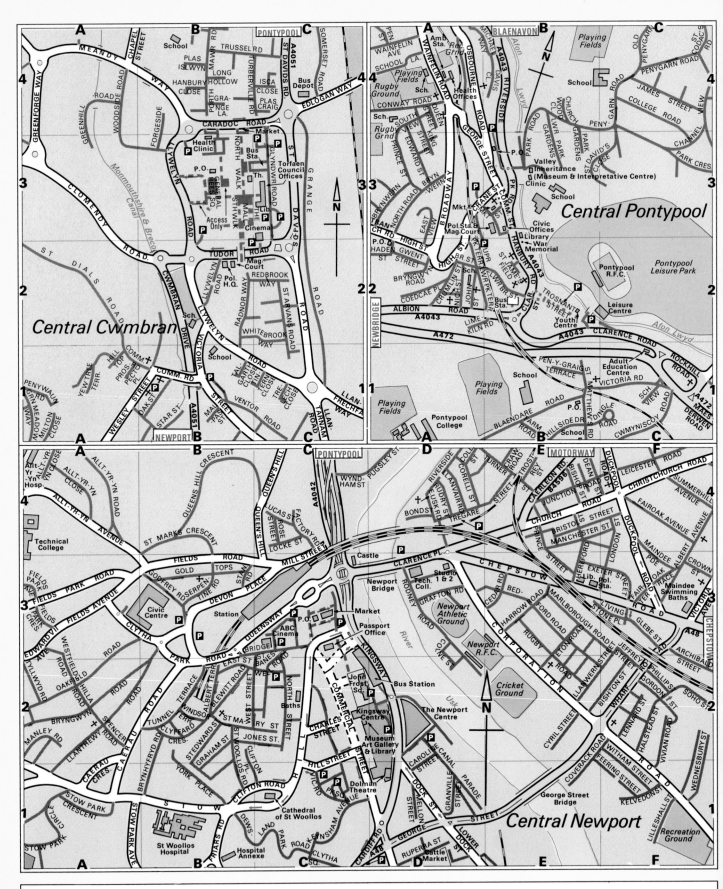

Newport

When the Industrial Revolution hit South Wales Newport, on the River Usk, came into its own as a harbour for the export of the coal and iron products manufactured in the valleys. At the zenith of Newport's activity in the mid 19th century there were six miles of quays. Today it is still an important port but the range of industries using it has expanded as light industry has taken over.

The Civic Centre just to the west of the town centre is a rather striking development which is particularly well-known for a series of modern murals that illustrate the history of Monmouthshire (now part of Gwent). Further background to Newport, including the Chartist Riots of 1839, and the iron industry can be found in the town museum in John Frost Square. There is also an interesting section on the Roman history of the area, particularly concerning the nearby forts of Caerleon

and Caerwent. The city is relatively short of historic buildings, but St Woolos' Cathedral, crowning Stow Hill, dates back to Norman times. Its unusual name is believed to be a corruption of Gwynllyw, a local baron who built the first church on this site.

Perhaps Newport's most remarkable structure is the Transporter Bridge which is one of just two left in Britain – the other is at Middlesbrough. The bridge consists of a suspended moveable platform which carries cars and pedestrians across the river.

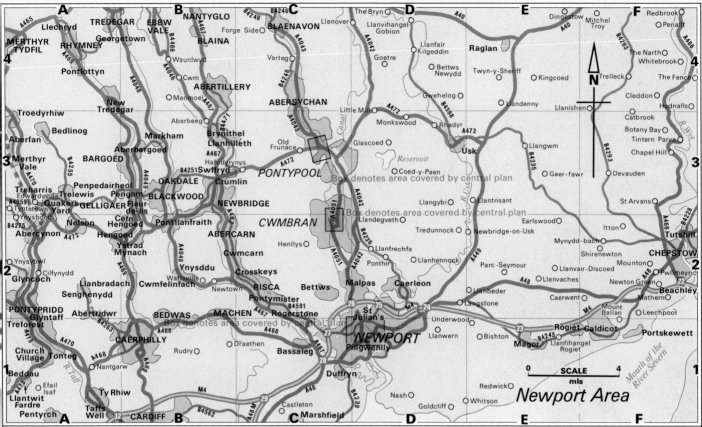

LEGEND

Town Plan
- AA recommended route
- Restricted roads
- Other roads
- Buildings of interest — Hall
- Car parks — P
- Parks and open spaces

Area Plan
- A roads
- B roads
- Locations — Redwick
- Urban area

Street Index with Grid Reference

Newport

Albert Avenue	F3-F4
Albert Terrace	B2
Allt-yr-yn Avenue	A4-A3-B3-B4
Allt-yr-yn Close	A4
Allt-yr-yn Road	A4
Archibald Street	F2-F3
Baneswell Road	C2-C3
Bedford Road	E3
Bishop Street	E4
Bishton Street	E2-F2
Blewitt Road	B2
Bond Street	B2
Bridge Street	B3-C3
Bristol Street	E4-F4
Brynhyfryd Road	B1-B2
Brynwyn Road	A2-B2
Caerau Crescent	A1-A2
Caerau Road	A1-A2-B2
Caerleon Road	E4
Canal Parade	D1-D2
Cardiff Road	C1-D1
Caroline Street	D1-D2
Cedar Road	E3
Charles Street	C2
Chepstow Road	D3-E3-F3
Christchurch Road	F4
Church Road	E4-F4
Clarence Place	C3-D3-D4
Clifton Place	B2-B1-C1
Clifton Road	B1-C1
Clyffard Crescent	B2
Clytha Park Road	A3-B3-B2-B3
Clytha Square	C1
Collier Street	D4
Colne Street	D2-D3
Commercial Street	C3-C2-C1-D1
Corelli Street	D4
Corporation Road	D3-E3-E2-F2-F1
Coverack Road	E1-E2-F2
Crawford Road	E4
Crown Street	F3
Cyril Street	E2
Dean Street	E4-F4
Dewsland Park Road	B1-C1
Devon Place	B3-C3
Dock Street	D1-D2
Duckpool Road	F3-F4
East Street	B2
East Usk Road	D4
Edward VII Avenue	A2-A3
Eton Road	E2-E3
Exeter Street	E3-F3
Factory Road	C4
Fairoak Avenue	F4
Fairoak Terrace	F3
Feering Street	E2-E1-F1
Fields Avenue	A3
Fields Road	B3-C3
Fields Park Avenue	A3
Fields Park Crescent	A3
Fields Park Road	A3
Friars Road	B1
George Street	C1-D1-E1
Glebe Street	F3
Godfrey Road	B3
Gold Tops	B3
Gordon Street	F2
Grafton Road	D3
Graham Street	B1-B2
Granville Street	D1
Halstead Street	F2
Harrow Road	E3
Hereford Street	E3-E4
Hilla Road	A2
Hill Street	C1-C2
Jeffrey Street	F2-F3
Jones Street	B2-C2
Junction Road	E4-F4
Kelvedon Street	F1
Keynsham Avenue	C1
Kingsway	C3-D3-D2
Leicester Road	F4
Lennard Street	F2
Lilleshall Street	F1
Livingstone Place	E3-F3
Llanthewy Road	A1-A2-B2
Llanvair Road	D4
Llanwern Street	E2-F2-F3
Locke Street	C4
London Street	F3-F4
Lower Dock Street	D1-D2
Lucas Street	C4
Maindee Parade	F3-F4
Manchester Street	E4-F4
Manley Road	A2
Marlborough Road	E3-F3
Mellon Street	D1
Mill Street	C3-C4
North Street	C2
Oakfield Road	A2-A3
Park Square	C1
Phillip Street	F2
Prince Street	E3-E4
Pugsley Street	C4-D4
Queen's Hill	C3-C4
Queens Hill Crescent	B4-C4
Queensway	B3-C3
Riverside	D4
Rodney Road	D3
Rose Street	C4
Rudry Street	D4
Rugby Road	E2-E3
Ruperra Street	D1
St Marks Crescent	B3-B4
St Mary Street	B2-C2
St Woollos Road	B1-B2
Serpentine Road	B3
Soho Street	F2
Spencer Road	A2
Stanley Road	B3
Steward Street	F2
Stow Hill	A1-B1-C1-C2-C3
Stow Park Avenue	A1
Stow Park Circle	A1
Stow Park Crescent	A1
Summerhill Avenue	F4
Tregare Street	D4-E4
Trostrey Street	E4
Tunnel Terrace	B2
Turner Street	D4-E4
Tyllwyd Road	A2
Queensway	B3-C3
Victoria Avenue	F3
Victoria Road	C1
Vivian Road	F1-F2
Wednesbury Street	F1-F2
Westfield Road	A2-A3
West Street	B2-C2-C3
Wharf Road	F2-F3
Windsor Terrace	B2
Witham Street	F1-F2
Wyndham Street	C4
York Place	B1-B2

Cwmbran

Abbey Road	B1
Caradoc Road	B4-C4
Chapel Street	A4-B4
Clomendy Road	A3-A2-B2
Commercial Road	A1-B1
Cwmbran Drive	B1-B2
Edlogan Way	B4
Forgeside	B3-B4
General Rees Square	B3
Glyndwr Road	C2-C3-C4
Grange Lane	B4
Grange Road	C1-C2-C3-C4
Greenforge Way	A3-A4
Greenhill Road	A3-A4
Green Meadow Way	A1
Hanbury Close	B4
Hill Top	A1
Isca Close	C4
Llanfrechfa Way	C1
Llantarnam Road	C1
Llywelyn Road	B3-B2-B1-C1
Long Hollow	B4
Malpas Street	B1
Meandy Way	A4-B4
Milton Close	A1
North Walk	B3
Oak Street	B1
Orchard Lane	C4
Penywaun Road	A1
Plas Craig	C4
Plas Islwyn	B4
Porth Mawr Road	B4
Prospect Place	A1
Radnor Way	B1-B2
Redbrook Way	B2-C2
St Arvans Road	C1-C2
St Davids Road	C1-C2-C3-C4
St Dials Road	A1-A2
Somerset Road	C4
South Walk	B2-B3
Star Street	B1
Talgarth Close	B1
The Mall	B3
Tintern Close	B1-C1
Trelech Close	C1
Trussel Road	B4-C4
Tudor Road	B2-C2
Turberville Road	C4
Ventor Road	B1-C1
Victoria Street	B2-B1-C1
Wesley Street	A1-B1
Whitebrook Way	B2-C2
Woodside Road	A3-A4
Yew Tree Terrace	A1

Pontypool

Albion Road	A2-B2
Blaendare Road	A1-B1
Bridge Street	A2
Broadway	A2-A3-A4
Bryngwyn Road	A2
Brynwern	A3
Channel View	C3-C4
Churchwood Close	B4
Clarence Road	B2-B1-B2-C2-C1
Clarence Street	B2
Coedcae Place	A4
College Road	C3-C4
Commercial Street	B3
Conway Road	A4
Crane Street	A3-B3
Crumlin Street	A2
Cwmynyscoy Road	C1
Davis Close	B4
Dingle Close	B1-C1
East View	A2-A3
Edward Street	A3-A4

Farm Road	B1
George Street	A4-A3-B3
Gwent Street	A2
Haden Street	A2
Hanbury Road	B2-B3
High Street	D2
Hillside Drive	B1
James Street	C4
John Street	A2
King Street	A3-A4
Lime Kiln Road	A2-B2
Lower Bridge Street	B2
Lower Park Gardens	B3-B4
Lower Park Terrace	A2-B2
Maesderwen Road	C1
Market Street	A3-B3
Michael Way	A4-B4
Nicholas Street	A2
North Road	A3
Old Penygarn	C4
Osbourne Road	A4-A3-B3-B4
Park Crescent	C3
Park Gardens	B3-B4
Park Road	B3-B4
Penygarn Road	B4-C4
Pen-y-Graig Terrace	B1
Penywain Street	A4
Prince Street	A3
Queen Street	A4
Riverside	B3-B4
Rockhill Road	C1
St Codac's Road	C4
St David's Close	B3-C3
St James's Field	B2
St Matthew's Road	B1
School Lane	A4
School View	C1
South View	A3-A4
Tranch Road	A2-A3
Trosnant Street	B2
Upper Park Terrace	A2-B2
Victoria Road	B1-C1
Wainfelin Avenue	A4
Wainfelin Road	A4

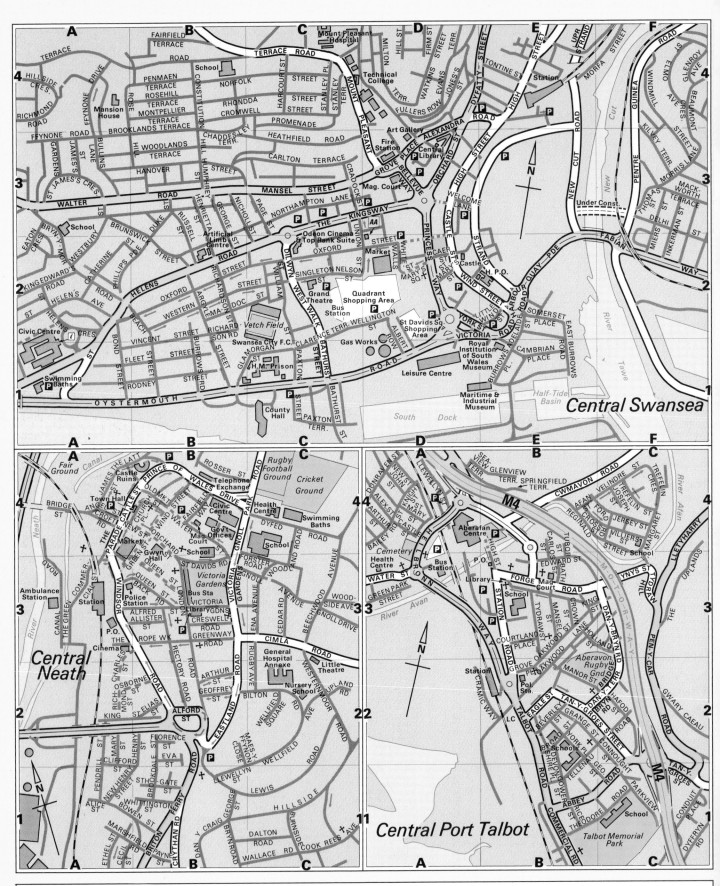

Central Swansea

Central Neath

Central Port Talbot

Swansea

Like nearly all the towns in the valleys and along the coast of Glamorgan, Swansea grew at an amazing speed during the Industrial Revolution. Ironworks, non-ferrous metal smelting works and mills and factories of every kind were built to produce the goods which were exported from the city's docks. There had been a settlement here from very early times – the city's name is derived from Sweyn's Ea – Ea means island, and Sweyn was a Viking pirate who had a base here. Heavy industry is still pre-eminent in the area, but commerce is of increasing importance and the university exerts a strong influence. Hundreds of acres of parkland and open space lie in and around the city, and just to the west is the Gower, one of the most beautiful areas of Wales. The history of Swansea is traced in the Maritime, Industrial and Royal Institution of South Wales Museums, while the Glynn Vivian Art Gallery contains notable paintings and porcelain.

Neath and **Port Talbot** are, like Swansea, dominated by heavy industry. Neath was once a Roman station, and later had a castle and an abbey, ruins of which can still be seen. Port Talbot has been an industrial centre since 1770, when a copper-smelting works was built. Steelworks and petrochemical works stretch for miles around Swansea Bay.

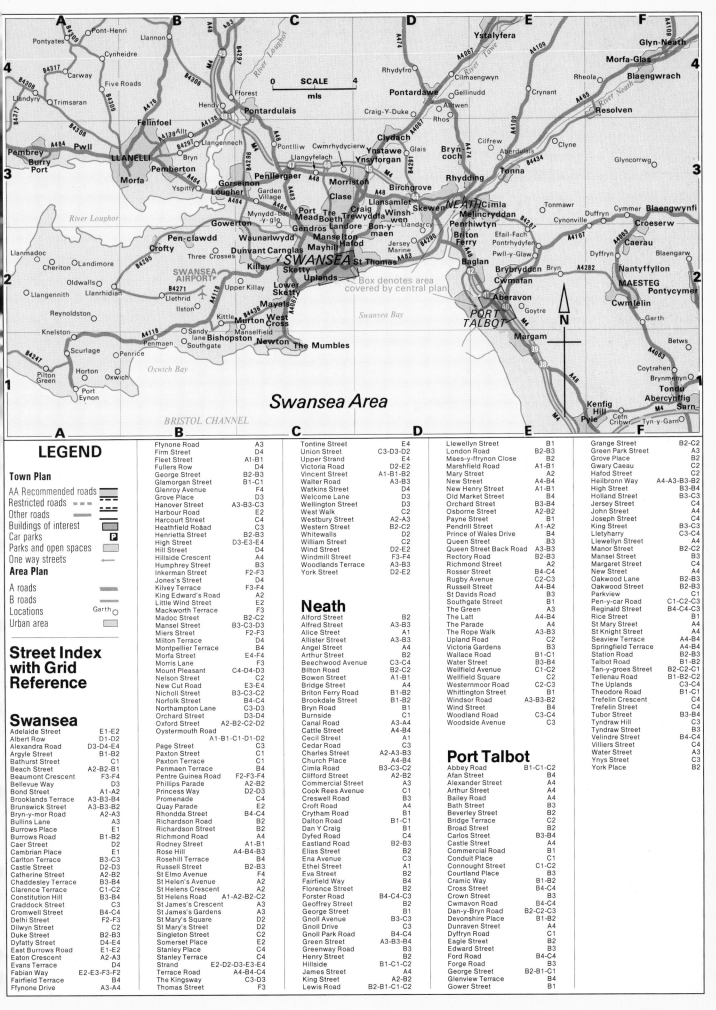

Swansea Area

LEGEND

Town Plan
- AA Recommended roads
- Restricted roads
- Other roads
- Buildings of interest
- Car parks
- Parks and open spaces
- One way streets

Area Plan
- A roads
- B roads
- Locations — Garth
- Urban area

Street Index with Grid Reference

Swansea

Adelaide Street	E1-E2
Albert Row	D1-D2
Alexandra Road	D3-D4-E4
Argyle Street	B1-B2
Bathurst Street	C1
Beach Street	A2-B2-B1
Beaumont Crescent	F3-F4
Bellevue Way	D3
Bond Street	A1-A2
Brooklands Terrace	A3-B3-B4
Brunswick Street	A3-B3-B2
Bryn-y-mor Road	A2-A3
Bullins Lane	A3
Burrows Place	E1
Burrows Road	B1-B2
Caer Street	D2
Cambrian Place	E1
Carlton Terrace	B3-C3
Castle Street	D2-D3
Catherine Street	A2-B2
Chaddesley Terrace	B3-B4
Clarence Terrace	C1-C2
Constitution Hill	B3-B4
Craddock Street	C3
Cromwell Street	B4-C4
Delhi Street	F2-F3
Dilwyn Street	C2
Duke Street	B2-B3
Dyfatty Street	D4-E4
East Burrows Road	E1-E2
Eaton Crescent	A2-A3
Evans Terrace	D4
Fabian Way	E2-E3-F3-F2
Fairfield Terrace	B4
Ffynone Drive	A3-A4

Ffynone Road	A3
Firm Street	D4
Fleet Street	A1-B1
Fullers Row	D4
George Street	B2-B3
Glamorgan Street	B1-C1
Glenroy Avenue	F4
Grove Place	D3
Hanover Street	A3-B3-C3
Harbour Road	E2
Harcourt Street	C4
Heathfield Roàad	C3
Henrietta Street	B2-B3
High Street	D3-E3-E4
Hill Street	D4
Hillside Crescent	A4
Humphrey Street	B3
Inkerman Street	F2-F3
Jones's Street	D4
Kilvey Terrace	F3-F4
King Edward's Road	A2
Little Wind Street	E2
Mackworth Terrace	F3
Madoc Street	B2-C2
Mansel Street	B3-C3-D3
Miers Street	F2-F3
Milton Terrace	D4
Montpellier Terrace	B4
Morfa Street	E4-F4
Morris Lane	F3
Mount Pleasant	C4-D4-D3
Nelson Street	C2
New Cut Road	E3-E4
Nicholl Street	B3-C3-C2
Norfolk Street	B4-C4
Northampton Lane	C3-D3
Orchard Street	D3-D4
Oxford Street	A2-B2-C2-D2
Oystermouth Road	A1-B1-C1-D1-D2
Page Street	C3
Paxton Street	C1
Paxton Terrace	C1
Penmaen Terrace	B4
Pentre Guinea Road	F2-F3-F4
Phillips Parade	A2-B2
Princess Way	D2-D3
Promenade	C4
Quay Parade	E2
Rhondda Street	B4-C4
Richardson Road	B2
Richardson Street	B2
Richmond Road	A4
Rodney Street	A1-B1
Rose Hill	A4-B4-B3
Rosehill Terrace	B3
Russell Street	B2-B3
St Elmo Avenue	F4
St Helen's Avenue	A2
St Helens Crescent	A2
St Helens Road	A1-A2-B2-C2
St James's Crescent	A3
St James's Gardens	A3
St Mary's Square	D2
St Mary's Street	D2
Singleton Street	C2
Somerset Place	E2
Stanley Place	C4
Stanley Terrace	C4
Strand	E2-D2-D3-E3-E4
Terrace Road	A4-B4-C4
The Kingsway	C3-D3
Thomas Street	F3

Tontine Street	E4
Union Street	C3-D3-D2
Upper Strand	E4
Victoria Road	D2-E2
Vincent Street	A1-B1-B2
Walter Road	A3-B3
Watkins Street	D4
Welcome Lane	D3
Wellington Street	D3
West Walk	C2
Westbury Street	A2-A3
Western Street	B2-C2
Whitewalls	D2
William Street	C2
Wind Street	D2-E2
Windmill Terrace	F3-F4
Woodlands Terrace	A3-B3
York Street	D2-E2

Neath

Alford Street	B2
Alfred Street	A3-B3
Alice Street	A1
Allister Street	A3-B3
Angel Street	A4
Arthur Street	B2
Beechwood Avenue	C3-C4
Bilton Road	B2-C2
Bowen Street	A1-B1
Bridge Street	A4
Briton Ferry Road	B1-B2
Brookdale Street	B1-B2
Bryn Road	B1
Burnside	C1
Canal Road	A3-A4
Cattle Street	A4-B4
Cecil Street	A4
Cedar Road	C3
Charles Street	A2-A3-B3
Church Place	A4-B4
Cimla Road	B3-C3-C2
Clifford Street	A2-B2
Commercial Street	A3
Cook Rees Avenue	C1
Creswell Road	B3
Croft Road	A4
Crytham Road	B1
Dalton Road	B1-C1
Dan Y Craig	B1
Dyfed Road	C4
Eastland Road	B2-B3
Elias Street	B2
Ena Avenue	C3
Ethel Street	A1
Eva Street	B2
Fairfield Way	B2
Florence Street	B2
Forster Road	B4-C4-C3
Geoffrey Street	B2
George Street	B1
Gnoll Avenue	B3-C3
Gnoll Drive	C3
Gnoll Park Road	C3-C4
Green Street	B4-C4
Greenway Road	B3
Henry Street	B2
Hillside	B1-C1-C2
James Street	A4
King Street	A2-B2
Lewis Road	B2-B1-C1-C2

Llewellyn Street	B1
London Road	B2-B3
Maes-y-ffrynon Close	B2
Marshfield Road	A1-B1
Mary Street	A2
New Street	A4-B4
New Henry Street	A1-B1
Old Market Street	B4
Orchard Street	B3-B4
Osborne Street	A2-B2
Payne Street	B1
Pendrill Street	A1-A2
Prince of Wales Drive	B4
Queen Street	B3
Queen Street Back Road	A3-B3
Rectory Road	B2-B3
Richmond Street	A2
Rosser Street	B4-C4
Rugby Avenue	C2-C3
Russell Street	A4-B4
St Davids Road	B3
Southgate Street	B1
The Green	A3
The Latt	A4-B4
The Parade	A4
The Rope Walk	A3-B3
Upland Road	C2
Victoria Gardens	B3
Wallace Road	B1-C1
Water Street	B3-B4
Wellfield Avenue	C1-C2
Wellfield Square	C2
Westernmoor Road	C2-C3
Whittington Street	B1
Windsor Road	A3-B3-B2
Wind Street	B4
Woodland Road	C3-C4
Woodside Avenue	C3

Port Talbot

Abbey Road	B1-C1-C2
Afan Street	B4
Alexander Street	A4
Arthur Street	A4
Bailey Road	A4
Bath Street	B3
Beverley Street	B2
Bridge Terrace	C2
Broad Street	B2
Carlos Street	B3-B4
Castle Street	A4
Commercial Road	B1
Conduit Place	C1
Connought Street	C1-C2
Courtland Place	B3
Cramic Way	B1-B2
Cross Street	B4-C4
Crown Street	B3
Cwmavon Road	B4-C4
Dan-y-Bryn Road	B2-C2-C3
Devonshire Place	B1-B2
Dunraven Street	A4
Dyffryn Road	C1
Eagle Street	B2
Edward Street	B3
Ford Road	B4-C4
Forge Road	B3
George Street	B2-B1-C1
Glenview Terrace	B4
Gower Street	B1

Grange Street	B2-C2
Green Park Street	A3
Grove Place	B2
Gwary Caeau	C2
Hafod Street	C2
Heilbronn Way	A4-A3-B3-B2
High Street	B3-B4
Holland Street	B3-C3
Jersey Street	A4
John Street	C4
Joseph Street	C4
King Street	B3-C3
Lletyharry	C3-C4
Llewellyn Street	A4
Manor Street	B2-C2
Mansel Street	B3
Margaret Street	C4
New Street	A4
Oakwood Lane	B2-B3
Oakwood Street	B2-B3
Parkview	C1
Pen-y-car Road	C1-C2-C3
Reginald Street	B4-C4-C3
Rice Street	B1
St Mary Street	A4
St Knight Street	A4
Seaview Terrace	A4-B4
Springfield Terrace	A4-B4
Station Road	B2-B3
Talbot Road	B1-B2
Tan-y-groes Street	B2-C2-C1
Tellenau Road	B1-B2-C2
The Uplands	C3-C4
Theodore Road	B1-C1
Trefelin Crescent	C4
Trefelin Street	C4
Tubor Street	B3-B4
Tyndraw Hill	C3
Tyndraw Street	B3
Velindre Street	B4-C4
Villiers Street	C4
Water Street	A3
Ynys Street	C3
York Place	B2

Legend to Atlas

Motorway with number	AA Centre (24 hours)	Urban area Village
Junctions with and without numbers	AA Centre (normal office hours)	National boundary
Junctions with limited entries or exits	AA Motorway Information Centre	County boundary
Service area	AA Road Service Centre	Distance in miles between symbols
Motorway & junction under construction	AA Port Service Centre	Spot height in feet
Primary route	AA & RAC telephones	
Other A roads	BT telephones in isolated areas	River and lake
B roads	Picnic site	Sandy beaches
Unclassified	Steep gradient (arrows pointing downhill)	Overlaps and numbers of continuing pages
Dual carriageway	Road toll. Level crossing	Numbers of adjacent Touring Guides listed below:-
Road with limited entries or exits	Vehicle ferry in Great Britain	The West Country
Under construction	Continental vehicle ferry	Central England & East Anglia
Scotland: narrow roads with passing places	Airport	The North Country

Abbey or Cathedral	Coastal Launching Site	Nature Trail
Ruined Abbey or Cathedral	Surfing	Wildlife Park (mammals)
Castle	Climbing School	Wildlife Park (birds)
House and Garden	County Cricket Ground	Zoo
House	Gliding Centre	Forest Drive
Garden	Artificial Ski Slope	Lighthouse
Industrial Interest	Golf Course	Tourist Information Centre
Museum or Collection	Horse Racing	Tourist Information Centre (summer only)
Prehistoric Monument	Show Jumping/Equestrian Centre	Long Distance Footpath
Famous Battle Site	Motor Racing Circuit	AA Viewpoint
Preserved Railway or Steam Centre	Cave	Other Place of Interest
Windmill	Country Park	Boxed symbols indicate tourist attractions in towns
Sea Angling	Dolphinarium or Aquarium	

The National Grid

The National Grid provides a system of reference common to maps of all scales. The grid covers Britain with an imaginary network of 100 kilometre squares. Each square is identified by two letters, *eg* TR. Every 100 kilometre square is then sub-divided into 10 kilometre squares which appear as a network of blue lines on the map pages. These blue lines are numbered left to right 0-9 and bottom to top 0-9. These 10 kilometre squares can be further divided into tenths to give a place reference to the nearest kilometre.

Key to Road Maps

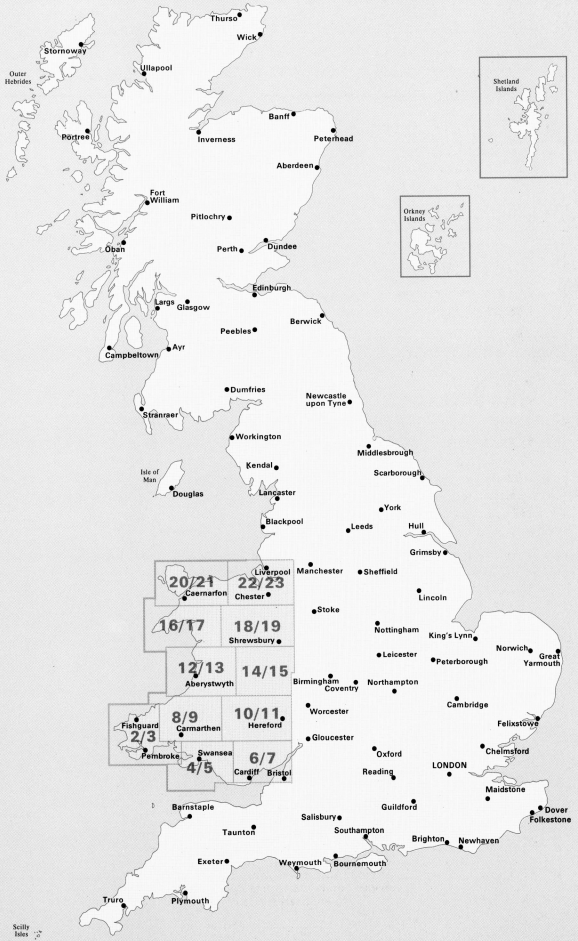

Stornoway

Outer
Hebrides

Portree

Ullapool

Thurso

Wick

Banff

Inverness

Peterhead

Aberdeen

Fort
William

Pitlochry

Oban

Perth

Dundee

Edinburgh

Largs

Glasgow

Peebles

Berwick

Campbeltown

Ayr

Dumfries

Newcastle
upon Tyne

Stranraer

Workington

Kendal

Middlesbrough

Scarborough

Isle of
Man

Douglas

Lancaster

York

Blackpool

Leeds

Hull

Grimsby

20/21

Liverpool

Caernarfon

Manchester

Sheffield

Lincoln

22/23

Chester

Stoke

Nottingham

16/17

18/19

Shrewsbury

King's Lynn

Norwich

Leicester

Peterborough

Great
Yarmouth

12/13

14/15

Aberystwyth

Birmingham

Coventry

Northampton

Cambridge

Worcester

Felixstowe

Fishguard

8/9

10/11

Carmarthen

Hereford

Gloucester

Chelmsford

2/3

Pembroke

Swansea

6/7

Cardiff

Bristol

Oxford

Reading

LONDON

Maidstone

4/5

Barnstaple

Guildford

Dover

Salisbury

Folkestone

Taunton

Southampton

Brighton

Newhaven

Exeter

Weymouth

Bournemouth

Truro

Plymouth

Scilly
Isles

Shetland
Islands

Orkney
Islands

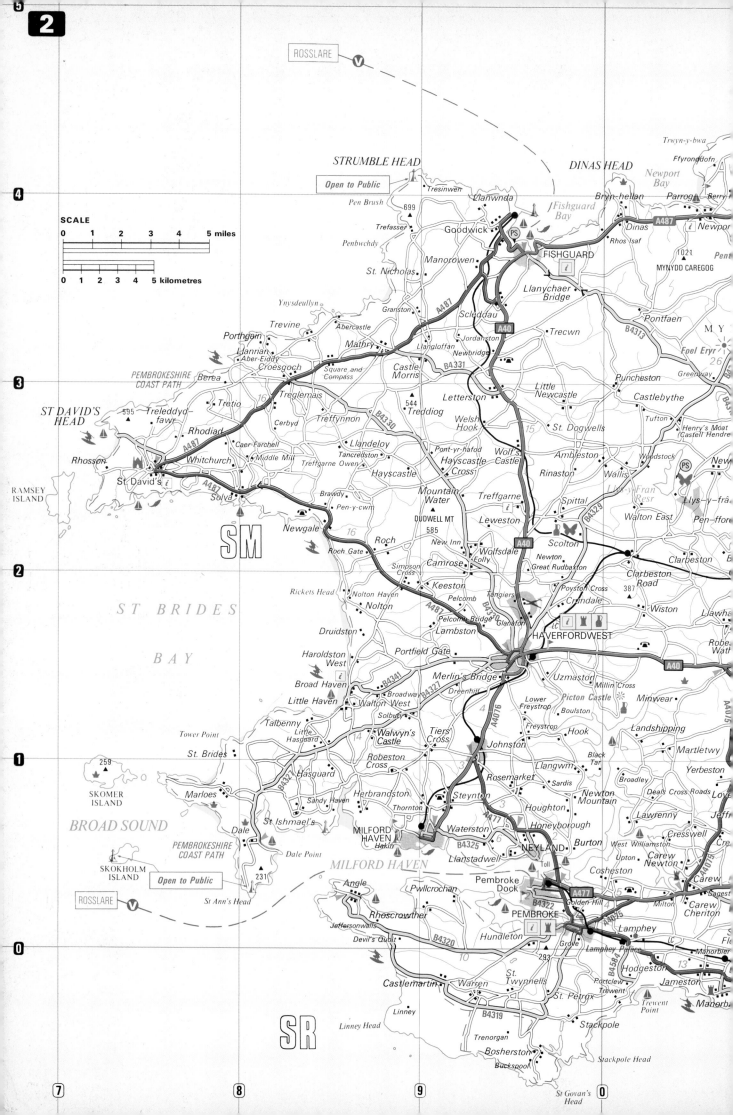

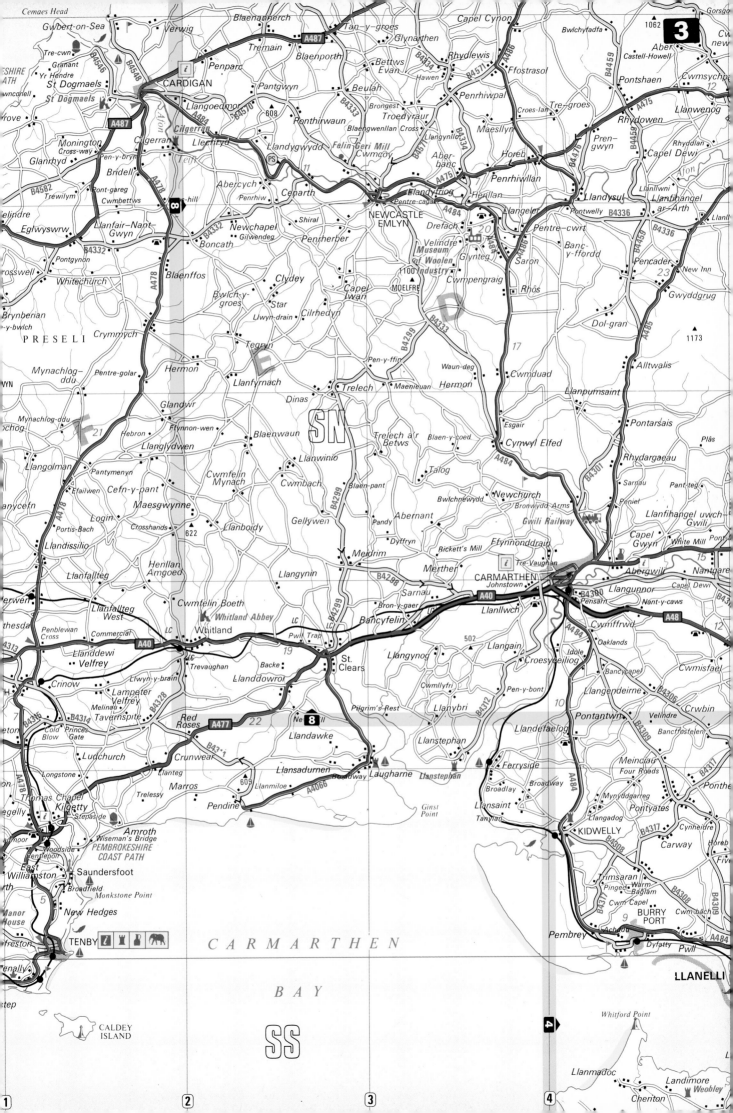

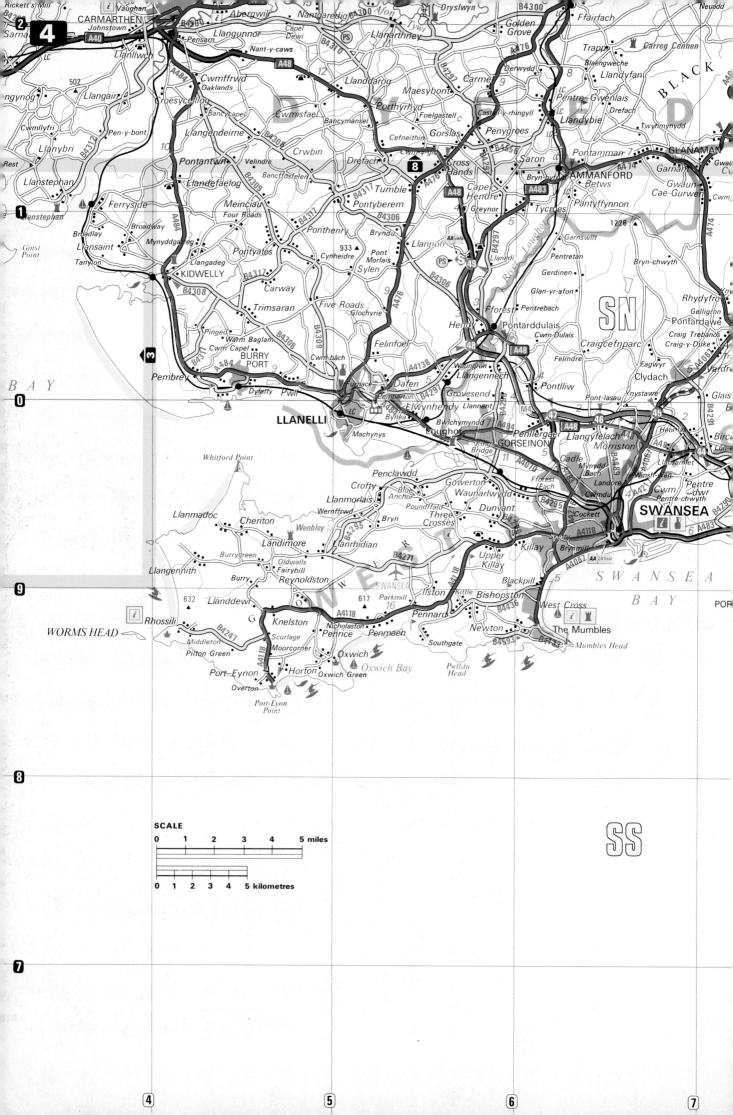

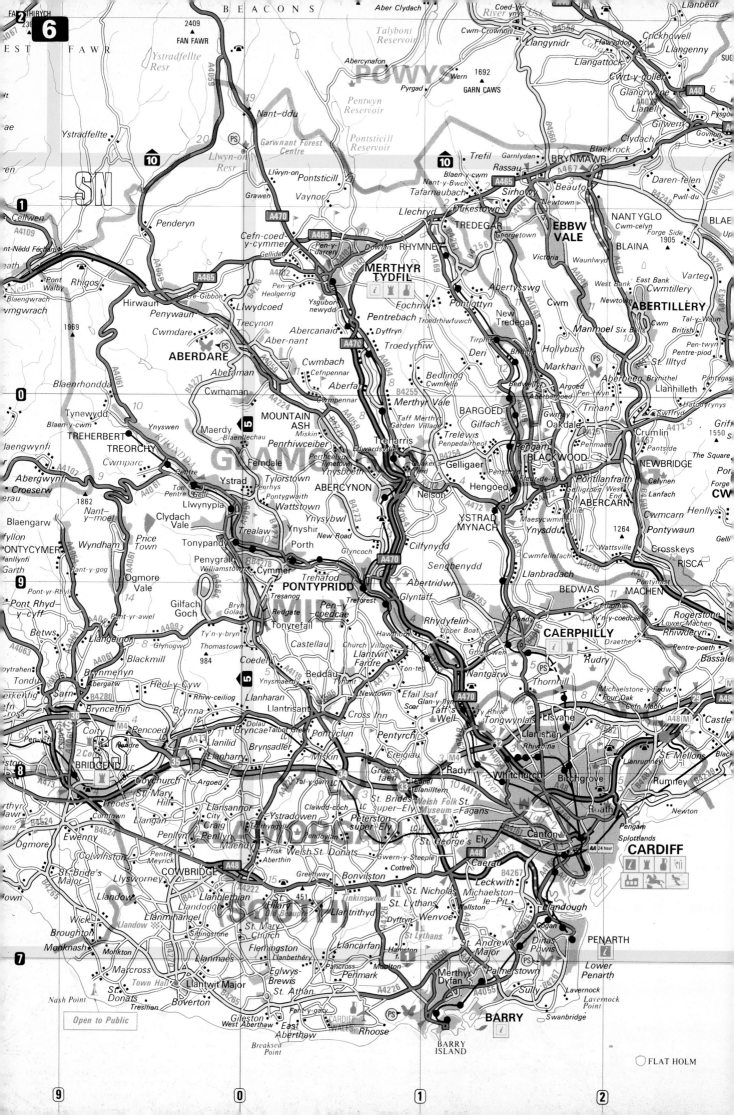

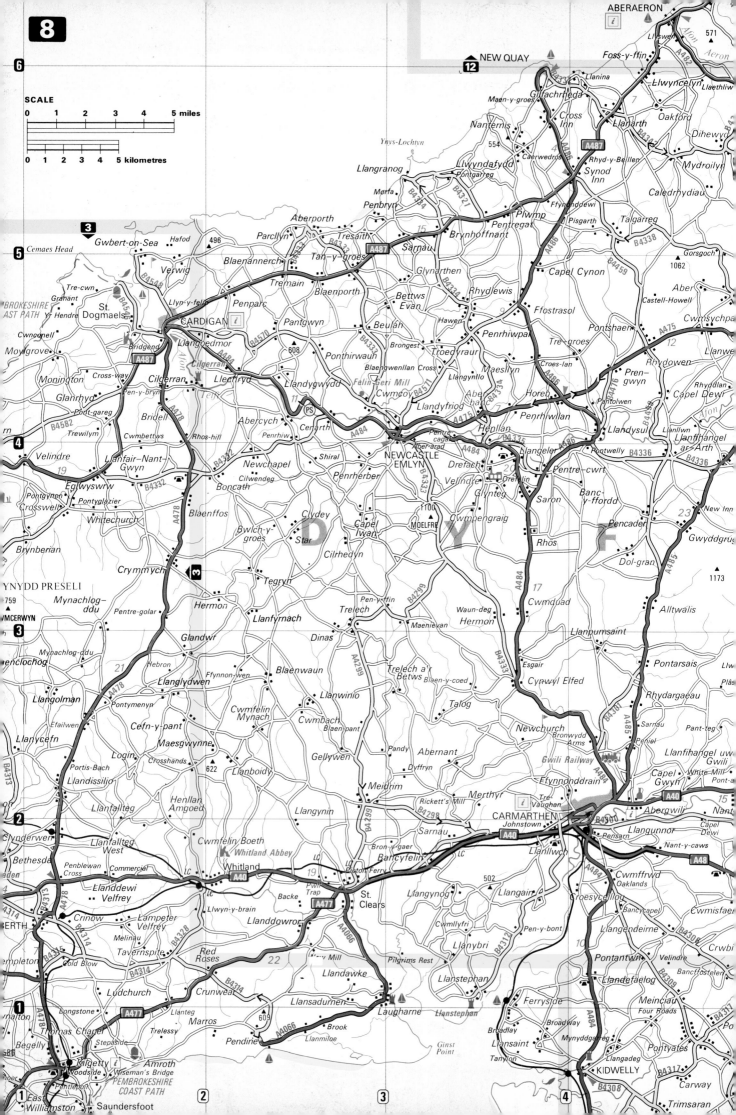

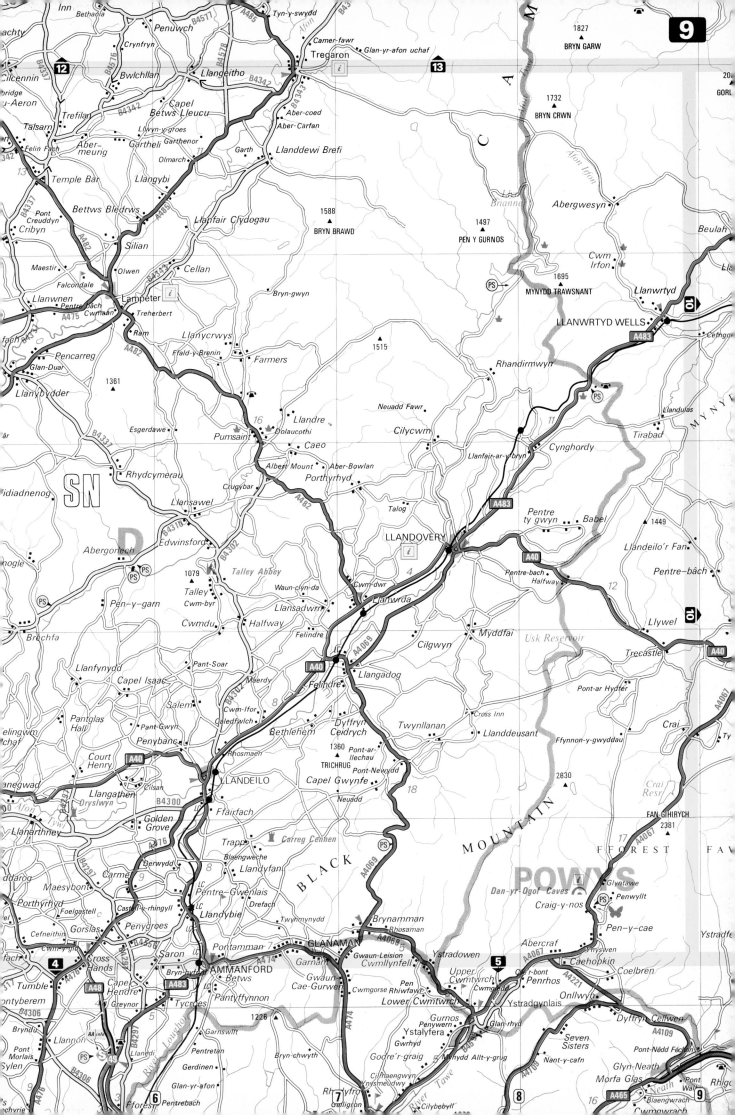

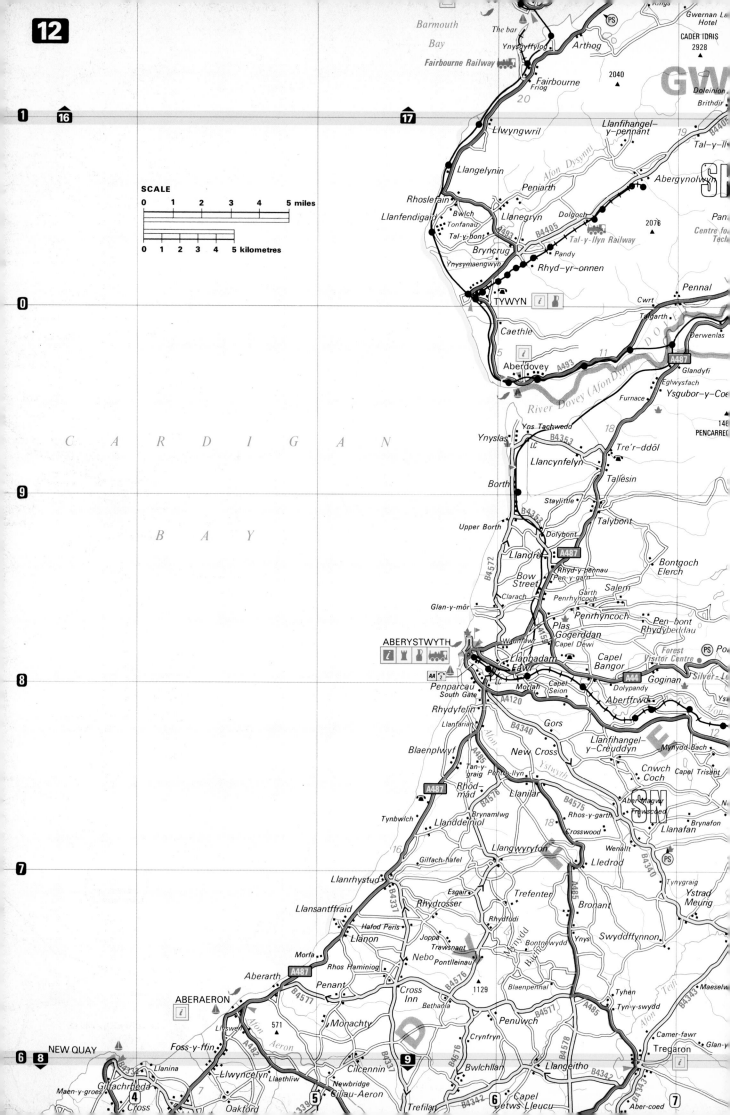

SCALE

0   1   2   3   4   5 miles

0 1 2 3 4 5 kilometres

CADER IDRIS
2928

Barmouth Bay

The bar

Ynysgyffylog

Fairbourne Railway

Arthog

Fairbourne

Friog   2040

Doleinion

Brithdir

GW

16   17

Llwyngwril

Llanfihangel-
y-pennant

Tal-y-ll

19

Llangelynin

Afon Dysynni

Peniarth

Abergynolwyn

SK

Rhoslefain

Bwlch

Llanegryn

Dolgoch

2076

Pan

Centre fo
Tech

Llanfendigaid

Tonfanau

Tal-y-bont

Tal-y-llyn Railway

Bryncrug

Pandy

Ynysymaengwyn

Rhyd-yr-onnen

Pennal

TYWYN

Cwrt

Talgarth

Derwenlas

Caethle

11

DO

A487

Glandyfi

Aberdovey   A493

Eglwysfach

Ysgubor-y-Coe

River Dovey (Afon Dyfi)

Furnace

PENCARRE

146

C A R D I G A N

Yns Tachwedd

Ynyslas

LC

B4353

Tre'r-ddôl

Llancynfelyn

Taliesin

Borth

Staylittle

Talybont

9

B A Y

Upper Borth

Dolybont

B4353

Llandre

A487

Rhyd-y-pennau
Pen-y-garn

Bontgoch
Elerch

B4572

Bow
Street

Garth
Penrhyncoch

Salem

Clarach

Glan-y-môr

Penrhyncoch

Pen-bont
Rhydybeddau

Plas
Gogerddan

Capel Dewi

Forest
Visitor Centre

PS

Po

ABERYSTWYTH

Waunfawr

Capel
Bangor

Llanbadarn
Fawr

A44

Goginan

Silver-Le

8

LC

Morfah

Capel
Seion

Dolypandy

Aberffrwd

Ys

Penparcau
South Gate

A4120

Rhydyfelin

A487

Blaenplwyf

B4340

Llanfarian

Gors

Llanfihangel-
y-Creuddyn

Mynydd Bach

A485

Tan-y-graig

Pentre-llyn

New Cross

Ystwyth

Cnwch
Coch

Capel Trisant

SN

Rhôd-
mâd

B4576

Llanilar

Aber-magwr

Trawscoed

B4575

Tynbwlch

Brynamlwg

Rhos-y-garth

Brynafon

Llanafan

Llanddeiniol

Crosswood

18

Llangwyryfon

Wenallt

PS

7

Gilfach-hafel

Lledrod

B4340

Llanrhystud

Trefenter

Tynygraig

Ystrad
Meurig

Llansantffraid

B4337

Esgair

Rhydrosser

Bronant

A485

Swyddffynnon

Hafod Peris

Rhydfudi

Ynys

Llanon

Joppa
Trawsnant

Bontnewydd

Morfa

Rhos Haminiog

Nebo
Pontlleinau

A487

Aberarth

Penant

B4576

1129

Blaenpennal

Tyhen

Tyn-y-swydd

A485

ABERAERON

B4571

Cross
Inn

Bethania

B4577

Penuwch

Teifi

Camer-fawr

Glan-i

Monachty

571

Crynfryn

Aber-coed

Tregaron

NEW QUAY

8   9

Foss-y-ffin

Afon Aeron

A482

Cilcennin

B4337

Bwlchllan

Llangeitho

B434

7

Maen-y-groes

Gilfachrheda

Llanina

Llwyncelyn

Laethliw

Newbridge
Ciliau-Aeron

Trefilan

Betws Lleucu

4   5   6

Cross

Oakford

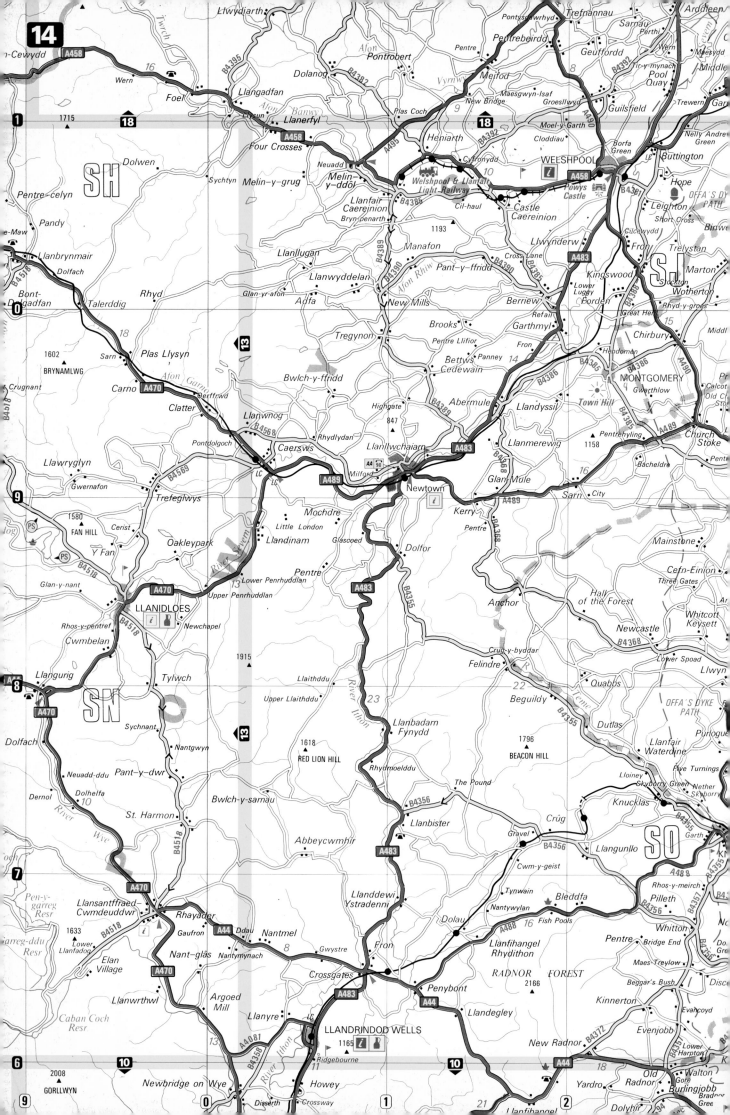

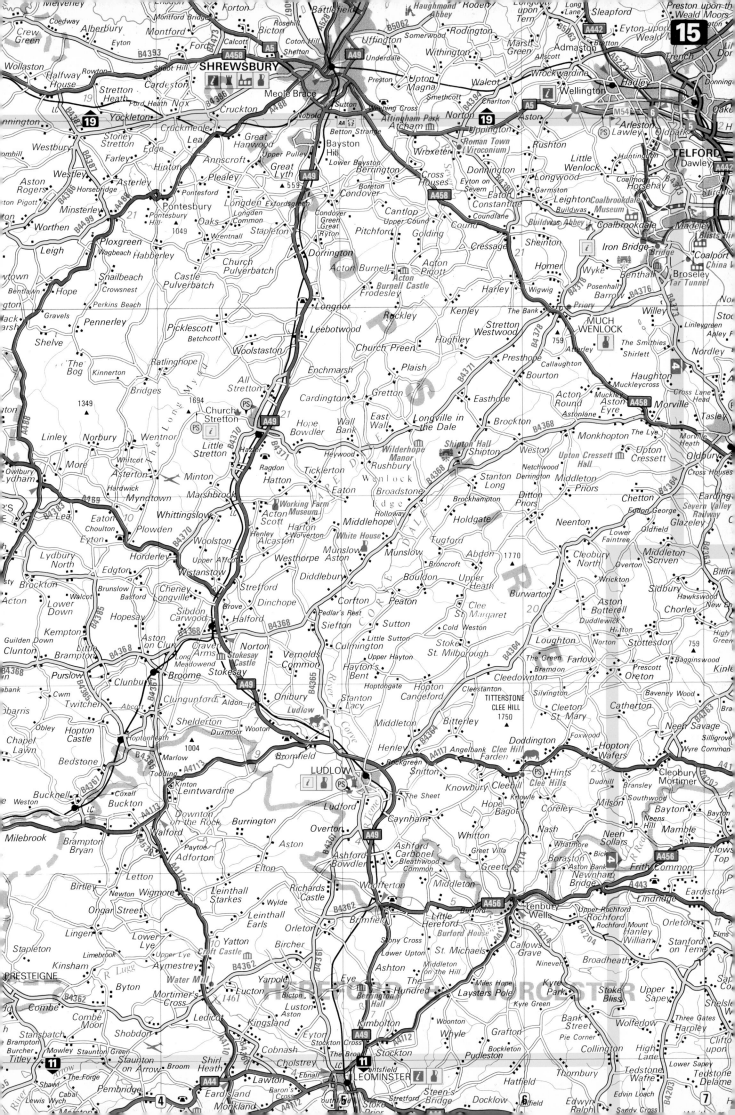

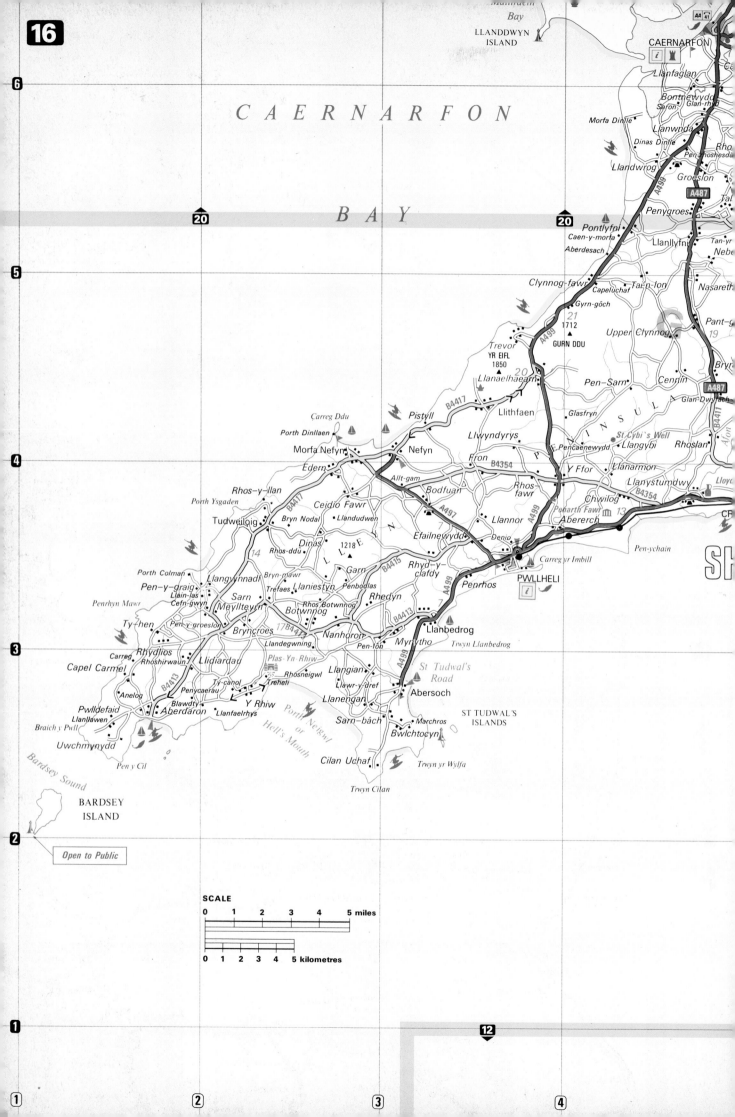

16

MENAI
Bay

LLANDDWYN
ISLAND

CAERNARFON
ⓘ

C A E R N A R F O N

Llanfaglan

Bontnewydd
Saron · Glan-rhyd

Morfa Dinlle

Llanwnda

Dinas Dinlle

Pen-rhoshesda

B A Y

Llandwrog

Groeslon

20

20

Pontllyfni

Penygroes

Caen-y-morfa

Llanllyfni

Tan-yr-

Aberdesach

Nebe

Clynnog-fawr

Capeluchaf

Tai'n-lon

Nasareth

Gyrn-goch

21
1712
▲
GURN DDU

Upper Clynnog

Pant-G

19

Trevor
YR EIFL
1850
▲

20

Pen-Sarn

Cennin

Bryn

A487

Llanaelhaearn

B4417

Llithfaen

Glasfryn

Glan-Dwyfach

B4411

Carreg Ddu

Pistyll

Llwyndyrys

St Cybi's Well

Rhoslan

Afon

Porth Dinllaen

Nefyn

E. Pencaenewydd

Llangybi

Morfa Nefyn

Fron

B4354

Y Ffor

Llanarmon

Edern

Bodfuan

Allt-gam

Rhos-
fawr

Llanystumdwy

B4354

Lloyd

Rhos-y-llan

Ceidio Fawr

Llannor

Penarth Fawr

Chwilog

13

CR

Porth Ysgaden

Bryn Nodal

Llandudwen

A497

Denio

Abererch

Tudweiloig

7

Efailnewydd

Dinas

1218
▲

Garn

Rhyd-y-
clafdy

Pen-ychain

Porth Colman

Rhos-ddu

L L E Y N

Penbodlas

B4415

PWLLHELI
ⓘ

SH

Llangwnnadl

Bryn-mawr

Llaniestyn

Penrhos

Carreg yr Imbill

Pen-y-graig

Trefaes

Rhedyn

7

Llain-las
Cefn-gwyn

Sarn
Meyllteyrn

Rhos Botwnnog

Botwnnog

B4413

Penrhyn Mawr

Ty-hen

Pen-y-groeslon

Bryncroes

17 B4417

Nanhoron

Llanbedrog

Myrtho

Trwyn Llanbedrog

Rhydlios

Llandegwning

Pen-lôn

A499

3

Carreg

Llidiardau

Rhoshirwaun

Plas-Yn-Rhiw

*St Tudwal's
Road*

Capel Carmel

Ty-canol

Rhosneigwl

Llangian

Penycaerau

Treheli

Llawr-y-dref

Abersoch

Anelog

Blawdty

*ST TUDWAL'S
ISLANDS*

Pwlldefaid

Llanllawen

Aberdaron

Y Rhiw

Llanfaelrhys

Llanengan

Sarn-bâch

Marchros

*ST TUDWAL'S
ISLANDS*

Braich y Pwll

*Porth Neigwl
or
Hell's Mouth*

Bwlchtocyn

Uwchmynydd

Cilan Uchaf

Trwyn yr Wylfa

Pen y Cil

Trwyn Cilan

Bardsey Sound

**BARDSEY
ISLAND**

2

Open to Public

SCALE

0   1   2   3   4   5 miles

0 1 2 3 4   5 kilometres

1

12

① ② ③ ④

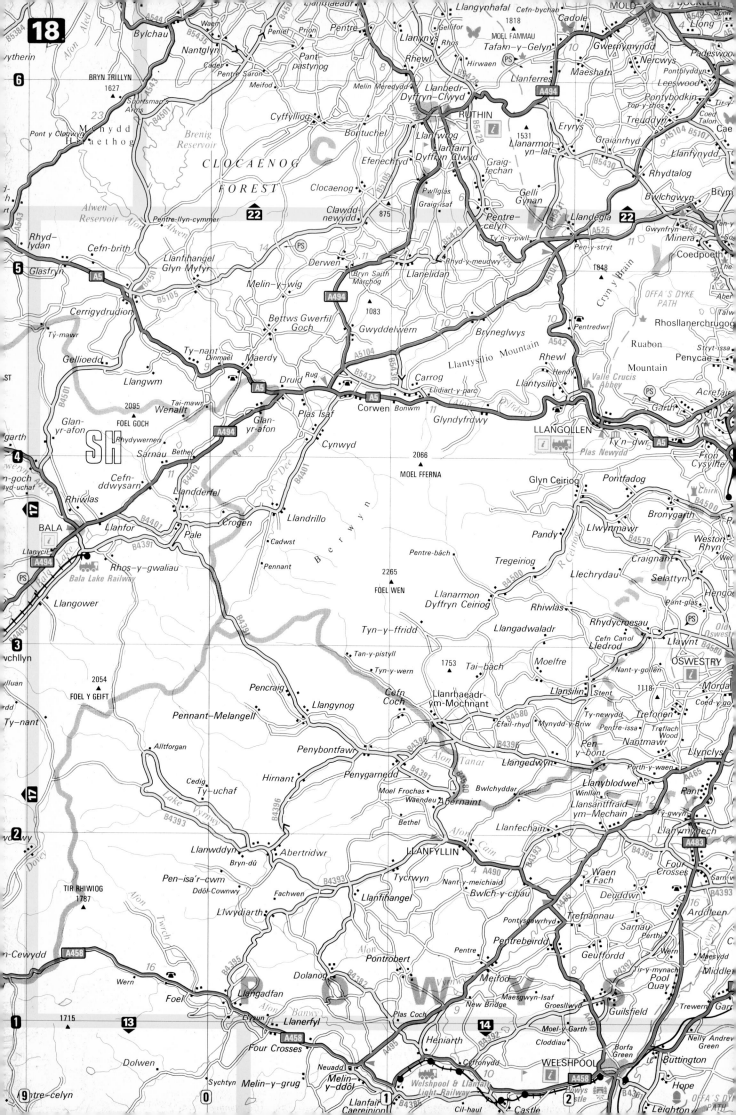

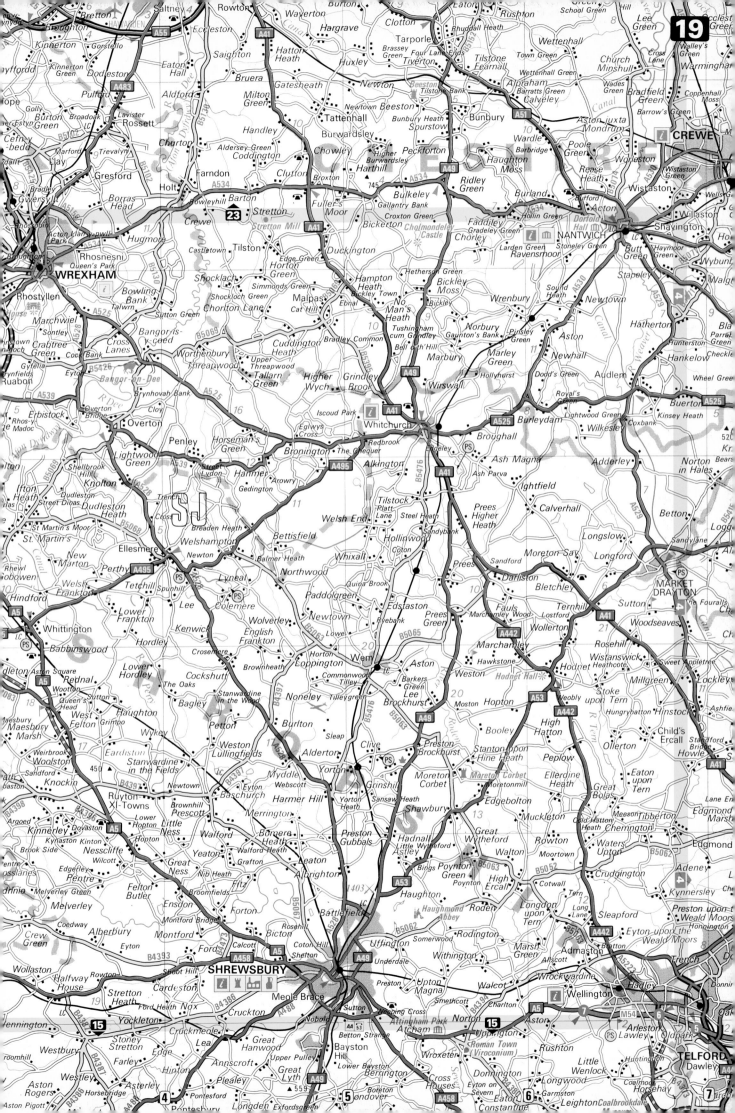

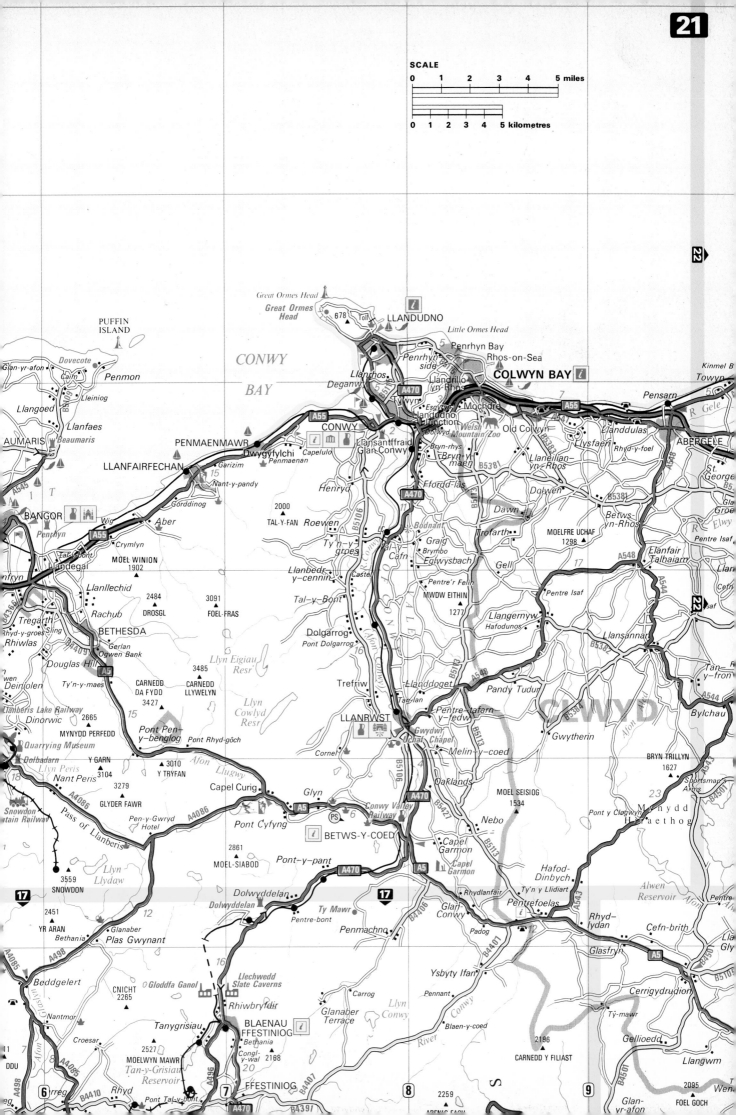

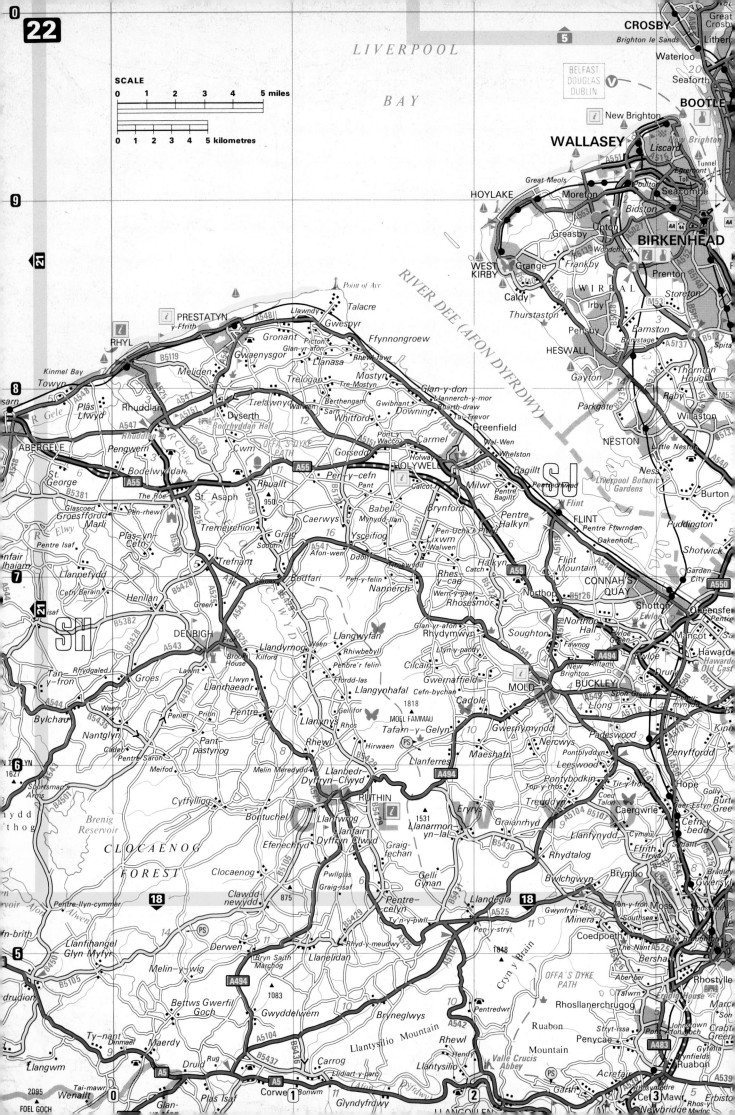

INDEX

As well as the page number of each place name the index also
includes an appropriate atlas page number together with a four figure
map reference (see National Grid explanation on page 112).

In a very few instances place names appear without a map reference.
This is because either they are not shown on the atlas or they lie just
outside the mapping area of the guide. However, each tour does
include a detailed map which highlights the location of all places
mentioned on the route.